# Every girl should travel alone...
# at least once.

You don't need a boyfriend, a travel partner or anyone's approval to travel the world. And you don't need a massive bank account or an entire summer off work.

All you need is that wanderlust in your blood and a good guidebook in your hands.

If you've doubted yourself for one moment, remember this:

Millions of girls travel across the globe all by themselves every damn day and you can, too.

You are just as capable, just as smart, and just as brave as the rest of us. You don't need permission – this is your life.

Listen to your gut, follow your heart and remember that the best adventures start with the simple decision to go.

# SEATTLE

## AND THE
## PACIFIC NORTHWEST

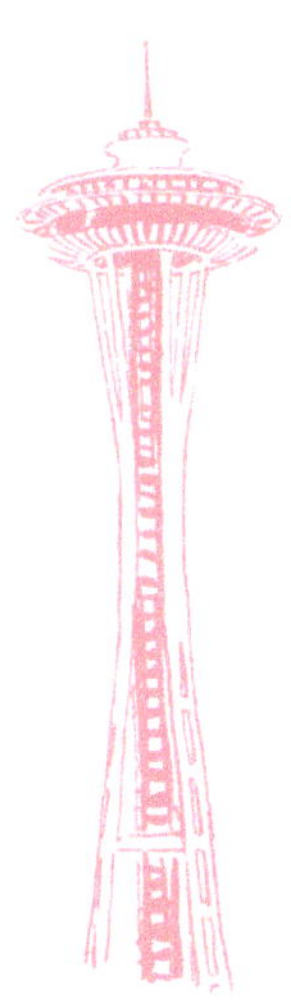

ALEXA WEST GUIDES

# Hey, I'm your
# Seattle Travel Guide...

**Hey, it's me, Alexa**—though you can call me Lexi.

By the time this book was published, I'd already written 12 best-selling travel guides—but never one for my own country.

That changes now. This Seattle guide is the first in a series that covers not just my home country, but my hometown! You guys, this is my city.

While I grew up in a little fishing village called Gig Harbor, about an hour south of Seattle on the Olympic Peninsula, I grew up coming to "the big city" to see the ballet, to go shopping downtown at Christmas when it was all lit up, to take dance classes, and to attend hockey games (yeah, I had a thing for hockey players in high school). This city has always been a bit magical to me.

So naturally, I fell head over heels for Seattle and applied to only one university: The University of Washington in Seattle. Thank goodness they let me in.

My college years were spent darting around the city at night, high heels on, fake ID in hand. Discovering the best late night hot dog trucks.

Then, I joined the Peace Corps and left the country for a decade...until I met a Seattle boy who swept me off my feet. Now, I live here (again).

Oh and by the way, my boyfriend is born and raised in *Seattle Seattle* - like right in the city. The man is full of city secrets - many of which I've been permitted to share with you. On that note, expect this edition of The Solo

Girl's Travel Guide to have more romance and dating stuff.

As I've returned to this city as this award-winning travel guide writer, I've spent the past three years studying my city as I'd study any other city I have written a travel guide for: through food, beauty, public transportation, cheap nights out, romance, talking to locals and getting lost.

All of this is to say, I don't just know Seattle—I am Seattle. This is going to be my best book yet.

♥ Follow my Seattle adventures on Instagram, TikTok and YouTube @SoloGirlsTravelGuide

 **Want me to help you plan your Seattle trip?** Meet me at:

Alexa-west.com/services

⇨ And now, let me introduce you to my travel bestie and podcast partner, Emilia Igartua, all the way from Mazatlán, Mexico...

Emy stayed with me for five weeks while we explored every corner of Seattle together, pouring our hearts into this guidebook. You're going to love the energy she brings! ☞

# Meet the designer...

**Hiii! I'm Emilia, but my friends call me Emy...**

I'm the person behind making this book (and all of ours books!) so pretty. I'm Lexi's partner in crime in everything Solo Girl's Travel Guide, but I'm also a creative chameleon.

I love art, travel and photography, and when I'm not creating travel guides or recording podcast episodes with Lexi (at True Crime Travelers!), you'll find me going on travel adventures, camera in hand. Or, making art in my home studio in Spain, where I live.

I hope you love this book as much as we do and that Seattle brings you as much magic as it brought me. I can't wait to enjoy more of what this amazing city has to offer.

Con amor,

Emilia

♥ Follow Emilia's adventures on Instagram and Tiktok at @__helloemilia — and find her art at holaemilia.com

# HOW THIS BOOKS WORKS:

**This book is both for visitors and people who live in or are moving to Seattle!**

So while I write with visitors in mind, this book will also be filled with super local tips, adventures and recommendations that people living here need to know! Like which hidden parks make for the best sunset picnics (Jack Block Park, West Seattle).

So here's how to approach this book:

### ▸ Step 1: Create Your Bucket List

**Grab your highlighter** and go through this book **highlighting and ear-marking adventures that excite you.** Note which neighborhood holds the most important adventures that appeal to you. Look out for "Adventure Pairings" throughout the book (nearby activities grouped together for easy planning!)

### ▸ Step 2: Choose Your Stay

Pick a neighborhood close to your planned adventures because **where you stay can make or break your trip.** I have an entire hotel chapter waiting to guide you.

### ▸ Step 3: Get Ready to Go

Use the Survival Guide to **prep, pack, connect and go.**

♥ Remember, if you're nervous about this trip, remember that you're not alone!

### ☞ JOIN GIRLS IN SEATTLE

You can drop a message of anxiety or boredom or whatever in **Girls in Seattle** at any time and one of us will answer.

Scan this code ☞

...or head to: **facebook.com/groups/ girlsinseattle**

### ☞ PEP TALK WITH ALEXA

Call me for a 30-minute girl chat about travel plans, dating in Seattle, moving here, general travel nerves! I'm the queen of dissolving fear.

### ☞ BROWSE ITINERARIES

Grab the itineraries Alexa gives to her family and friends when they visit Seattle.

Scan the code to book your call and browse itineraries:

# *Seattle*

## TABLE OF CONTENTS

Ps. You will find maps in this book - but general maps to give you general ideas. For detailed maps on your phone that will ACTUALLY help you find the things in this book, scan this code:

# Seattle

**To truly understand this city, you must understand where it came from.**

## QUICK SEATTLE HISTORY

### Before the 1900s: Duwamish Land

Long before skyscrapers and tech giants, Seattle was the land of the Duwamish Tribe, led by Chief Si'ahl (Seattle's namesake). The Duwamish lived along the shores of Elliott Bay, with villages at the mouths of rivers like the Duwamish River. They fished the waters, cultivated the land, and built a community that thrived for thousands of years.

✳ **Fun Fact:** You can still visit the Duwamish Longhouse & Cultural Center today, which serves as a space for cultural education and honoring the history of the Duwamish people.

☞ **Learn More:** <u>duwamishtribe.org</u>

# SEATTLE TIMELINE: 1900s TO 2024

▶ **1900s: Klondike Gold Rush Fuels Growth**

Seattle morphs into a bustling launchpad for gold seekers heading to Alaska, bringing a wave of new wealth and transforming the city into a gateway to the north.

▶ **1916: Boeing Takes Off**

Boeing sets up shop, launching its first seaplanes and planting the seeds for Seattle's future as an aerospace powerhouse.

▶ **1920s: Prohibition and Speakeasies**

Prohibition hits, but Seattle doesn't stop the party—hidden bars and speakeasies keep the good times rolling, turning the city into a haven for secret nightlife

▶ **1930s: Building Through the Great Depression**

Despite the tough times, Seattle pushes ahead with projects like the Ballard Locks and the Seattle Art Museum, laying the groundwork for the city's future growth.

▶ **1940s: Wartime Boom**

World War II transforms Seattle into a war machine, with bustling shipyards and Boeing's factories working non-stop to fuel the war effort.

▶ **1950s: Suburbs and Aerospace Boom**

Boeing's expansion sends Seattle soaring, with suburbs spreading out and the city embracing a wave of post-war optimism.

▶ **1962: World's Fair and Space Needle**

The World's Fair puts Seattle on the map, gifting the city its iconic Space Needle and Monorail. It's a moment where Seattle embraces its futuristic spirit and sets the standard for cool.

▶ **1970s: Environmental Awakening**

Seattle begins to protect its natural beauty, cleaning up Lake Washington and adding new green spaces. Nature and city life start to blend in a way that feels uniquely Seattle.

▶ **1980: Mount St. Helen's Eruption**

When Mount St. Helens erupts, an ash cloud drifts over Seattle, reminding the city that Mother Nature calls the shots in the Pacific Northwest.

### ▸ 1990s: Grunge, Protests and Dot-Com Boom

Nirvana and Pearl Jam put Seattle on the musical map with the rise of grunge. The decade also sees the "Battle in Seattle" WTO protests, where tens of thousands flood downtown, turning it into a scene of both peaceful demonstrations and clashes. It's a defining moment for the city's activist spirit.

### ▸ 2000s: Tech Titans Rise

Amazon and Microsoft turn Seattle into a tech epicenter, reshaping the skyline and drawing in fresh talent. The city's transformation is fast and furious.

### ▸ 2010s: Beer, Food and Urban Revival

Seattle's craft beer scene explodes, and the food scene follows, with farm-to-table restaurants and food trucks everywhere. Neighborhoods like Capitol Hill and Ballard become playgrounds for beer lovers and foodies.

### ▸ 2020: Covid and Adapting to Change

The pandemic shifts Seattle's vibe to remote work and outdoor living, with streets turned into dining spots.

### ▸ 2021: Alexa West Moves Back Into Town

The biggest event of the 21st century.

### ▸ 2023: Pickleball Craze

Pickleball becomes the city's new obsession, with courts popping up everywhere.

### ▸ 2024: Writing Seattle's New Chapter

Seattle stands at the edge of whatever comes next—tech, culture, and the spirit of reinvention ready to keep the city moving forward.

### ▸ 2025: Writing Seattle's Next Chapter

The Link Light Rail will continue to grow, with new stations opening in **2024-2025** in **Bellevue, Redmond**, and **Lynnwood**, making Seattle's suburbs more accessible.

### ▸ 2026: FIFA World Cup 2026

Seattle will host matches at Lumen Field!

# Seattle 101

### ▸ THE FOOD

Seattle is known for **fresh-caught salmon, bountiful mushrooms, and Seattle Dogs** (hot dogs with cream cheese and grilled onions). But what truly sets Seattle apart is its **Asian cuisine**, thanks to vibrant Asian communities, making up around **18% of the population**. Head to the International District for **pho, hand-shaved noodles,** and **Chinese dumplings.**

With **100,000**+ Mexican Americans, Seattle also has a fantastic Mexican food culture with a heavy **Oaxacan** influence in the south of Seattle. You'll find **tamales** and **taco trucks** galore.

### ♥ NOTE FROM ME...

Ps. I'm gatekeeping my favorite Oaxacan Taco stand because I don't want to ruin it for myself. But if you leave a review for this book on Amazon, send me a screenshot on Instragram @sologirlstravelguide...I'll tell you my secret taco spot.

And yes, Seattle's coffee obsession is real. With **1,700+ coffee shops,** it's a city that takes its brew seriously. The **Pike Place Starbucks** (opened in 1976) is the oldest surviving location, but the true first Starbucks opened in **1971** at **2000** Western Avenue. So don't stand in that super-long line at Pike Place, I beg of you. Instead, for a different slice of history, check out **Monorail Espresso,** Seattle's **first espresso cart from 1980**, now a beloved café.

Lastly, let's talk beer. Seattle has been a craft beer leader since the **1980s**, with **70+ breweries** in the city and over 170 in the area. I'm a beer lover, so get ready for lots of beer recommendations.

### ▸ THE WEATHER

Don't worry—it doesn't rain as much as you think! And when it does rain, it's more of a gentle drizzle than a heavy downpour. The city averages around 150 rainy days a year, but most of this is light rain or mist, contributing to the lush green landscapes Seattle is famous for.

Seattle's weather is actually a true celebration of the four seasons. Spring bursts with vibrant flowers and fresh produce, perfect for farmers' markets. Summer offers long, sunny days that are ideal for kayaking on Lake Union or hiking in the Cascades. Fall is cozy season perfect for live music in a dim bar. Winter, while mild, brings the opportunity for snow sports just a short drive away in the mountains.

I'll dive into more details about Seattle's weather and how to make the most of it in just a minute.

### ▸ THE PEOPLE

Have you heard of the so-called **"Seattle Freeze?"** It's this phenomenon where people are polite and helpful on the surface but might not go out of their way to make new friends quickly. Don't take it personally; it just takes a little longer to break the ice here.

That said, once you do connect with locals, you'll find them to be warm, inclusive, and

## QUICK FACTS

▸ **Language:**
English

▸ **Population:**
Over 750,000 (city proper)

▸ **Total Area:**
142 square miles

▸ **Currency:**
U.S. Dollar

▸ **Time Zone:**
Pacific Daylight Time (GMT -7)

▸ **Religion:**
Diverse (Christianity, Buddhism, Secular, etc.)

♥ If you see someone with an **SGTG Flamingo Sticker on their laptop - it is an open signal to SAY HI.**

Be a **travel friend magnet** by traveling with our **Solo Girls Travel Gear.**

Get yours at:
**alexa-west.com/travel-shop**

or scan this code ☞

passionate about their city. Seattle is a tech hub, so you'll meet plenty of people working in software, startups, and other high-tech industries. We call these people "transplants" and they are much more eager to make friends than the small-circle Seattle locals. I have resources to help you  break the freeze and make friends in a later chapter.

### ▸ THE CRIME

Seattle's **crime rates** are on par with many other major U.S. cities of similar size. So let me start by saying that Seattle is solo-girl-approved when it comes to safety, but like any big city, it has areas that require a bit more caution. **Property crimes** and **car break-ins** are the most common crimes here, especially in **Downtown**, the **International District**, and parts of **Rainier Valley**—be mindful here, especially after dark. I still love these spots, just better to visit during the day.

**Recent trends** show a rise in **motor vehicle thefts** and smash-and-grabs in high-traffic areas like South Lake Union and near trailheads. **Lock your car, park in well-lit areas**, and **keep valuables out of sight** to avoid any issues. **Avoid Little Saigon.** Drugs have hit this area hard.

All in all, Seattle remains **a pretty safe city,** particularly in vibrant neighborhoods like Capitol Hill, Fremont, Ballard, North Beacon Hill and The U-District. Always keep your phone charged, stick to well-lit streets, and trust your instincts. And don't worry, I have a **full safety section** for you later in this book to make sure you're prepared!

### ▸ THE EARTHQUAKES

Seattle is located in an earthquake-prone region known as the Pacific Ring of Fire. While major earthquakes are rare, it's good to be aware that they can happen. Most of the time, these seismic events are small and go unnoticed, but it's always smart to know what to do in case of a larger quake.

Let me teach you what we learn in middle school about what to do when an earthquake hits. The safest actions are to "Drop, Cover, and Hold On." This means dropping to the ground, taking cover under a sturdy table or desk, or standing in a doorway if no better protection is available, and holding on until the shaking stops. These simple steps can make a big difference in staying safe during an earthquake.

## ▸ THE GROWTH

Seattle is a city on the rise, with a rapidly growing population that's reshaping the urban landscape. Over the past decade, the city has seen a significant increase in new residents, mostly thanks to Amazon, Microsoft and the booming tech industries here, leading to a surge in townhouse developments and a revitalization of neighborhoods. This growth has brought new energy to the city, especially downtown, where a vibrant mix of new restaurants, shops, and more frequent happy hours are drawing people back into the heart of the city.

As Seattle expands, so does its social scene. The influx of residents has led to a boom in local businesses, creating a lively atmosphere across the city. Whether you're enjoying a craft cocktail during happy hour in Belltown or exploring the newly revitalized Pioneer Square, there's always something happening in Seattle. The city's ongoing transformation is bringing new life to downtown and beyond, making it an exciting time to visit or live here.

## ▸ THE VOLTAGE

Seattle uses standard U.S. voltage at 120 Volts / 60 Hz frequency. If you're traveling from outside North America, you might need a power adapter, but for those from the U.S. or Canada, you're all set.



Do you have any specific questions about Seattle? As your designated local guide, I'm here to help! Shoot me your questions at:

♥ @sologirlstravelguide / alexa@thesologirlstravelguide.com



Seattle is named after **Chief Si'ahl** (often anglicized as Chief Seattle), a respected leader of the **Duwamish and Suquamish tribes.** He played a key role in advocating for peaceful relations with early settlers in the area.

# Check the Weather

**Fun Fact:** Seattle gets about 37 inches of rain annually—less than cities like New York or Miami!

## When to Visit:

Seattle's climate is classified as a "marine west coast climate," which means cool, wet winters and mild, dry summers. While the rain might get a lot of attention, the truth is, Seattle's weather is varied and often beautiful. You'll experience misty mornings, crisp afternoons, and gorgeous summer evenings.

## A SEASONAL BREAKDOWN

### SPRING

Spring in Seattle is lovely, with temperatures ranging from the mid-40s to the 60s°F. The rain starts to taper off, and the city bursts into color as cherry blossoms and tulips bloom. It's a perfect time to explore parks and gardens. A light jacket will suffice during the day, but evenings can be cool.

### SUMMER

Summer is the best-kept secret of Seattle! From June to September, you'll enjoy warm, dry days with temperatures often in the 70s and low 80s°F. This is prime time for outdoor activities—hiking, kayaking, and rooftop happy hours. Rain is rare, but it's always wise to carry a light layer for cooler evenings.

### FALL

Fall brings a return of the rain, especially in October and November, but it also ushers in beautiful autumn colors. Temperatures range from the mid-40s to 60s°F. This is sweater weather at its finest, perfect for cozying up in a café or taking a scenic drive through the surrounding forests.

## WINTER

Winter is cool and wet, with temperatures typically between the mid-30s and 50s°F. While snow is rare in the city, the nearby mountains offer excellent skiing and snowboarding. Seattle's holiday season is magical, with festive lights and events all over town. Don't forget a warm coat for those chilly nights.

♥ **Alexa's Vote on the Best Time to Visit...**

### Spring (April-June)

The city is in bloom, the rain is less frequent, and it's an ideal time to explore Seattle's gardens and outdoor attractions without the summer crowds. And...

### Summer (June-September)

I'm not supposed to tell the whole world this but...Seattle has the most beautiful summers on this planet! Take a ferry ride on the Puget Sound, go camping, go for a hike around Mt. Rainer, have a picnic at the beach. The temps are amazing. You will need this guidebook, however, to out run the crowds.

## QUICK GUIDE TO SEATTLE WEATHER:

**"Official" Best Time to Visit:**
July- September

**Busiest Time to Visit:**
June - August

**High Season**
*(The Most Tourists):*
July - September

**LowSeason**
*(The Least Tourists):*
January - March

**Warmest Weather:**
July - August

**Coldest Weather:**
December - February

**Coldest Month:**
January

**Driest Month:**
July

**Rainiest Month:**
November

**Life is better with the right soundtrack, so I made you a Seattle Playlist.**

**Find it here!** ☞ 

# Seattle at a Glance

Ps. All the maps in this book were hand-made by Emy! And you can get this map as a print at: holaemilia.com/quick-links

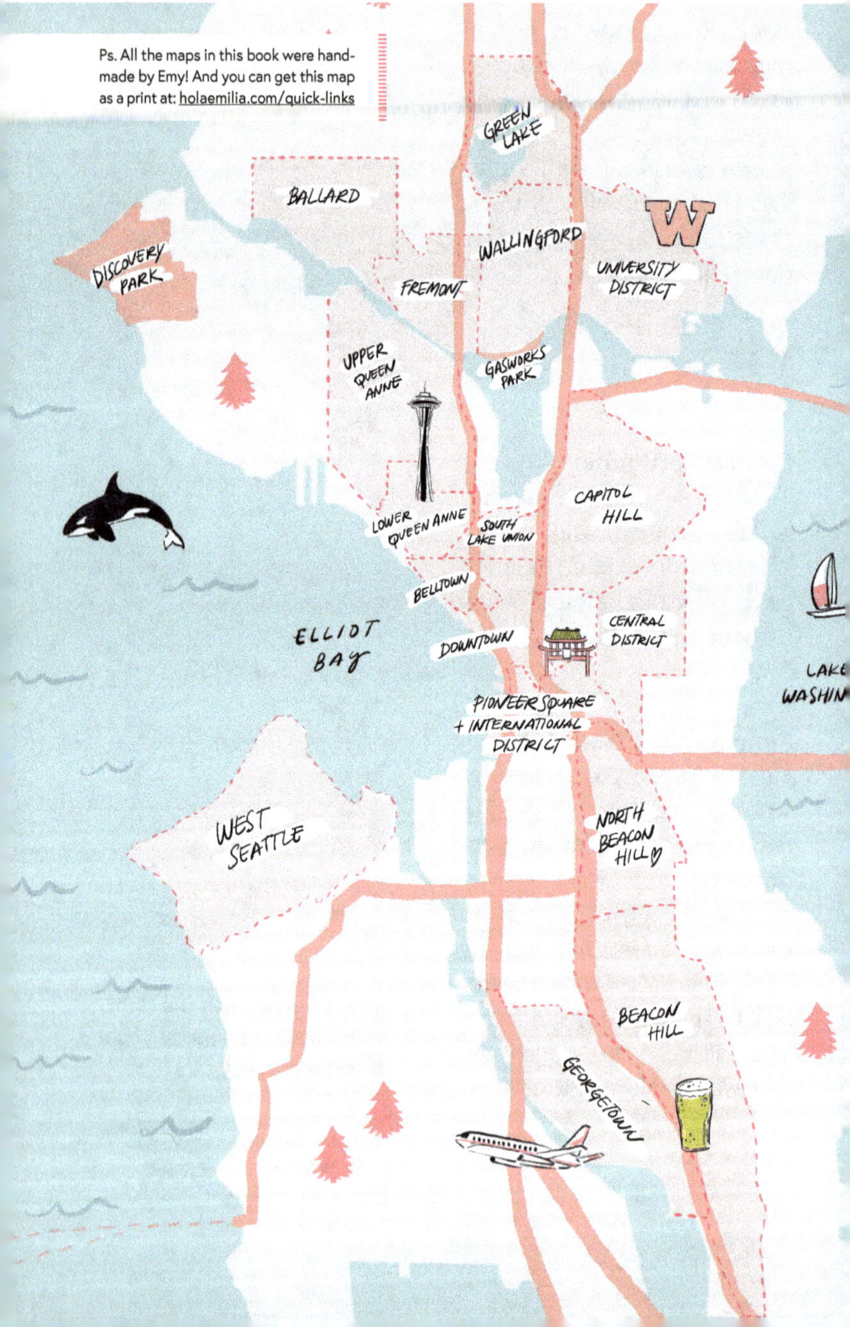

### ▸ DOWNTOWN

The heart of the action. From the iconic Pike Place Market to the city's sports stadiums, this is where locals and tourists collide. You'll find high-end shopping, cultural spots, and maybe even catch a glimpse of the famous fish-tossing at the market.

★Best for:
Shopping and touristy things

### ▸ BELLTOWN

Just north of Downtown, Belltown is where nightlife meets trendy urban living. Known for its swanky bars, top-notch restaurants, and indie music venues, it's a hub for young professionals and Seattleites looking to enjoy the city after dark. The streets are lined with cool boutiques, art galleries, and plenty of spots to grab a drink. Plus, it's a stone's throw from the waterfront, offering some killer sunset views over Elliott Bay.

★Best for:
Hotels and cocktail bars

### ▸ SOUTH LAKE UNION

Welcome to tech central. South Lake Union, often called SLU, is home to Amazon HQ and the heart of Seattle's tech boom. You'll find modern buildings, trendy coffee shops, and waterfront green spaces like Lake Union Park. The area is buzzing with young professionals, cyclists, and people enjoying happy hour along the lake. It's also a great spot to catch a seaplane or rent a kayak for an afternoon paddle.

★Best for:
Outdoor activities

### ♀ LOWER QUEEN ANNE + UPPER QUEEN ANNE = SEATTLE CENTER

This is where you'll find Climate Pledge Arena (home to NHL and WNBA), the Space Needle, Chihuly Gardens and More. Why not just one Queen Anne? The simple answer: hills. The hills are so steep that it feels like two worlds, upper and lower.

### ▸ LOWER QUEEN ANNE

Referred to as "Uptown" by some folks, Lower Queen Anne is home to the Space Needle, museums, Climate Pledge Arena and .... Amazon territory (or tech in general), where sleek, modern glass towers mix with bustling new restaurants and waterfront parks. The vibe is young professional.


Sporting events and touristy things

## ▶ UPPER QUEEN ANNE

Perched atop one of Seattle's steepest hills, Upper Queen Anne is a residential neighborhood known for its historic homes, tree-lined streets, and the most quienesstial views of Seattle's skyline from Kerry Park.

★Best for:
Pretty and peaceful strolls with retail.

## ▶ CAPITOL HILL

Gays, tattoos, dive bars! When I'm in the mood to throw on my most glittery and hit the town, Capitol Hill is always my go-to. It's the heart of Seattle's LGBTQ+ scene and where creativity runs wild. From drag shows to neon-lit dive bars, there's always something happening. By day, it's all about quirky coffee shops and a stroll through Volunteer Park, but by night, Capitol Hill transforms.

★Best for:
Quirky nightlife and karaoke
.

## ▶ CENTRAL DISTRICT

Lots of great food and drinks, but more residential. There are cute shops, grocery stores and restaurants galore, but the Central District isn't loud enough to get its own chapter. Instead, you'll find pieces of the Central District in the Cap Hill chapter; they're close enough together.

★Best for:
Moving here

## ♀ South Seattle

## ▶ INTERNATIONAL DISTRICT (ID) / CHINATOWN / PIONEER SQUARE

The city's multicultural hub, full of Asian groceries, dim sum, and hidden gems. ID and Pioneer Square offer a peek into Seattle's past, with cobblestone streets, old brick buildings, and the birthplace of the city's coffee culture.

★Best for:
Stuffing your face

## ▶ BEACON HILL

Up-and-coming and residential, Beacon Hill is a mix of quiet streets and amazing hidden restaurants. Jefferson Park is an idyllic location for a picnic with unbeatable views of downtown Seattle

Cozy neighborhood dining



## ▶ WEST SEATTLE

West Seattle feels like a beach town within the city. Alki Beach is a must for sunset views, beach bonfires, and casual strolls. With ferry access and a slower pace, it's the ideal escape without leaving the city limits.


Beach Walks

## ♀ North Seattle

## ▶ FREMONT & GREENLAKE

Known as "The Center of the Universe" (literally—it's on a sign), Fremont is your go-to for quirky, artsy vibes. There's a troll under a bridge, offbeat boutiques, and enough weird public art to keep your camera busy. Want to move to Seattle? This is the place if you're looking for community and excitement. The heart of the area is called Greenlake where you can eat, shop, walk, kayak, and intermingle with the community.


Feeling a sense of community

## ▶ U-DISTRICT

Home to the University of Washington, this area buzzes with college energy. Think cheap eats, indie coffee shops, and a youthful scene. Don't miss the cherry blossoms in spring! There is an upscale side to the U-District, however, called U-Village.


Student life and cheap eats

## ▶ BALLARD / PHINNEY RIDGE

Old Scandinavian fishing village meets trendy, hipster haven. Ballard boasts waterfront views, cool breweries, and a Sunday farmer's market that's worth the trip. And it's a trip. Ballard is about a 25-minute drive from Pike Place, but if you're moving here, I promise you'll spend time in Ballard. A connector neighborhood, Phinney Ridge, just a skip away, is a charming residential area, perfect for low-key vibes and parks with stunning city views.


Bougie dinners and cocktails

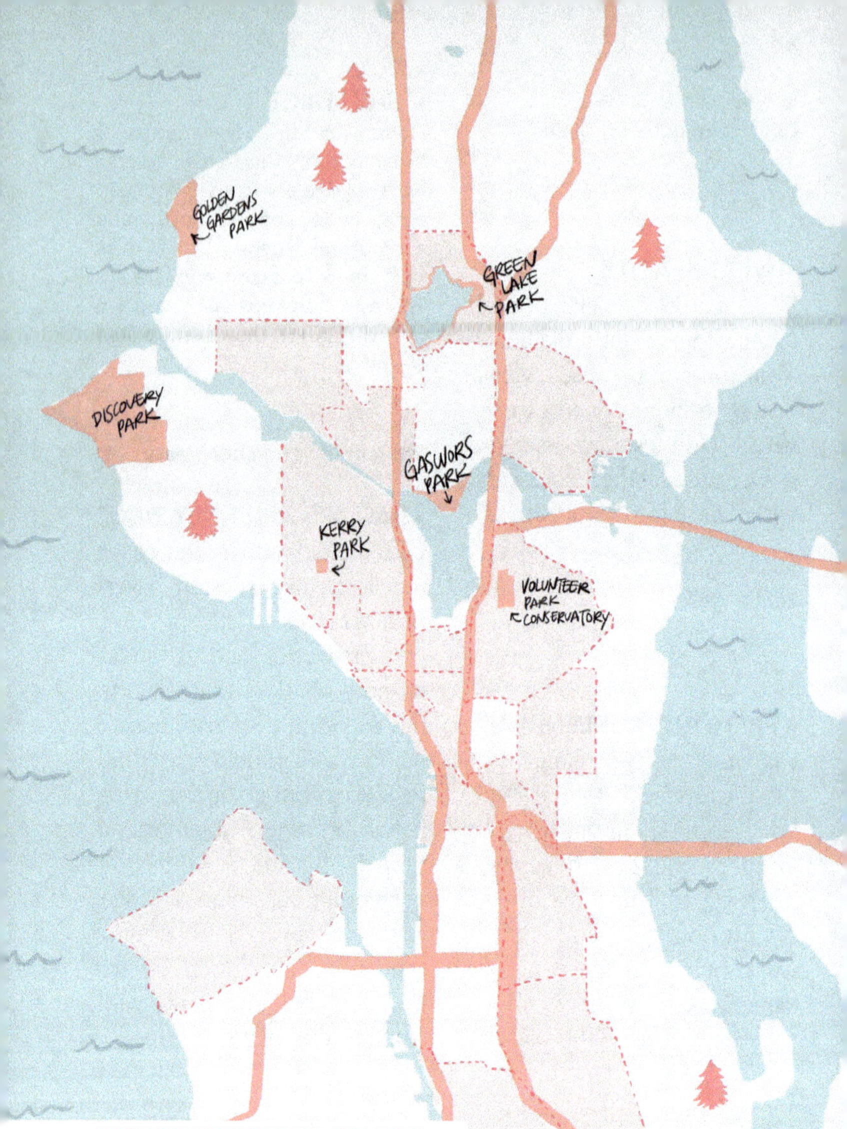




# Parks & Green Spaces in Seattle

My favorite thing to do in Seattle is to grab food to-go and spend time outside. This is just the tip of the iceberg, I have so many more greenspace recommendations at alexa-west.com/seattle

## ▶ GAS WORKS PARK

Opened in 1975, Gas Works Park is a 20-acre park on Lake Union's north shore built on the site of a former gasification plant. It offers remnants of old industrial structures alongside grassy hills and picnic areas, with sweeping views of the Seattle skyline and Lake Union.

♥ Pro Tip! The park is a prime spot for viewing the Fourth of July fireworks over Lake Union…. but it gets so packed!

☞ Learn More: seattle.gov/parks/find/parks/gas-works-park

## ▶ KERRY PARK

Established in 1927, Kerry Park is a small viewpoint located on the south slope of Queen Anne Hill. It's known for offering some of the best panoramic views of downtown Seattle, the Space Needle, and even Mount Rainier on clear days.

♥ Pro Tip! The park is especially beautiful at night when the city lights reflect off Elliott Bay.

☞ Learn More: seattle.gov/parks/find/parks/kerry-park

## ▶ GREEN LAKE PARK

Established in 1908, Green Lake Park is a 323-acre urban oasis centered around a 2.8-mile loop trail that wraps around Green Lake. It's a favorite among locals for walking, jogging, biking, and rollerblading, offering scenic views, abundant wildlife, and spots for picnicking. The park also has boat rentals and fishing piers and one of the biggest and busiest pickleball courts in the city.

♥ Pro Tip! Rent a kayak or paddleboard from the Greenlake Boathouse and explore the lake from the water.

✳ Fun Fact: Green Lake was carved by a glacier around 50,000 years ago.

☞ Learn More: seattle.gov/parks/find/parks/green-lake-park

## ▶ DISCOVERY PARK

Opened in 1973, Discovery Park is Seattle's largest green space, spanning 534 acres on the shores of Puget Sound in the Magnolia neighborhood. It features miles of walking trails, sandy beaches, and stunning views of the Olympic Mountains and Mount Rainier on clear days. The West Point Lighthouse, situated on the park's beach, is a popular spot for photographers and sunset watchers.

♥ Pro Tip! Take the Loop Trail, a 2.8-mile route that provides a great overview of the park's diverse ecosystems, from meadows to forests to coastal bluffs. Don't forget to explore the beach area for a peaceful retreat by the water.

✳ **Fun Fact:** The park is on the site of the former Fort Lawton, a military installation established in 1900. You can still see some of the historic buildings scattered throughout the park.

☞ Learn More: seattle.gov/parks/find/parks/discovery-park

## ▸ VOLUNTEER PARK CONSERVATORY

Opened in 1912, the Volunteer Park Conservatory is a Victorian-style greenhouse featuring five display houses filled with tropical plants, succulents, and seasonal flowers. It's in Volunteer Park, which also houses the Seattle Asian Art Museum and a historic water tower with panoramic views of the city.

♥ **Pro Tip!** Admission is free on the first Thursday and Saturday of each month, making it an ideal time to visit without a fee.

✳ **Fun Fact:** The conservatory's structure is made from original glass panels imported from Belgium over a century ago.

☞ Learn More: volunteerparkconservatory.org

## ▸ LEXI'S SECRET WATERFRONT SPOT IN BALLARD

If I print the name of this park inside this book I will be kicked out of Seattle. It's a small, lesser-known waterfront access point offering peaceful views of Elliott Bay and downtown Seattle, perfect place to bring a coffee and a journal and contemplate life.

Want the name? Send me a photo with you + this book on Instagram @SoloGirlsTravelGuide and Ill give you the GoogleMaps link.

## ▸ GOLDEN GARDENS PARK

Established in 1907, Golden Gardens Park is a stunning beachfront park located in Ballard, offering sandy beaches, rocky tide pools, and sweeping views of Puget Sound and the Olympic Mountains. It's a popular spot for beachgoers, picnics, and bonfires, especially during Seattle's warmer months.

♥ **Pro Tip!** Bring your own firewood and cozy up around one of the beach fire pits, which are available on a first-come, first-served basis.

✳ **Fun Fact:** Golden Gardens is home to some of Seattle's best tide pools—visit during low tide to spot starfish, crabs, and sea anemones.

☞ Learn More: seattle.gov/parks/find/parks/golden-gardens-park

# The Seattle Bucket List

**Hey! Tick the bucket list here** ☞ **Alexa-West.com/Seattle**

## TOP 10 THINGS TO DO

**01.** **Morning Breakfast Tour** with Savor Seattle

**02.** Stroll **Pike Place Market**

**03.** Ride **The Great Wheel**

**04.** Play **Pickleball** with the Locals

**05.** Visit **The Seattle Aquarium**

**06.** Take the Ferry to **Alki Beach**

**07.** **Hot Tub Boats** on South Lake Union

**08.** Attend a **Seattle Kraken Game** or **Seattle Sounders Game**

**09.** Join **Alexa's Glow Up Happy Hours**

**10.** Try a **Japanese Head Spa**

## TOP 10 RESTAURANTS

**01. Dick's Drive-In,** visit their locations in Capitol Hill, Belltown or Wallingford)

**02. Umi Sake House,** Capitol Hill

**03. Canlis,** Queen Anne

**04. DoughZone,** ID

**05. E-Jae Pak Mor,** ID

**06. El Legendario Mexican Restaurant,** Fremont

**07. Woodshop BBQ,** Capitol Hill

**08. Taylor Shellfish Oyster Bar,** Capitol Hill

**09. Westward,** Freemont

**10. Rochambeau,** Queen Anne

☞ **CONFESSION:**

I am gate-keeping my favorite restaurant in the entire city of Seattle because I don't want there to be huge lines when I want to go!

But if you **leave a review for this Seattle Travel Guide on Amazon and send me a screenshot on @SoloGirlsTravelGuide**…I'll reply with the restaurant name and my favorite thing to order.

# BEST SEATTLE TOURS

See the city and meet new people! I pick the best tours (even if you hate tours).

 **01. Morning Breakfast Tour with Savor Seattle**

**02. Seattle Under-ground Walking Tour** 

 **03. Whale and Orca Boat Tour near Seattle**

**04. Mount Rainier National Park Guided** 

 **05. Viking Beer Crawl in Ballard**

**06. 3-Hour City Tour** 

 **07. Gourmet Comfort Food Restaurant Tour**

**08. Visit Snoqualmie Falls and Hike to Twin** 

 **09. Woodinville: Wine Tasting Tour**

**10. Pike Place Market Plant-Based Food Tour** 

 **11. Pike Place Market: Ghost Hunting & Booze**

# ALEXA'S FAVORITE HOTELS

**01. W Seattle**, Downtown

**02. The Edgewater**, Belltown

**03. Cecil Bacon Manor**, Capitol Hill

**04. Maxwell Stay Pineapple**, Lower Queen Anne

**05. Pali Hotel**, Downtown

Quick links to these hotels ☞ 

# MUST-VISIT MUSEUMS

**01.** The Museum of Flight

**02.** Seattle Art Museum (SAM)

**03.** MoPop Museum (Music)

**04.** Chihuly Garden and Glass

**05.** Burke Museum of Natural History and Culture

***FUN FACT!**

**Washington State is officially the UFO capital of the United States!** It ranks #1 for the highest number of UFO sightings per capita, with reports coming in from every corner of the state—from the peaks of Mount Rainier to the streets of Seattle! The modern UFO era even began here, with the famous 1947 sighting over Mount Rainier.

# Best Farmers & Vintage Markets in Seattle

## U-DISTRICT FARMERS MARKET

What to Expect: Seattle's longest-running farmers market, offering a wide variety of fresh, local produce, artisan cheeses, and flowers. This is a staple for those looking to experience the best of Seattle's farm-to-table culture.

⊙ When: Saturdays, 9 AM – 2 PM

♥ Location: University Way NE

## FREMONT SUNDAY MARKET

What to Expect: An eclectic mix of vintage finds, crafts, antiques, and local food vendors. A vibrant and quirky market perfect for treasure hunters and those seeking one-of-a-kind items.

⊙ When: Sundays, 10 AM – 4 PM

♥ Location: 3410 Evanston Ave N

## CAPITOL HILL FARMERS MARKET

What to Expect: A great urban farmers market featuring fresh produce, local meats, and artisanal goods. The market has a community feel, perfect for grabbing fresh ingredients or a quick local bite.

⊙ When: Sundays, 11 AM – 3 PM

♥ Location: Broadway & Pine

## SODO FLEA MARKET

What to Expect: Specializing in vintage goods, SODO Flea offers a wide range of retro and antique furniture, clothing, and collectibles. This is a must for those looking to add unique flair to their home.

⊙When: 2nd Saturday of every month, 10 AM – 4 PM

♥ Location: 3701 7th Ave S

## BALLARD FARMERS MARKET

What to Expect: A lively market known for its fresh seafood, organic produce, and local crafts. Ballard is a foodie haven, and this market is a reflection of that, offering the best of local flavors and artisan goods.

⊙ When: Sundays, 9 AM – 2 PM

♥ Location: Ballard Ave NW

## SOUTH LAKE UNION SATURDAY MARKET

**What to Expect:** A seasonal market offering food trucks, fresh produce, and handmade crafts. It's a smaller market with a relaxed vibe, great for a quick Saturday stroll while grabbing fresh bites.

⊙ **When:** Saturdays, May through September, 11 AM – 4 PM

⚲ **Location:**  410 Terry Ave N

## SEATTLE ANTIQUE MARKET

**What to Expect:** Located near Pike Place Market, this spot is a hidden gem for those in search of unique vintage treasures, including furniture, home decor, and quirky collectibles. It's a perfect stop for travelers looking to bring home a piece of Seattle's history.

⊙ **When:** Open daily, 10 AM – 6 PM

⚲ **Location:** 1400 Alaskan Way (across from the Seattle Aquarium)

## LATE NIGHT VINTAGE MARKET

**What to Expect:** Hours of spectacular vintage shopping! A wonderful selection of unique finds! Not the cheapest, but the most magical. (gosh I sound like a hippie, but it's true.)

⊙ **When:** Wed – Fri, 3 PM – 12 AM, Sat - Sun 12PM –2AM

⚲ **Location:** 517 E Pike St.

## THE BEST BREWERIES IN SEATTLE

01. Cloudburst Brewing, Downtown
02. Fast Fashion, SoDo
03. Mirage, Georgetown
04. Single Hill, Ballard
05. Fremont Brewing, Fremont
06. Holy Mountain Brewing, Interbay
07. Georgetown Brewing, Georgetown
08. Ravenna Brewing Co., U- District (ish)
09. Yonder Cider + Bale Breaker Brewing Co., Ballard
10. Fair Isle Brewing, Ballard (If you like sour beer)

**BONUS!**

My favorite bottle shop with local beers on tap and in cans is **Full Throttle Bottles** in Georgetown (this place is super solo-female-friendly, albeit super dim and divey).

Plus! You can buy signed copies of my books here.

♥ IG: @fullthrottlebottles

# Best Happy Hours in Seattle

To make dining alone less awkward, I love to find a restaurant with a bar where I can order food, have a drink and possibly meet some new people.

## FOOD-SPECIFIC

### UMI SAKE HOUSE

My #1 go-to happy hour in Belltown. Sit at the bar or the sushi bar, order a "sushi set" and a draft Sapporo beer.

✳ Happy Hour: Daily, 4 PM–6 PM, and late-night 10:30 PM–close

✳ Specials: Discounts on sushi sets, draft beers, and select small plates

📍 Location: Belltown

### MATT'S IN THE MARKET

Listen, this place is typically pricey (and worth every damn penny) so take advantage of the happy hour! You can only sit at the bar, so no crazy views, but crazy delicious food fresh from the market below. This place is iconic.

✳ Happy Hour: Monday–Friday, 5 PM–6 PM

📍 Location: Belltown, Pike Place Market

### THE COLUMBIA TOWER CLUB

Perched atop Seattle's tallest building, the Columbia Tower Club offers stunning views that make for a memorable happy hour. Expect a bit of an adventure getting there—you'll navigate a vertical maze with two separate elevators to reach the 75th floor. It's worth it for the panorama alone. Order the Smash Burger during happy hour (4 PM–6 PM), then stick around for a co-working session with a breathtaking backdrop.

✳ Happy Hour: Monday–Friday, 4 PM–6 PM

📍 Location: Downtown

🌐 Visit: Alexa-West.com/Seattle for a tutorial on how to find your way up.

### THE MATADOR

A sexy little spot, The Matador serves up spicy margaritas and delicious Tex-Mex.

* **Happy Hour:** Daily, 4 PM–6 PM, and 10 PM–1 AM

* **Specials:** $6 house margaritas, $5 tacos, and $1 off drafts

♀ **Location:** Ballard and West Seattle

## VINDICKTIVE BAR & WINGS WINGS

Trivia on Tuesday, 99-cent wings on Wednesdays and karaoke on Thursdays. It's easy to make friends here and the food is great.

* **Happy Hour:** Monday–Friday, 3 PM–6 PM

* **Specials:** you must try the wings on wednesdays!

♀ **Location:** Belltown

## OSTERIA LA SPIGA

This Italian spot in Capitol Hill is known for its vibrant atmosphere, amazing pasta, and cozy happy hour. Coming solo? Sit and eat at the bar.

* **Happy Hour:** Daily, 4 PM–6 PM

* **Specials:** $7 wines, $5 beers, $8 cocktails, discounted small plates

♀ **Location:** Capitol Hill

## PERIHELION BREWERY

This neighborhood gem is a laid-back hangout best enjoyed on the outdoor patio, preferably a seat with a fire! Wonderful food and dessert.

* **Happy Hour:** Monday–Friday, 3 PM–6 PM

* **Specials:** $1 off pints, discounted appetizers

♀ **Location:** Beacon Hill

## BIG TIME BREWERY & ALEHOUSE

Seattle's oldest brewpub is popular with the university crowd and offers rotating craft beers (and wood-fired pizzas, too).

* **Happy Hour:** Monday–Friday, 3 PM–6 PM

* **Specials:** $1 off pints, discounted pizzas

♀ **Location:** U-District

### DRINK-SPECIFIC

## FREMONT BREWING

Cozy and warm, even if you're outside underneath the heated lamps. The atmosphere is great, the beer is fantastic.

* **Happy Hour:** Tuesday–Thursday, 4 PM–6 PM

* **Specials:** $1 off beers

♀ **Location:** Fremont

♥ **Did you know?**
Seattle was the first major city in the U.S. to have a female mayor!

## BATHTUB GIN & CO.

A speakeasy hidden away in an alley, offering a sophisticated yet relaxed ambiance. The bartenders are known for their well-crafted cocktails.

✳ **Happy Hour:** Daily, 5 PM–7 PM

✳ **Specials:** $8 rotating cocktails, $5 house wine, $3 off select appetizers

📍 **Location:** Belltown

## RUMBA

If you're into rum cocktails and Caribbean vibes, Rumba is the place to be. (Weird) date-night approved!

✳ **Happy Hour:** Monday–Friday, 5 PM–6 PM

✳ **Specials:** $7 house daiquiris, $1 off all cocktails, discounted small plates

📍 **Location:** Capitol Hill

## THE TIN TABLE

Woman-owned, located inside the Century Ballroom! Come have dinner and drinks before you dance!

✳ **Happy Hour:** Daily 5-6 PM

✳ **Specials:** Deals on drink plus discounted menu items like their Floozy Burger.

📍 **Location:** Capitol Hill

# MOVIE-THEMED MUSTS

### 01. GREY'S ANATOMY

**Adventure:** Visit Kerry Park for that classic Seattle skyline shot featured in nearly every season. Then, stop by the "Seattle Grace Hospital" exterior, which is actually KOMO Plaza near the Space Needle. End at Joe's Bar (aka The Edgewater Hotel) for a drink, the inspiration for the bar where the doctors hang out.

### 02. TWILIGHT

**Adventure:** Drive out to Forks, WA, and explore Twilight filming locations like Bella's house, the lush forests, and La Push beaches.

### 03. 10 THINGS I HATE ABOUT YOU

**Adventure:** Head to Gas Works Park, where the famous paintball scene was shot. Then visit the Fremont Troll.

### 04. SLEEPLESS IN SEATTLE

**Adventure:** Stroll through Pike Place Market and dine at The Athenian, both featured in Sleepless in Seattle.

### 05. FRASIER

**Adventure:** Stroll through Volunteer Park and see its iconic conservatory, a backdrop in Frasier scenes.

# Free Things to Do in Seattle

## PIKE PLACE MARKET

Established in **1907**, Pike Place Market is one of the oldest continuously operating public farmers' markets in the United States. It features fresh produce, seafood, crafts, and over 200 unique shops. Visitors can watch the famous fish-throwing at Pike Place Fish Co. and explore local artisans.

☉ **Best Time to Visit:** Early weekday mornings to avoid the crowds.

⊕ **Learn More:** pikeplacemarket.org

## SEATTLE FREE WALKING TOUR

Go on a guided tour through historic and cultural neighborhoods like Pioneer Square and Pike Place Market, providing insights into Seattle's history and hidden gems. Tours typically last around 90 minutes.

♥ **Pro Tip:** While the tour is free, tipping is encouraged, as guides rely on donations to keep the program running.

✴ **Fun Fact:** Pioneer Square is considered the birthplace of Seattle, dating back to 1852 when the city's founders settled there.

⊕ **Learn More:** walk-seattle.com

## SEATTLE CENTRAL LIBRARY

Designed by architect Rem Koolhaas and opened in 2004, the Seattle Central Library is an 11-story glass and steel building that has become a modern architectural landmark.

♥ **Pro Tip:** Visit the 10th-floor Reading Room for panoramic views of downtown Seattle, and check the events calendar for free workshops, author talks, and art exhibits.

✴ **Fun Fact:** The library's glass exterior is made up of 9,994 panels, making it a striking addition to the Seattle skyline.

⊕ **Learn More:** spl.org

## VISIT THE FREMONT TROLL

Installed in 1990 as a part of an art competition, the Fremont Troll is a quirky public art installation located beneath the Aurora Bridge in the Fremont neighborhood. It was inspired by the Scandinavian folklore of trolls living under bridges. The

**18-foot-tall troll** clutches a real Volkswagen Beetle, making it a unique photo spot and a quirky landmark in Seattle.

♥ **Pro Tip:** Combine your visit with a stroll through the Fremont neighborhood, known for its eclectic shops, street art, and the nearby Fremont Sunday Market.

⊕ **Learn More:** fremont.com/troll

## PLAY PICKLEBALL

Ya'll, I travel the world with my Pickleball Paddle! It's the best way to meet new people and stay active while traveling! Seattle is home to numerous outdoor and indoor pickleball courts, making it easy to join a game of the sport that originated right here in **Washington in 1965.** Pickleball is a mix of tennis, badminton, and ping-pong, perfect for staying active and meeting new people.

♥ **Pro Tip:** Visit Alexa-West. com/Seattle to find a list of "open-play" PickleBall times and locations.

✳ **Fun Fact:** The sport was named after **Pickles**, a dog that used to chase the ball during early games.

♥ **Hiii! Emy here...**

Did you know that when I'm not creating travel guides or recording podcast episodes with Lexi... I'm usually taking photos or making travel-inspired art?

Find everything I create, including Seattle paintings and art, at:

holaemilia.com/quick-links

Or just scan this code ☞ 

# Seattle Girl Specific

## SEATTLE SOCIAL

**Listen, the idea of solo travel isn't to be solo forever.**
The idea is to go into the world and find your people. Let
me help you find your people. Or since our mascot is a
flamingo - let me help you find your flock.

### ☆ This Book Has Magic Powers...

See a girl with this book? Say hi!  Want to make friends?
**Keep this book visible**, either on your dinner table or
next to you at the park. It's a green light for other girls
in the flock to approach.

### ☞ Look for Friends in the Wild...

Often, girls in the flock find each other by carrying the
Solo Girls Travel Guide tote bag or displaying the SGTG
Flamingo sticker on their water bottle or laptop. Look
for it when you're out. See all the merch at alexa-west.
com/shop

### ♥ Communities to Join

▸ **Girls in Seattle Facebook Group:**
facebook.com/groups/girlsinseattle

▸ **Solo Girls Travel Facebook Group:**
facebook.com/groups/sologirlstravelguide

**Need Seattle advice ASAP?**
**Want me to book your trip?**
w alexa-west.com/services 

 Ps. I made you a **Seattle music playlist.**

# Top 5 Safe Girl Spots

I'm gonna make this city feel real safe and cozy for you, my babe. I'm connecting you to local businesses that make me feel safe. I've worked with the owners of the places below and they know to expect my solo girls - whether you're here for a date, popping in solo or want to show your girlfriends around - you're super safe here.

## RACHEL'S GINGER BEER
Pike Place, p. 173

A welcoming space with lots of natural light and a breeze in Post Alley, this is the perfect place to pop in for a cool-down after wandering Pike Place or the U-Village.

♥ IG: @rgbsoda

☺ Hours: Mon–Thu 10-8 PM, Fri–Sat 10-9 PM, Sun 10-8 PM

## CLOUDBURST BREWING
Downtown, p. 79

Just a short walk from Pike Place, cozy yet breezy, this is a safe space to have a beer and ponder life. Not super social, but very calming energy for a brewery!

♥ IG: @cloudburstbrew

☺ Hours: Mon–Thu 12-10 PM, Fri–Sat 12-11 PM, Sun 12-9 PM

## VINDICKTIVE BAR & WINGS
Belltown, p. 30

The owners, two brothers, are often hanging around and seem to really enjoy their staff. The vibe is just so upbeat and welcoming. Sit at the bar, befriend strangers.

♥ IG: @vindicktive_wings

☺ Hours: Mon–Thu 3-11 PM, Fri 3-12 AM, Sat 12-12 AM, Sun 12-10 PM

## FULL THROTTLE BOTTLES
Georgetown, p. 154

A beer spot. My home-away-from-home. I come here even when I'm not in the mood for a beer but just want to chit chat with the bartenders (and end up drinking a beer). Very "Always Sunny" vibes.

♥ IG: @fullthrottlebottles

☺ Hours: Mon–Fri 12-8 PM, Sat 12-7 PM, Sun Closed

# Solo Girl Approved Date Ideas

**Ps. Self love is love, too. Take your self out on a solo date.**

## PICNIC & PADDLING ON LAKE UNION

Rent a kayak or paddleboard from Moss Bay Kayak, Paddle Board, and Sail Center in South Lake Union. From here, you can explore the calm waters of Lake Union, paddling past the iconic houseboats, and watch seaplanes fly over your head and land next to you.

***Food:** Lunch or dinner at I Love Sushi on Lake Union with beautiful views of the lake from their cozy patio—perfect for continuing the waterfront vibe of your date.

**♥ Commitment Level: Mid**
Unless you can paddle away really fast, you're committed to hanging out on the water; this allows you to have some physical distance while hanging out.

**♥ Alternative Location:** Rent from Agua Verde Paddle Club and eat at Agua Verde Café in the U-District

## COFFEE, BOOKS, & ICE CREAM AT U-VILLAGE

Grab a coffee at Joe Coffee Bar and take a leisurely stroll through University Village, an open-air shopping center with charming pathways and cozy vibes.
Bookstore Stop: Wander into Third Place Books, where you can browse shelves together, share book recommendations, and discover hidden literary gems.

***Ice Cream:** Treat yourselves to a scoop (or two!) at Molly Moon's—their local flavors are perfect for sharing as you explore.

**♥ Commitment Level: Low**
No dinner involved. No sitting down unless you want to. Public space, plenty of people around.

## PICNIC AT GASWORKS PARK

Pick up picnic essentials like fresh sandwiches, salads, and snacks from PCC Community Market in Fremont or a poke bowl from Fremont Bowl.

✳ **Food:** Spread out a blanket at Gasworks Park and enjoy your meal with a view of the Seattle skyline and boats passing by on Lake Union.

♥ **Commitment Level: Low**...You can leave at any time. No bill to pay.

## FERRY, BEER, & SUNSET AT ALKI BEACH

Hop on the ferry from downtown Seattle to West Seattle. Walk or jump in a free shuttle (Route #775 runs along Alki Beach) to Alki Beach. Have a drink at **Future Primitive Beach Bar's** outdoor area, facing the water. Walk hand-in-hand along Alki Beach, taking in the sea breeze.

✳ **Food:** Head to **Cactus Alki Beach** for shrimp tacos and margaritas with a waterfront view.

✳ **Sunset:** Find a cozy spot with a blanket and watch the sun dip behind the city, turning the skyline golden.

♥ **Commitment Level: High**
If you've come over here together on the ferry, then hypothetically you need to return together on the ferry. You can always Uber, but it will be expensive going over the West Seattle Bridge. Make this a second-date spot.

## ART & TAPAS IN CAPITOL HILL

Visit the **Seattle Asian Art Museum** in Volunteer Park, where you can explore beautiful art and take in the city views from the nearby Volunteer Park Conservatory.

✳ **Food:** Head to **Osteria La Spiga** afterward for an intimate meal of Italian tapas and pasta, paired with a glass of wine. Their warm, inviting atmosphere makes for a perfect romantic evening.

♥ **Commitment Level: Mid**
This is a more structured and intimate date.

## KENMORE SEAPLANE OVER THE CITY + DINNER ON THE WATER

Take off with a **Kenmore Seaplane** from Lake Union for a thrilling aerial tour of Seattle, complete with sweeping views of the city, Puget Sound, and Mount Rainier.

✳ **Dinner:** After landing, head to **Westward** on Lake Union for waterfront dining. Enjoy fresh seafood like oysters or their famous clam chowder while taking in the beautiful sunset.

♥ **Commitment Level: High**
You're in a plane together but honestly the views are so beautiful and your adrenaline will be so high that it doesn't even matter if you don't like this person.

## BREWERY HOPPING IN GEORGETOWN

Hop around the smallest little beer district with amazing food. Here's your **Brewery Bucket List:** Great Notion, Mirage Brewing, Jellyfish Brewing and Full Throttle Bottles. Drink water in-between.

**✳Food:** Grab a cheap(ish) chirashi bowl at Donburi Station or go blow your mind at Ciudad.

**♥ Commitment Level: Low.**
You can Uber out of there at any time.

## LUNCH + SPA DAY AT BANYA 5

Adventure: Start with a healthy lunch at Portage Bay Café in South Lake Union, where you can build your own delicious bowls and enjoy fresh, organic ingredients.

**◗ Relax:** Head to Banya 5, a Russian-style spa, for an afternoon of hot and cold plunge pools, steam rooms, and sauna relaxation. Finish with a warm herbal tea in the lounge area.

**♥ Commitment Level: High**
...and half-naked. You'll be in your swimsuit and you want to be relaxed. Make this a 2nd or 3rd date.

## THE SMITH TOWER

Your date starts on the first floor with some Seattle history from the 20's. Then take the elevator up to the 35 floor. Welcome to the bar and observatory with 360 degree views of the city.

**✳Food:** Come for happy hour (and plan to eat dinner here.)

**♥ Commitment Level: Mid**
You are on the 35th floor but it's just dinner. Might be awkward waiting for the elevator if you want to leave, though.

**♥ Want to find the love of your life in Seattle?**

I did. And this is how...

I made you a totally free Dream Partner Visualization.

Go to:
alexa-west.com/free-things

or scan this code ☞ 

---

📷 ♥

**SEATTLE IGS TO FOLLOW**

@SecretSeattle_

@SeattleMag

@SeattleFoodScene

@VisitSeattle

@SeattleRefined

@Seattle.food.diva

# Seattle Wellness + Beauty Guide

Consider making a beauty appointment as an adventure pairing! Museum and massage? Waxing and wine? Hair and happy hour?

## Central

### SKIN TREATMENTS:

**Bellora Medical Aesthetics, _Downtown Seattle_**

Specializes in Botox, fillers, facials, microneedling, and more for skin rejuvenation.

♥ IG: @belloramedicalaesthetics

### HAIRCUT AND COLOR:
**Blonde and Gold Salon, _Queen Anne_**

Known for balayage and blonding techniques and color correction services.

♥ IG: @blondeandgoldsalon

### HAIRCUT AND COLOR:

**Gary Manuel Salon, _Downtown_**
The place that has been recommended to me most by Seattle girls.

♥ IG: @garymanuel

### A GOOD BLOWOUT:
**Sugar and Shears, _Capitol Hill_**
Get a trim, as well. Then hit the town hot. Make an appointment well in advance.

♥ IG: @sugarandshears

### NAILS AND FACIALS:

**Leila Klein, _Belltown_**
A one-on-one spa experience for classy manicures, pedicures and facials.

♥ IG: @leilaklein10

### WAXING:

**Sugar Plum Spa, _South Lake Union_**
Offers organic sugaring for a natural waxing alternative, ideal for sensitive skin.

♥ IG: @sugarplumsugaring

## Southend

### WAXING, FACIALS, AND LASHES:
**Treat YourSelf Studios, _Columbia City_**
Known for customized facials, lash lifts, and sugar waxing.

♥ IG: @treatyourselfstudios

### CHEAP TRIM:
**Vy's Salon, _North Beacon Hill_**
Offers affordable haircuts, starting at $20.

♥ Website: vyshairsalon.com

**MASSAGE:**
**Little Red Day Spa, _SoDo_**
Offers customizable couples massages in private rooms with soaking tubs.

♥ IG: @littlereddayspa

**Thai Massage**
Trained in Thailand, this massage therapist works out of his house and is in high demand! For that reason, I'm keeping him kinda secret. The key to unlock it and get his info?

♥ Leave us a review for this book on Amazon, send me a screenshot on Instagram @ SoloGirlsTravelGuide and I'll give you my guy. $170 per hour and worth it.

## ⚲ North End

**HEAD SPA:**
**RS Head Spa, _Greenlake_**
Offers Japanese head spa treatments with scalp massages, deep cleansing, and a neck and shoulder massage.

☆Girls in Seattle
Happy Hour Spa Edition:
Tuesday & Thursday between 11 AM - 3 PM, use **Code GIRLSINSEATTLE for 10% off.**

♥ IG: @rsheadspa

**SPIRITUAL BATH HOUSE, MASSAGES, AND REIKI:**
**Sacred Rain Healing Center, _Ballard_**
Offers shamanic healing baths, reiki energy work, and deep tissue massages.

♥ IG: @sacredrainhealing

**FLOAT THERAPY:**
**Float Seattle, _Greenlake_**
Features sensory deprivation tanks with salt water for deep relaxation.

♥ IG: @floatseattle

## ⚲ West Seattle

**HAIR:**
**La Luna Hair Studio**
This is my girl. She is great with blondes and fun colors and the queen of bangs. Consider a Seattle makeover.

♥ IG: @lalunaonalkisalon

**EYELASHES:**
**Skylash Studio _West Seattle_**
Specializes in classic, hybrid, and volume lash extensions.

♥ IG: @skylashstudio3280

**BOTOX:**
**Forever Young Aesthetics**
Your go-to for botox and injections in a boutique-medical setting.

♥ IG: @foreveryoungseattle

## SKIN TREATMENTS
### Aesthetix Beauty

Leave looking 20 years younger with microneedling, peels and lasers.

⊕ Visit: aesthetixbeautyseattle.com

## MASSAGES + FACIALS:
### Head to Toe Day Spa

Massages, facials and a sauna make for the perfect rainy spa day.

♥ IG: @headtotoedayspaws

## BATH HOUSES
### Banya 5, *South Lake Union*

A Russian-style bathhouse with steam rooms, cold plunges, and a saltwater hot tub.

♥ FB: facebook.com/Banya5

### Olympus Spa, *Lynnwood*

A women-only Korean-style spa with jjimjilbang rooms, hot and cold pools, and exfoliating body scrubs.

♥ IG: @olympusspa_lynnwood

### Sacred Rain Healing Center, *Ballard*

Offers ritual baths with herbs and essential oils for emotional and spiritual balance.

♥ IG: @sacredrainhealing

♥ Have beauty recommendations? Lemme know @SoloGirlsTravelGuide



# Check the Calendar

See if you can align your visit with any of these events…

## BEST FOOD & DRINK SEASONS:

### ▸ WOODINVILLE WINE SEASON

The best time to visit Woodinville is during harvest season in **September and October** when vineyards are in full swing and the scenery is stunning.

♥ Where to Drink: **Chateau Ste. Michelle** offers guided tours and often hosts musical guests in their outdoor amphitheater. **DeLille Cellars** is perfect for enjoying Bordeaux-style blends in a cozy setting.

♥ Where to Eat: Try **The Herbfarm** for a multi-course, farm-to-table experience, or **The Commons Kitchen & Bar** for comfort food with a local twist.

★ Adventure: Woodinville is **25 miles** from Seattle (30-45 minutes by car). Uber fares run about $40-$70. Stay at **Willows Lodge** and explore during **Harvest Wine Weekend** for special tastings and live music.

Want to go Wine Tasting but just for the afternoon? Join this tour ☞

▶ **SALMON SEASON**

The best time for fresh wild-caught salmon is from May through September, coinciding with the annual salmon runs in the Pacific Northwest.

📍 **Where to Eat:** I highly recommend you go to the **fishmongers in Pike Place market** and ask for **"Salmon Jerky"**; it will change your salmon-loving life. Also, try **Matt's in the Market** for salmon cooked how god intended. Want to buy some salmon and cook at home? Order it from the fishmongers and have them throw it for ya'.

★ **Adventure: Take the Bainbridge Island Ferry** to the Olympic Peninsula. Drive the **US-101** which offers stunning views of the Hood Canal and forests. Your destination is **Hama Hama Oyster Saloon** for local seafood. Or go fishing for wild salmon and **All Star Fishing Charters**, based out of Seattle and Edmonds, know the best place to look for em.

🌐 **Website:** allstarfishing.com

## ▶ DUNGENESS CRAB SEASON

Peak season for Dungeness crab is from December through February, although it can extend into spring in some areas.

📍 **Where to Eat:** Check out **The Walrus and the Carpenter** in Ballard for fresh crab dishes, or head to **Etta's Seafood** near Pike Place Market for their famous crab cakes.

*Confession: My freezer is always full of Dungeness Crab clusters from Costco. Best prices ever.*

★ **Adventure:** Head to **Port Angeles** in mid-October for the **Dungeness Crab & Seafood Festival**, where you can enjoy freshly caught Dungeness crab, live music, cooking demos, and local seafood vendors. Check out crabfestival.org for event details.

Or book a guided crabbing trip with **Seattle Fishing Charter**, departing from **Shilshole Bay Marina** in Ballard. They provide all the gear and guidance you need for a successful crabbing adventure in the waters of Puget Sound.

🌐 **Website:** seattlefishingcharter.com.

## ▶ CHANTERELLE MUSHROOM SEASON

Chanterelles are best harvested from late summer through early fall, typically August through October. I just bought an off-grid cabin in the woods surrounded by chanterelles! The best places to find them are in the dense, mossy forests of the Olympic Peninsula, Mount Rainier National Park, and the Cascade Mountains.

 **Nell's Restaurant** in Green Lake, or head to **The Pink Door** in Pike Place Market, known for incorporating chanterelles into their pasta and risotto.

★ Adventure: Head to the **Olympic Peninsula** or **Mount Rainier National Park** for a chanterelle foraging trip. Look for them **1-3 days after a rain**, in dense, mossy forests under coniferous trees like firs and hemlocks. Stop by **Finnriver Cidery in Chimacum** afterward for a cider flight. For safe foraging, bring a guidebook or hire a local expert.

## ▶ MOREL MUSHROOM SEASON

Morels are most commonly found from April through June, especially after a forest fire the previous year. Prime locations for morel hunting include the eastern slopes of the Cascade Mountains, particularly in areas with recent burns (like forests after fires), and in the Gifford Pinchot National Forest and the Methow Valley.

♀ **Where to Eat:** Try **Spinasse** in Capitol Hill, which frequently highlights seasonal morels in their refined Italian dishes or again, **Nell's in Greenlake**. Keep an Eye Out: Morels often **pop up on pizza menus** across Seattle.

★ Adventure: Head to **Gifford Pinchot National Forest** or **Methow Valley** for a morel foraging trip. Focus on areas with recent burns for the best chance of finding these elusive fungi. Camp at **Pearrygin Lake State Park in Methow Valley** and cook your harvest over a campfire.

## ▶ FRESH HOP BEER SEASON

**Mid-September to mid-October.**

Did you know that 75 percent of the hops for all U.S. beers are grown in Washington? Year-round, beer is typically made using dried hops, but during fresh hop season, breweries use hops right after harvest, creating uniquely vibrant beers that I nerd out on.

♀ **Where to Drink:** Visit **Chuck's Hop Shop** in the Central District for a wide selection of fresh hop beers from local breweries. Or head to **Fremont Brewing.**

★ Adventure: Take a road trip to Yakima, Washington's hop-growing hub. Visit **Bale Breaker Brewing Company**, which is surrounded by hop fields, and try their fresh hop brews right from the source. Plan your trip around the **Fresh Hop Ale Festival in Yakima**, held in early October, to sample beers made with freshly harvested hops from dozens of local brewers. (Yakima Airbnbs on <u>alexa-west.com/yakima</u>.)

► JANUARY
## Lunar New Year in the International District
*January/February*

Celebrate Lunar New Year with dragon and lion dances, martial arts, and traditional music filling the streets of the International District.

★ **Best Places to Celebrate: Hing Hay Park** is the center of festivities, with performances and celebrations all around.

♀ **Where to Eat:** Enjoy dim sum at **Dough Zone**, or savor authentic Taiwanese dishes at **Henry's Taiwan.** For a classic experience, try **Tai Tung**, Seattle's oldest Chinese restaurant.

♥ **Pro Tip:** Arrive early for the dragon dance, then explore local shops for festive treats and traditional gifts.

⊕ Learn More: seattlechinatownid. com

► FEBRUARY
## Northwest Flower & Garden Festival

The largest garden show on the West Coast, offering stunning display gardens, educational seminars, and a sprawling marketplace for everything plant-related. It's a burst of greenery in the middle of winter, perfect for inspiration as you plan your spring garden.

★ **Best Places to Celebrate:** Washington State Convention Center, Downtown Seattle.

♥ **Pro Tip:** Come early to beat the crowds, and bring a notebook to jot down tips from expert gardeners. Don't miss the plant market for rare finds and unique garden décor.

⊕ Learn More: gardenshow.com

► MARCH
## Skagit Valley Daffodil & Tulip Fields, *March & April*

Kick off spring with the bright yellow daffodils of **Skagit Valley** in March, followed by the famous **Skagit Valley Tulip Festival** in April. Wander through golden daffodil fields as a prelude to the stunning rainbow of tulip blooms that take over the valley in early to mid-April, transforming the landscape into a floral paradise.

☺ **Best Time to Visit:** Mid to late March for daffodils, and early to mid-April for peak tulip season. You might even catch a few early tulips in late March.

♀ **Where to Go:** Visit **Roozengaarde Display Garden** for daffodils and continue to Roozengaarde and **Tulip Town** for the tulips. Both spots offer curated displays and perfect photo ops.

♥ **Pro Tip:** Pack a picnic to enjoy

among the flowers, and visit on a weekday for fewer crowds and better light in the early morning hours.

⊕ Learn More: <u>tulipfestival.org</u>

## ► APRIL
### <u>Alexa's Birthday Specials</u> - *on my website.*

### <u>Seattle Restaurant Week,</u>
*April & October*

Twice a year, Seattle Restaurant Week offers three-course meals at some of the city's best restaurants at a fraction of the price. Scroll through a list of over 165 participating locations and book meals with set-prices.

♥ **Pro Tip:** Make reservations early—these deals draw crowds. It's also a perfect time to try new spots you've been eyeing without breaking the bank.

⊕ Learn More: <u>srweek.org</u>

## ► MAY
### <u>Seattle International Film Festival (SIFF)</u>, *May-June*

North America's largest film festival, featuring hundreds of screenings from international films and local indie projects, all over the city.

★ **Best Places to Celebrate:** SIFF Cinema Uptown, Egyptian Theatre, and other theaters that sound fancy.

♥ **Pro Tip:** Get a pass, see as many films as possible.

⊕ Learn More: siff.net

## ► JUNE
### Fremont Solstice Parade

To celebrate the start of summer, the **Fremont Solstice Parade** is famous for its body-painted cyclists, larger-than-life floats, and wild, imaginative performances. Expect naked people.

★ **Parade Viewing:** Find a spot near **Fremont Brewing** on N 34th Street—it's a great place to grab a beer and watch the parade roll by. Or, stand near the **Fremont Troll** on N 36th Street for a classic Fremont vibe and a view as the parade winds through the neighborhood.

★ **After the Parade:** Stick around for the **Fremont Fair**, where you'll find local artisans, food vendors, and live music at the heart of the neighborhood.

♥ **Pro Tip:** Arrive early to snag a seat at **Fremont Brewing's** outdoor patio before the parade starts—it fills up fast but offers a perfect view.

⊕ Learn More: <u>fremontfair.com</u>

The next time you're nervous to do something big, <u>listen to this song</u> ☞ 

## Seattle Pride Parade & Festival

Seattle goes all out for Pride. The parade is epic, filled with colorful floats, lively music, and the best people watching you will ever see.

★ **Parade Viewing:** Find a spot near **Westlake Park** at 4th Avenue and Pine Street for a central view with lots of energy. Or, head to **Denny Way and 4th Avenue** for a less crowded spot to see the parade as it begins.

★ **After Party:** Capitol Hill is the place to be after the parade, with **Cal Anderson Park** turning into a hub of activity and impromptu celebrations. **Neumos on Pike Street** is a great venue for post-parade shows and events, while **Unicorn/Narwhal on 11th Avenue** offers drinks and dancing with a quirky vibe.

♥ **Pro Tip:** Bring tequila in your purse, and a water bottle.

⊕ **Learn More:** seattlepride.org

## ► JULY
## Capitol Hill Block Party

A three-day music festival that takes over Capitol Hill, with multiple stages featuring local and national bands, food trucks, and art installations.

★ **Best Places to Celebrate:** Pike/Pine corridor—basically, if it's not loud, you're in the wrong spot.

♥ **Pro Tip:** Get a weekend pass to fully immerse yourself in the experience.

⊕ **Learn More:** capitolhillblockparty.com

## ► AUGUST
## Seafair *(July-August)*

Seattle's signature summer celebration, featuring hydroplane races on Lake Washington, the Blue Angels air show, and a series of parades and community events.

★ **Best Places to Celebrate:** For the best views of the Blue Angels, head to Lake Washington (Genesee Park is a good area) early to secure a spot along the shore at any park.

♥ **Pro Tip:** Afterwards, don't miss the **Torchlight Parade** downtown for a family-friendly evening of fun.

⊕ **Learn More:** seafair.org

## ► SEPTEMBER
## Bumbershoot
*(Labor Day Weekend)*

Bumbershoot is Seattle's iconic music and arts festival, featuring a mix of big-name acts, local talent, and art installations. It's a multi-day celebration of creativity that attracts crowds from all over.

★ **Best Places to Celebrate:** Seattle Center, especially near the main stage and art installations.

♥ **Pro Tip:** Purchase your tickets early, as they often sell out. Consider taking public transportation to avoid parking hassles, and be sure to explore the art exhibits and food vendors in between sets.

⊕ Learn More: bumbershoot.com

## ▸ OCTOBER
## Oktoberfest
*(Late September/October)*

Raise a stein and join the festivities at Seattle's Oktoberfest celebrations. From traditional German beer and bratwurst to live music and lederhosen contests, it's a lively celebration of all things Bavarian.

★ **Best Places to Celebrate:** neighborhood, especially around **Lagunitas Brewing Taproom** and **Peddler Brewing Company**, where beer gardens and festivities spill into the streets.

♥ Pro Tip: There is a **stein-holding competition...**

⊕ Learn More: fremontoktoberfest. com

## Seattle Restaurant Week
*(see April)*

## ▸ NOVEMBER & DECEMBER
## Seattle Girl Fest

In 2025, it's just an idea. Next year, maybe it will be a fall festival. Want to help? Join my newsletter at alexa@alexa-west.com for updates and ideas.

## WildLanterns at Woodland Park Zoo *(November to January)*
**Woodland Park Zoo** transforms into a glowing dreamscape with massive lanterns and twinkle lights. Wander through illuminated paths under the glow of snow leopards, sea creatures, and vibrant flowers—perfect for a cozy winter date night.

♥ Pro Tip: Visit on a weeknight for fewer crowds. Grab a hot cocoa and take your time exploring the lights. Bring mini wines in your purse.

🎟 Cost: $30-$35 per person.

◷ Hours: Open nightly from **4:00 PM to 9:00 PM.**

♥ Location: Woodland Park Zoo, Seattle, WA

⊕ Learn More: zoo.org/wildlanterns

## New Year's at the Space Needle
Get ready for a spectacular fireworks show launched from the Space Needle.

★ Best Places to Watch the Fireworks:
**Rooftop Bars:** Head to The Nest at the Thompson Seattle, or **Mbar** for some of the best rooftop views in town.
**Queen Anne:** Kerry Park offers sweeping views of the Space Needle and the Seattle skyline. It's popular, so get there early to secure a spot.

♥ Pro Tip: Check out Alexa-West. com/Seattle when it comes time to find Seattle NYE events.

# Seattle Sports Seasons & Game Day Itineraries

### SEATTLE SEAHAWKS (NFL)

September through January, with playoffs extending into February if the team qualifies at Lumen Field

◷ **Game Day Itinerary:** Take the Light Rail to Stadium Station. Eat and pre-game at Hatback Bar & Grille.

♥ **Pro Tip:** Want a great view of the game without breaking the bank? The Hawks Nest seats in the north end zone offer affordable tickets and an unbeatable crowd vibe.

☞ **See the Schedule:** seahawks.com/schedule

### SEATTLE MARINERS (MLB)

April through September, with potential playoffs in October at T-Mobile Park

◷ **Game Day Itinerary:** Take the Light Rail to Stadium Station. Walk to Fast Fashion Brewing in SoDo for a local beer before the game. On your way to the stadium, keep an eye out for food trucks selling Seattle Dogs—a hot dog topped with cream cheese and grilled onions.

♥ **Pro Tip:** Want to be social while you watch the game? Head straight to The 'Pen—the lively bar area in center field right by the bullpen. You'll find a variety of beers, batch cocktails, and mixed drinks flowing here, along with Edgar's Cantina, a popular standing-room bar that fills up fast.

☞ **See the Schedule:**
mariners.com/schedule

## SEATTLE KRAKEN (NHL)

October through April, with playoffs extending into June if the team qualifies at Climate Pledge Arena

◎ **Game Day Itinerary:** Take the Monorail from Westlake Station to Seattle Center—it drops you right by the arena. Head to Queen Anne Beerhall for a spacious spot with plenty of local beers and giant pretzels before walking over to the game. At the game, the cheapest beers in the arena are the "Beer of the Week" specials at stands near Section 11 on the main concourse.

♥ **Pro Tip:** Head to the American Express Lounge for a DJ, great vibes, and a view of the rink. It's a popular spot for socializing.

☞ **See the Schedule:**
nhl.com/kraken/schedule

## SEATTLE SOUNDERS FC (MLS)

February through October, with playoffs extending into November at Lumen Field

◎ **Game Day Itinerary:** Take the Light Rail to International District/Chinatown Station and walk a few blocks to Lumen Field. Eat dinner at Dough Zone then have pre-drinks at Elysian Fields.

♥ **Pro Tip:** Join the March to the Match from Occidental Park, where fans gather to walk together to Lumen Field, chanting and waving scarves.

☞ **See the Schedule:**
soundersfc.com/schedule

## SEATTLE STORM (WNBA)

May through September, with playoffs in September and October at Climate Pledge Arena

◎ **Game Day Itinerary:** Take the Monorail from Westlake to Seattle Center. Dine at The Masonry and walk to the game. Arrive early to catch player warm-ups.

☞ **See the Schedule:**
storm.wnba.com/schedule

✳ **FUN FACT!**

Seahawk's fans have the Guiness World Record for the loudest crowd roar at a sport stadium. I wonder if they've been debunked by Swifties yet!

# Safety and Crime in Seattle

Hey there, let's talk about staying safe in Seattle. Just like all other places on the planet, explore well-lit areas, don't walk alone at night, watch your drink, and stay sober enough to remain vigilant.

Then understand that Seattle is a safe city...but one with a drug problem, particularly downtown around Third Avenue, in Little Saigon (an area I don't recommend in this book) and parts of Pioneer Square. That drug problem has led to an increase in **Property Crimes** in Seattle, such as:

⚠ **Car Break-Ins:** This is common in touristy spots like downtown, Capitol Hill, and near popular parks like Discovery Park and Golden Gardens. If you're driving, don't leave anything valuable in your car where it's visible—thieves are always on the lookout. Keep your things out of eye-sight and you'll be fine.

## AREAS TO USE CAUTION

⚠ **Pioneer Square:**
While historic and interesting during the day, Pioneer Square can be less safe at night, particularly due to its higher rates of drug activity and homelessness.

⚠ **Third Avenue (between Pike and Pine):** This area can be sketchy, especially after dark. It's known for loitering and some drug-related activities.

⚠ **Parts of Belltown:** Although Belltown is a trendy neighborhood, certain blocks can feel unsafe, especially late at night.

## SEATTLE'S SAFEST AREAS

♥ **Capitol Hill:** A lively, walkable neighborhood known for its vibrant nightlife and diverse community. While it's busy, it's generally safe, especially around well-trafficked areas like Broadway and Pike/Pine.

♥ **Queen Anne:** A picturesque neighborhood with stunning views and a family-friendly vibe. It's quiet and safe, making it a great area for solo travelers.

♥ **Ballard:** This neighborhood has a small-town feel with plenty of trendy shops, restaurants, and cafes. It's safe and popular with young professionals and families.

♥ **Fremont:** A very, progressive family-friendly neighborhood with low crime.

♥ **North Beacon Hill:** The main strip of Beacon Hill is lined with intimate bars and restaurants that draw a "let's have dinner and be in bed by 10pm" kind of crowd. Good people, safe place.

♥ **Green Lake:** A peaceful, residential neighborhood centered around a beautiful lake, perfect for walking, jogging, or just relaxing. Always someone around to help.

☞ **Visit Alexa-West.com/safety**

## Safety To-Do's

◯ **Carry your Birdie Alarm**

◯ **Carry pepper spray**

◯ **Share your live location with a friend at all times**

♥ **Do you have The One-Way Ticket Plan yet?**

For my entire breakdown on how to stay safe while traveling the world or your own country, read **Chapter 6: Safety and Scary Things** in my new book, The **One-Way Ticket Plan: Find and Fund Your Purpose While Traveling the World.**

# How to Get Around Seattle

### #1 Way to Get Around:
## LINK LIGHT RAIL

The Link Light Rail is Seattle's top public transportation option, connecting key areas of the city, including the airport, downtown, Capitol Hill, and the University District.

💵 **Cost:** $3 Flat Rate.

♥ **Pro Tip:** The Link is clean, and reliable. It's the best way to avoid traffic and get around quickly. Avoid traveling late at night, especially when alone, or at least have your pepper spray in your hand just in case…sometimes we've got some crazies on the link. Don't worry, there is security.

## WALKING

Seattle is walkable, especially within neighborhoods like Capitol Hill, Ballard, and Fremont. The hills can be tough, though! Bring comfy shoes. I don't recommend stilettos in this city.

♥ **Pro Tip:** Stick to well-lit streets, especially at night. Downtown and Pike Place Market are great for strolling during the day; **avoid Pioneer Square after dark.**

## UBER & LYFT

Convenient for when public transit isn't an option.

💵 **Cost:** $10-$45 for most city rides

## SEATTLE YELLOW CAB

A reliable taxi service with an app that makes hailing a cab easy. Taxis are available citywide, especially downtown and at the airport.

💵 **Cost:** I've found that Seattle Yellow Cab is often cheaper than Uber!

♥ **Pro Tip:** Download the Seattle Yellow Cab App

### Best Avoided:
## LIME SCOOTERS

2-wheeled Lime scooters are available for rent throughout the city, but they can be dangerous, especially on Seattle's hilly and often wet streets. I've had multiple friends hit by cars or hit a bump and break something.

💵 **Cost:** $1 to unlock, $0.36 per minute.

♥ **Pro Tip:** Only use if you're super sober on a well-lit road. Avoid hills. I approve of using scooters at Alki Beach in West Seattle.

## LIME BIKES

These electric-assist bicycles can be rented citywide.

☞ **Cost:** $1 to unlock, $0.36 per minute.

♥ **Pro Tip:** Lime bikes are a great way to explore flatter neighborhoods like South Lake Union and the waterfront. Wear a helmet and use bike lanes whenever possible.

## STREETCAR:

### South Lake Union & First Hill Lines

Seattle's streetcars connect downtown with South Lake Union and Capitol Hill, offering a smooth ride through key neighborhoods.

☞ **Cost:** $2.25 per ride.

♥ **Pro Tip:** The streetcar is a great way to get between South Lake Union and downtown or Capitol Hill and the International District. Avoid riding late at night when streets are less populated.

⊕ Learn more: seattlestreetcar.org

### Quick Access to Seattle Center

## MONORAIL

The Seattle Monorail connects downtown's Westlake Center with Seattle Center, home to attractions like the Space Needle and MoPOP.

☞ **Cost:** $3 one-way.

♥ **Pro Tip:** The Monorail is a fun and quick way to get to the Seattle Center. It's especially convenient if you're staying downtown and want to visit the Space Needle or the Chihuly Garden and Glass.

⊕ Learn more: seattlemonorail.com

## BUSES (King County Metro)

Seattle's bus system covers the entire city and surrounding areas.

☞ **Cost:** $2.75 per ride

♥ **Pro Tip:** Avoid buses that pass through Pioneer Square's "free zone" late at night, as they can attract a rougher crowd.

⊕ Learn more: kingcounty.gov

☞ Download the OneBusAway which provides real-time arrival info to avoid long waits.

☞ Find transportation tutorials at Alexa-West.com/Seattle

☞ **Hey! Planning to take public transportation in Seattle?**
Use their official trip planning app!
⊕ tripplanner.kingcounty.gov

**Find it here** ☞ 

# To and From the Airport ✈

Getting to and from Seattle-Tacoma International Airport (SEA) is straightforward, but your choice of transportation can significantly impact your budget. Here's what you need to know:

## OPTIONS FOR GETTING TO AND FROM THE AIRPORT:

### LINK LIGHT RAIL

🎟 **Cost:** $3 per ride

🕓 **Time:** 35-40 minutes to downtown Seattle

☞ **What to Expect:** The Link Light Rail is the most affordable option for getting to and from the airport. It's safe, clean, and runs frequently. The Light Rail connects SEA directly to downtown Seattle, making it a convenient choice.

♥ **Pro Tip:** Avoid peak travel hours to ensure you get a seat and travel comfortably.

**Emilia and I made an Airport Light Rail tutorial for you - get it on Alexa-West.com/Seattle**

### UBER/LYFT

🎟 **Cost:** $25-$40 for a 30-minute ride (non-peak hours)

🕓 **Time:** 20-30 minutes to downtown Seattle

☞ **What to Expect:** Uber and Lyft are the most convenient options for getting to and from the airport. They offer door-to-door service, and you can avoid the hassle of public transportation or waiting for a shuttle.

♥ **Pro Tip:** Use your travel credit card to take advantage of any Lyft or Uber credits you may have. Compare prices with Seattle Yellow Cab, which is often cheaper for airport rides.

# How to Budget for Seattle

As of 2024, Seattle is one of the most expensive cities in the USA. But don't worry—I'm here to show you how to explore this beautiful city without breaking the bank. Whether you're on a shoestring budget or looking to splurge, there's a Seattle experience for you.

When it comes to traveling, there are always 3 spending routes you can take:

## BUDGET 

 Stay in budget hotels or hostels, enjoy happy hour specials, explore free attractions, and use public transportation.

## BALANCED

Mix budget-friendly activities with a few splurges, such as staying in mid-range hotels or Airbnbs, dining out at local restaurants, and mainly using rideshares.

## BOUGIE

Indulge in luxury hotels, gourmet dining, private tours, and spa treatments. But don't miss out on the city's local charm—take a ferry ride, visit the iconic Pike Place Market, and treat yourself to some Seattle classics.

♥ **TRAVEL EXPERT ADVICE:** Don't book your hotels, flights or transportation with a debit card. Use a travel credit card and start collecting points and miles to use towards free travel. This is how I travel for free.

Search "credit" on my blog at Alexa-West.com/Blog.

## BUDGET 💵

**$90-$150 per day**

→ **Meals:** $25 (street food, food trucks, cheap eats)
→ **Coffee & Snacks:** $5 (local coffee shops)
→ **Transportation:** $10 (Link Light Rail, bus pass)
→ **Activities:** $10 (free attractions like parks, self-guided walking tours)
→ **Drinks/Nightlife:** $10 (happy hour deals, dive bars)

---

## BALANCED 💵 💵

**$175-$250 per day**

→ **Meals:** $60 (sit-down casual restaurants, local favorites)
→ **Coffee & Snacks:** $15 (specialty drinks and pastries)
→ **Transportation:** $20 (mix of public transit and occasional Uber/Lyft)
→ **Activities:** $40 (museum admissions, guided tours)
→ **Drinks/Nightlife:** $40 (cocktails at trendy spots, local breweries)

---

## BOUGIE 💵 💵 💵

**$350+ per day**

→ **Meals:** $120+ (fine dining, multi-course meals, wine pairings)
→ **Coffee & Snacks:** $30+ (brunch cafes, artisanal bakeries)
→ **Transportation:** $50+ (private car services, Uber/Lyft rides everywhere)
→ **Activities:** $100+ (private tours, wine tasting, special experiences)
→ **Drinks/Nightlife:** $100+ (upscale bars, cocktail lounges, club entry)

## ON A BUDGET?

### TIPS TO SPEND LESS IN SEATTLE

💵 **Visit during the shoulder season** (spring and fall) when accommodation prices are lower, and crowds are smaller.

💵 **Use public transportation** — the Link Light Rail is your best friend for getting around the city without spending a fortune.

💵 **Take advantage of happy hours** — many restaurants and bars offer discounted drinks and appetizers in the early evening.

💵 **Explore free attractions** — there are plenty of parks, markets, and scenic spots that don't cost a dime.

**Your biggest expenses will be:** Accommodation + Dining Out

Everything else can be adjusted to fit your wallet.

Okay my love, you're ready to start exploring and planning. ♥

## CHAPTER ONE

# Where to Stay in Seattle

**Where you stay will make or break your trip!** Because this city is so spread out, it's essential to carefully select where you stay based on what you want to experience. Pick the right home base, and you'll have a seamless adventure — pick wrong, and you might spend more time commuting than sightseeing.

But remember, you don't need to pick a hotel until after you've read this whole guide — circle the adventures that stand out to you and fit your budget. You can circle back later once you've got a bucket list.

**STEP 1:**

## Prioritize Your Adventures

Get your highlighter ready and mark the experiences you don't want to miss.

**STEP 2:**

## Pick Your Hotel with Your Adventures in Mind

I've organized your options by neighborhood, so you can match your adventures to hotels easily.

Whether you're here for a weekend or a longer stay, this chapter will guide you through the best places to select as your home-base.

## HOTELS BY NEIGHBORHOOD

Links to all these hotels + bonus Airbnbs at:

Alexa-West.com
/Seattle-Hotels

## CENTRAL SEATTLE

📍 *Downtown*

### THOMPSON SEATTLE

Stay here for a swanky rooftop bar and waterfront views. Thompson Seattle is home to Nest rooftop bar, a popular spot for both locals and tourists, serving craft cocktails with some of the best sunset views in the city. The hotel throws social parties (you're invited) and happy hours - making it easy to socialize! Ps. Their brunch is great.

💸 Budget: $$$

♥ IG: @thompsonseattle

## W SEATTLE

This is the hotel I chose for Emilia and I when we first visited Seattle together and began planning this book. We stayed in the Presidential Suite with a jacuzzi tub, a Peloton bike, a lounge area and sweeping 180 degree views of the city. Even if you don't spring for the suite, every room here is luxury. The location is perfect. You're a short walk from Pike Place Market, the Seattle Art Museum, and some of the city's best dining. After a day of exploring, head back for a cocktail at the Living Room Bar (inside the hotel) before hitting the town.

🎟 **Budget:** $$$$

♥ **IG:** @wseattle

## FAIRMONT OLYMPIC HOTEL

Opened in 1924, the Fairmont Olympic isn't just a place to stay—it's like a mini city of its own, with a spa, an indoor pool, and a lounge bar. Stay here if you're the traveler who enjoys plush robes, room service, and a little vintage glamor without giving up modern comforts. And for a treat, pop by George (their restaurant) for Northwest dishes, or hit up The Founders Club (their bar) to sip something fancy before heading out.

🎟 **Budget:** $$$$

♥ **IG:** @fairmontolympic

## HOTEL THEODORE

Originally opened in 1929 as the Roosevelt Hotel, this historic building has been thoughtfully updated, blending Art Deco details with contemporary design. Its location on Pine Street places you a few blocks from Pike Place Market, the flagship Nordstrom store, and the bustling retail core of downtown. Throughout the hotel, you'll find curated collections of local art, reflecting Seattle's rich history of innovation and craftsmanship—from aviation to music. The on-site restaurant,

Rider, is known for its Pacific Northwest cuisine!



♥ IG: @theodoreseattle

## GREEN TORTOISE HOSTEL SEATTLE

This one's for the true budget traveler. The location is unbeatable — right next to Pike Place Market — but be prepared for an outdated, vintage vibe with old carpet. It's a social spot with organized walking tours and communal dinners, great for meeting other travelers, but just don't expect a modern design or feel. Embrace the Seattle Grunge!

🎫 Budget: $

♥ IG: @greentortoiseseattle

## 📍 *Belltown*

I recommend staying in Belltown, by the way.

## THE EDGEWATER

The Edgewater is Seattle's only true waterfront hotel. With cozy fireplaces, log cabin vibes, and sweeping views, staying here feels like floating on the Puget Sound. The on-site Six Seven Restaurant is a must-visit, known for its fresh seafood like Dungeness crab and wild salmon, with floor-to-ceiling windows that let you soak in the waterfront scenery. It's just steps away from Pike Place Market and the waterfront, but you might find yourself too busy gazing at the Olympic Mountains from your room to leave.

🎫 Budget: $$$$

♥ IG: @theedgewater

## ACE HOTEL SEATTLE

Ace Hotel Seattle is one of those places that feels like a home away from home, with an eccentric charm that's hard to find elsewhere. Housed in a 1909 building in Belltown, this spot blends vintage vibes with modern minimalism. You'll notice the little details—art-filled walls, a communal breakfast area, and a front desk staff that feels more like a group of friendly locals ready to point you to the best hidden spots in the neighborhood. It's just a short walk from Pike Place Market!

🎫 Budget: $$

♥ IG: @acehotelseattle

## THE SOUND HOTEL

If you plan to go out for happy hours and cocktails, The Sound is in the perfect location. The rooftop terrace offers jaw-dropping views of the Space Needle and skyline, ideal for an evening drink as the sun sets over the city. Best of all, the soundproof walls ensure you get a great night's sleep no matter what party is happening in Belltown. P.S. They even have rooms with Pelotons, making it easy to squeeze in a workout—perfect for those rainy Seattle days.

💳 **Budget:** $$$

♥ **IG:** @thesoundhotel

## 📍 South Lake Union

### CITIZENM SEATTLE SOUTH LAKE UNION

Designed for the tech-savvy traveler, this Dutch-owned chain is known for its "smart" rooms, where everything from the lighting to the TV is controlled through a touchpad. Located near South Lake Union, the hotel puts you within walking distance of the Seattle Aquarium, the Museum of History and Industry (MOHAI), and the waterfront.

💳 **Budget:** $$

♥ **IG:** @citizenm

### MOXY SEATTLE

This pet-friendly spot in South Lake Union will make it easy for you to meet other travelers (and their pets). The cozy, industrial-chic rooms come with smart tech features like streaming TVs, and the open lobby is more like a living room with board games, cozy seating, and a full bar. You're just a short walk from the tech hubs of Amazon and Google, or a quick hop on the SLU Streetcar to downtown.

💳 **Budget:** $$

♥ **IG:** @moxyseattledowntown

### DENNY PARK HOTEL

I'm here for the soaking tubs. Absolute heaven after a day of running around town. If you can, spring for a room with a Space Needle view—it's worth it. You're right by South Lake Union, so you've got easy access to downtown and the waterfront. Ps. this hotel was previously called "Pan Pacific".

💳 **Budget:** $$$$

🌐 **Web:** DennyParkHotel.com

## 📍 Lower Queen Anne

### MAXWELL MEDITERRANEAN INN

Located a bit north in Lower Queen Anne but just a hop away from Belltown, this place is ideal for those who like to settle in and stay a while. The building itself has a classic charm, and each room comes with a kitchenette, perfect for prepping your own meals or snacks between adventures. Don't miss the rooftop deck with panoramic views of the Space Needle and Elliott Bay.

🏷 **Budget:** $$

🌐 **Web:** mediterranean-inn.com

## STAYPINEAPPLE HOTEL

Emilia and I stayed here while writing this book and wow, did we sleep well! Their Sleep Experience with European-style duvets, ultra-soft Staypineapple pillows, and mattresses make you feel like you're sleeping on a cloud. The location is ideal after a day of walking everywhere! Just a quick stroll from Seattle Center and Climate Pledge Arena, making it a perfect base for catching a game, concert, or exploring the Space Needle and MoPOP. It's also pet-friendly! I love that you have grocery stores nearby, helping you keep costs down with snacks and drinks for picnics or snacks to take back to your room.

🏷 **Budget:** $$$

♥ **IG:** @staypineapple

# Capitol Hill

Cap Hill (that's what the cool kids call it) doesn't have many hotels but on my website, you can find Airbnbs that I've selected for you based on walkability

☞ Alexa-West.com/Seattle-Hotels

## SEATTLE GASLIGHT INN

For a stay that feels like stepping into the past—without sacrificing modern comfort—**Seattle Gaslight Inn** is a fantastical retreat. Nestled in the heart of Capitol Hill, this historic gem from 1907 offers rooms dripping with vintage charm (think stained glass windows and antique furnishings), but with all the modern perks you love. Lounge by the outdoor pool in the summer or cozy up by the fire when it's chilly. With Seattle's best coffee spots and bars just a few steps away, you're never far from the action, but you'll feel like you're worlds away in this peaceful, eclectic oasis.

🏷 **Budget:** $$$

♥ **IG:** @the_seattle_gaslight_inn

## CECIL BACON MANOR

Want a homey feel? Sty at this historic Capitol Hill mansion where homemade breakfast is served every morning. For the nature lover, you're located right next to Volunteer Park, giving you immediate access to morning strolls, The Asian Art Museum and the delectable French Guys Bakery!

💸 **Budget:** $$$

♥ **IG:** @baconmanor

## SOUTH SEATTLE

### SoDo / Pioneer Square

**SONDER RAILSPUR**

Sonder RailSpur offers a unique, modern stay right in the heart of Pioneer Square, one of Seattle's oldest and most historic neighborhoods. You're close to Lumen Field for Seahawks games, T-Mobile Park for Mariners games, and tons of great bars and restaurants. Perfect for sports fans and history buffs alike. Ps. I typically tell you to avoid this area at night, but Sonder RailSpur is on the very southern border of Pioneer Square practically in SODO, so I consider it comfortable for a solo traveler.

💸 **Budget:** $$$

♥ **IG:** @sonderstays

### Georgetown

**GEORGETOWN INN**

Georgetown Inn is a female-friendly, safe, and cozy choice nestled in one of Seattle's most unique neighborhoods. The staff here is known for their warm hospitality, making solo travelers feel right at home. You'll be steps away from divey bars, art galleries, and local breweries. It's a great pick if you want to experience a more authentic side of Seattle, far from the crowds and tourist spots but close enough to easily reach downtown.

💸 **Budget:** $$

♥ **IG:** @georgetowninnseattle

## NORTHERN SEATTLE

### University District

**STAYPINEAPPLE AT UNIVERSITY INN**

This is the best place to stay when visiting the University of Washington or just looking to explore the U District. You're close to the UW Arboretum, the Burke Museum, and tons of great coffee shops. It's a lively area with a young vibe, perfect for exploring on foot. When you return, you will sleep like a princess and they have rooms with jacuzzi tubs!

 The very first night I met my boyfriend, he picked me up from this hotel and took me to Ravenna Brewing. *Memories.*

💳 Budget: $$

♥ IG: @staypineapple

## GRADUATE SEATTLE

Start your morning with a stroll through the University District. Grab a coffee at Cafe Allegro. Then, wander through the UW campus and take in the stunning architecture. Have lunch at Thai Tom's. Shop along "the ave". Then head back to the hotel and make your way up to The Mountaineering Club, the hotel's rooftop bar with views of Mount Rainier, Lake Union, and the Seattle skyline.

💳 Budget: $$

🌐 Web: graduatehotels.com/seattle

## ♀ *Ballard*

Hey, you'll find plenty of airbnbs in Ballard but just one hotel, so I'll put my favorite airbnbs on my website at alexa-west.com/seattle-hotels

## HOTEL BALLARD

If you're in town to be single and go on dates, this is your Bumble hub—you won't find a better location for meeting new people and exploring the best of Seattle. Hotel Ballard is for solo women who want a stylish, first-class stay in one of Seattle's most vibrant neighborhoods. The rooms are top-notch in both comfort and facilities, and the hotel has an amazing full-service gym and pool—a rarity in boutique stays. With great proximity to tons of restaurants, it's easy to walk to Ballard Locks, Discovery Park, and plenty of other local gems.

💳 Budget: $$$

Remember all these hotels are on:
🌐 Alexa-West.com/Seattle-Hotels

## CONSIDER HOUSESITTING

Go on **TrustedHousesitters.com** and search for homes that need you to stay for a weekend or a few weeks and look after their pets. I did a "garden sit" for a month in Greenlake and I felt so spoiled.

I wrote you an entire blog on to travel for free via housesitting - visit:

**Alexa-West.com /Travel-Paths**

♥ For travel tips on everything from booking your hotels and using the right travel credit cards to staying safe and making friends, check out my book **The One-Way Ticket Plan: Find and Fun Your Purpose While Traveling the World**

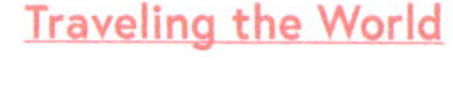

## APPS TO DOWNLOAD BEFORE YOU VISIT SEATTLE

▸ **Pay by Phone**

Use this app to pay for public street parking.

▸ **One Bus Away**

Never miss the bus again!

▸ **Transit Go App**

So that you can buy your ferry tickets and bus passes on the go.

▸ **MyOrca**

Keeps track of all your Orca Card (transportation) balances where you can add funds.

▸ **AlertSeattle**

Sends notifications about emergencies like severe weather, earthquakes, and safety incidents.

▸ **Find It, Fix It**

To report issues in the city like potholes and broken crosswalk signals (thrilling, right?)

▸ **Seattle Yellow Cab**

Often cheaper than Uber or Lyft, but not always available outside hotspots.

▸ **Merlin Bird ID**

Whenever you hear a bird, open the app and press play. It's like Shazaam for birds.

▸ **WTA Trailblazer AND Gaia**

For hiking enthusiasts.

▸ **TripIt**

I would die without this trip planning app. It organizes your flights and reservations in one timeline with reservation codes!

# CENTRAL SEATTLE



## CHAPTER TWO

# Downtown & Belltown

**DAYS NEEDED:**
2-3 to explore

*Downtown and Belltown are like that friend who's got their life together during the day—polished, professional, maybe a little buttoned-up. But when the sun sets, they are flirty, mischievous and a little drunk.*

Downtown and Belltown are Seattle's dynamic duo, each with its unique character and charm.

▶ **Downtown:** Born out of the Klondike Gold Rush, Downtown Seattle grew into a thriving cultural and commercial hub. It's where old meets new, with historic buildings standing alongside sleek skyscrapers. Today, it's the city's polished centerpiece, home to iconic landmarks, bustling markets, and cultural attractions that showcase the heart of Seattle.

▶ **Belltown:** Once the gritty epicenter of Seattle's music scene, Belltown has evolved into a vibrant neighborhood that still holds onto its edgy roots. It's where you'll find happy hours buzzing with locals, stylish cocktail lounges, and a thriving nightlife that keeps the neighborhood lively after dark. Connected by a seamless flow of streets, these two neighborhoods offer the best of Seattle's past and present.

This area is perfect for history buffs, foodies, and nightlife lovers, a day spent in Downtown and Belltown will leave you with a full itinerary—and a full heart.

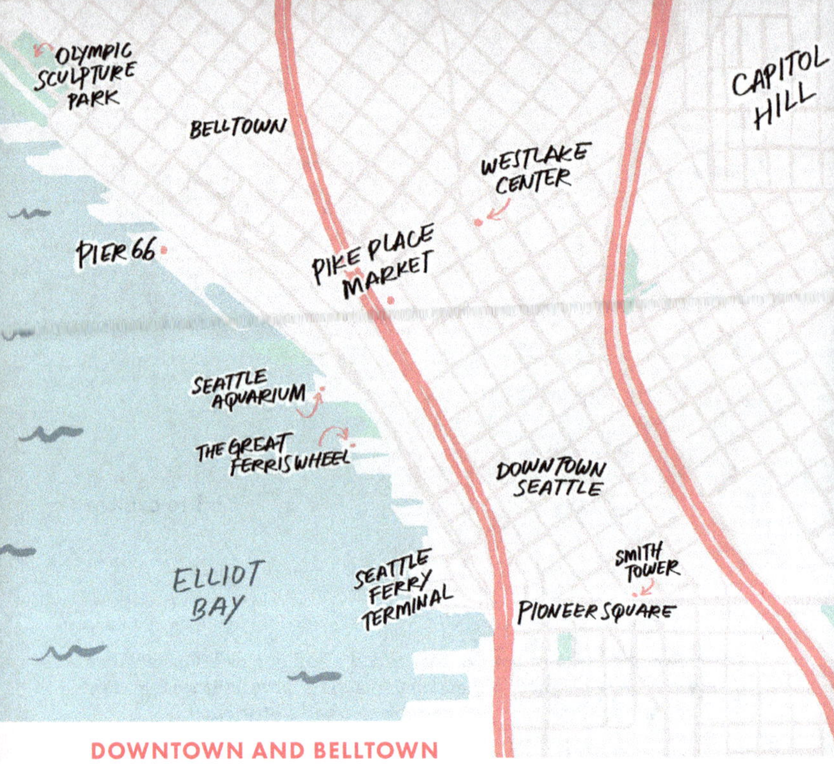




# Areas to Know

## DOWNTOWN

Downtown is home to Seattle's most famous sights including Pike Place Market. Stroll along the Seattle Waterfront for views of Elliott Bay, stop by the Seattle Art Museum or take in views from Smith Tower, Seattle's first skyscraper.

## PIKE PLACE MARKET

Founded in 1907, Pike Place Market is one of the oldest continuously operating public markets in the United States. Its creation was sparked by a simple desire: to give farmers a place to sell directly to customers, cutting out the middleman. Now, it's a bustling hub with over 500 shops, vendors, and craftspeople.

## WATERFRONT

Running along Elliot Bay, the waterfront has been a hub for trade and industry since the 1800s. Now, it's perfect for seafood lovers, with stunning views of the bay, waterfront restaurants, the Seattle Aquarium, and the Seattle Great Wheel—one of the best spots to catch a sunset over Puget Sound.

## BELLTOWN

Once the gritty center of Seattle's music scene, this area still holds that creative edge. This is where local legends like Nirvana and Pearl Jam began playing at venues like The Crocodile. Today, Belltown is synonymous with "happy hour".

## PIONEER SQUARE

Seattle's original downtown, dating back to 1852, is full of history with its red-brick buildings and cobblestone streets—but know that the nightlife scene can be a little sketchy after dark.

## WESTLAKE

Known more for function than flair, Westlake is Seattle's main transit hub. Here, you can catch the Light Rail or Monorail to zip around the city. There is also shopping here. Think Sephora.

♥ **PRO TIP!** <u>Scan the code to get the Seattle City Pass</u>  where you can bundle must-see destinations at a discount!

## ☞ How's the dating scene in Seattle?

I met my boyfriend on Bumble in Seattle. Emilia and I were in town to study the city for this book. We used Bumble to find tour guides, and I met him. That was easy. And dating in this city is getting easier. With so many tech transplants, the dating scene has evolved into a candy store of people from all backgrounds and cultures. Seattle is also less douchy than many big cities in the country. While you'll find you share of jerks anywhere in the world, I'd say that the humans who live and move here are high quality.

**♀ Where to Date?**
Bumble, Coffee Meets Bagel
**♥ Pro Tip!** Play Pickleball, especially at Greenlake Park; lots of single folk of all ages.

# Pike Place Mini Guide

## VISIT PIKE PLACE MARKET

Pike Place Market has been the heart of Seattle since 1907, starting as a humble farmers' market and evolving into an iconic 9-acre maze of shops, eateries, and local history. As you wander through the seafood and flower stalls, take a detour into Post Alley to discover quirky boutiques, or venture to the lower levels for old-world cafes like Freya and niche shops that still carry the market's early 20th-century charm. From its cobbled streets to hidden corners, Pike Place is not a tourist attraction. It is the true heart and soul of this city – and so, it gets its own mini chapter.

⊙ **Hours:** Daily, 9 AM – 6 PM (vendors often close around 4 PM)
📍 **Location:** 85 Pike St
🌐 **Visit:** <u>pikeplacemarket.org</u>

♥ **Pro Tip:** It's a common mistake to say "Pike's Place" instead of "Pike Place" — so to help you remember, listen our friend Matt's song in the QR Code (Skip to the 5:35 mark).



## MAIN ARCADE

**Aka where all the market stalls are!** This is where you'll find the classic fish-tossing spectacle at Pike Place Fish Market and rows of flower vendors, filling the air with fresh scents. You'll also find local produce stalls, artisanal honey sticks, and handcrafted goods—literally everything here is handmade.

📷 Photo by Emy! @__helloemilia

♥ **Pro Tip:** Come early (like 8am) to catch the fishmongers in action when it's less crowded.

▸**The FishMongers:** Known for fresh fish they throw in the air! This fish toss, established decades ago, has helped the fish market draw about 20,000 visitors daily. Ask to buy some salmon jerky from the fishmongers. It's smoked and fall-apart buttery. *(see picture on the opposite page)*

▸ **Market Spice:** Buy some honey sticks for your market stroll. Also, their Market Spice Tea is famous, take some home.

▸ **Matt's in the Market:** An iconic restaurant with dishes made with market ingredients.

▸ **Beecher's Handmade Cheese:** Watch cheesemakers at work through the window, then try their "World's Best" mac and cheese—rich, creamy, and perfect for a chilly Seattle day.

▸ **The Secret Garden:** With over 500 fresh herbs. Walk past the fishmongers and go left before Maximilien Restaurant.

▸ **Rachel the Piggy Bank:** Look for the big bronze pig in front of the fishmongers, make a wish and drop in a few coins—this iconic piggy bank supports the Pike Place Market Foundation

♥ **Pro Tip:** Head down the stairs near the "Pike Place Market" neon sign to find more local shops and the bathrooms.

Find all these destinations on The Solo Girl's Travel Guide Map

## POST ALLEY

Post Alley runs parallel to Pike Place for about five blocks, weaving its way through historic brick buildings and tucked-away cafes. It's not just an alley—it's a slice of Seattle's personality with a history dating back to the early 1900s when it served as a service corridor for market vendors.

*Must-see stops:*

▸ **The Gum Wall:** This sticky attraction began in the 1990s when theatergoers at the nearby Market Theater began sticking their chewed gum on the wall. Today, the wall is covered in thousands of pieces, creating a rainbow mosaic that's both gross and fascinating. Ps. They recently just scraped the wall in 2024, the first time in 10 years. So they need you to go contribute new gum.

▸ **Aditi Chai:** A mother-and-son-run chai stand offering rich, warming chai blends. Grab a cup and wander the market like a local.

▸ **Rachel's Ginger Beer:** A nice female-friendly space to rest your feet with locally-made ginger. Look for other solo girls traveling with this book while you're there.

▸ **Piroshky Piroshky:** Famous for their handheld pies—try the beef and cheese or the marzipan roll.

# #1 THING TO DO IN PIKE PLACE:

## SAVOR SEATTLE'S INSIDER'S BREAKFAST AND CULTURE TOUR

My biggest piece of travel advice is this: start every trip with a food tour! You get to eat, history, a local guide to ask all your questions to and a lay of the land so that by the end of the tour, you feel confident to explore on your own. And this tour is no different.

Savor Seattle's **Insider's Breakfast and Culture Tour** is the ultimate way to experience Pike Place Market and Seattle's culinary heartbeat. You'll meet your local guide (think of them as a new friend with serious insider knowledge) bright and early, before the market crowds arrive. As you wander, you'll taste some of the market's best breakfast bites, from fresh local pastries and smoked salmon to Seattle's perfect coffee, all while learning the hidden history and quirky stories that make Pike Place truly unique. This tour isn't just about food; it's your official introduction to Seattle's soul.

🎟 **Cost:** $60–$90

🕐 **Hours:** Starts at 8 AM, just as the market comes alive

📍 **Location:** Pike Place Market, Downtown

🌐 **Visit:** <u>savorseattletours.com</u>

# Top Things to Do in Downtown Seattle

## THE SEATTLE AQUARIUM

The Seattle Aquarium, located right on the waterfront, is home to all things Pacific Northwest marine life, from playful sea otters to intricate jellyfish displays. Recently, the aquarium expanded with the impressive Ocean Pavilion, a $170 million addition that immerses visitors in a 530,000-gallon reef ecosystem inspired by the Coral Triangle. You'll find incredible marine life, including sharks, rays, and over 1,000 fish species, all housed within expansive tanks with multi-story views and interactive education zones. For families, the Pavilion's tunnels and interactive displays offer an up-close way to learn about ocean conservation.

🎟 **Cost:** $35 for adults
🕑 **Hours:** Daily, 9:30 AM – 6 PM (last entry at 5 PM)
📍 **Location:** 1483 Alaskan Way, Pier 59, Seattle, WA 98101
🌐 **Visit:** seattleaquarium.org

## THE SEATTLE GREAT WHEEL

This **175-foot ferris wheel** has been spinning on the waterfront since 2012, offering views ranging from the **Olympic Mountains** to **Mount Rainier.** Its climate-controlled gondolas mean you'll be comfortable year-round.

♥ **Pro Tip:** Sunset rides are ideal. But you're up there for a while so bring wine and snacks in your purse (but be sneaky about it).
🎟 **Cost:** $17 for adults
🕑 **Hours:** Daily, 11 AM – 10 PM
📍 **Location:** 1301 Alaskan Way
🌐 **Visit:** seattlegreatwheel.com

## SMITH TOWER OBSERVATORY & BAR

While everyone flocks to the Space Needle, Smith Tower is Seattle's hidden gem for skyline views with a unique Prohibition-era twist. Opened in 1914 as the tallest building on the West Coast, this iconic skyscraper is full of charm. Take the vintage Otis elevator to the 35th-floor Chinese Room with its intricate woodwork and the famous Wishing Chair—legend has it, sitting here brings marriage luck. The Observatory Bar adds a speakeasy vibe, serving up craft cocktails and small bites against panoramic views of Elliott Bay and Mount Rainier.

🎟 Cost: $22
🕐 Hours: Wed–Sun, 11 AM – 11 PM
📍 Location: 506 2nd Ave, Seattle, WA 98104
🌐 Visit: smithtower.com

❤ Pro Tip: Come for happy hour from **3 PM – 6 PM**, Wednesday to Friday, where you can access the observatory and bar without the regular admission fee—as long as you're there to actually do happy hour.

## ARGOSY CRUISES

Operating since the 1940s, Argosy Cruises offers a variety of tours on Elliott Bay, from quick Harbor Cruises to scenic Locks Cruises that pass through the famous Ballard Locks, moving from freshwater to saltwater. These tours provide some of the best views of Seattle's skyline, waterfront landmarks, and surrounding mountains. For a quick taste of Seattle from the water, the **Harbor Cruise** is a solid pick.

🎟 Cost: $36 for adults
📍 Location: 1101 Alaskan Way, Pier 55
🌐 Visit: argosycruises.com

## MUSEUMS, CULTURE AND HISTORY

## OLYMPIC SCULPTURE PARK

This **9-acre open-air museum** transforms a former industrial site into a stunning blend of art and **nature along Elliott Bay.** It's home to large-scale sculptures like Alexander Calder's "Eagle" and Louise Bourgeois's "Father and Son", set against panoramic views of Puget Sound and the Olympic Mountains. Grab a coffee at Cherry Street Coffee House then walk the paths that wind through grassy areas and along the waterfront.







## SEATTLE ART MUSEUM (SAM)

Right downtown, the **Seattle Art Museum** is known for its blend of modern and classic art with a deep focus on Indigenous and Pacific Northwest pieces. Highlights include stunning Coast Salish and Tlingit carvings, and a jaw-dropping collection of Northwest Native masks. **Pro Tip:** First Thursdays are free—just be ready for a crowd, baby.









## THE SEATTLE PUBLIC LIBRARY (CENTRAL LIBRARY)

The Central Library, designed by Rem Koolhaas, is a glass and steel marvel that's part futuristic art piece, part literary treasure trove. It's known for its 11-story atrium, the vibrant Red Floor (it's like walking into an art installation), and the Book Spiral—a continuous ramp that displays the entire non-fiction collection. The 10th-floor reading room offers a quiet escape with sweeping views of downtown Seattle and Elliott Bay through the library's dramatic glass walls.

# Where to Eat

## BREAKFAST, BRUNCH & COFFEE

### STORYVILLE COFFEE

Known for its fluffy cinnamon rolls, this is my favorite little coffee shop gem where I take all my guests. Nestled in Pike Place Market, Storyville Coffee offers a cozy spot to enjoy expertly brewed coffee with a view of the waterfront.

◎ **Hours:**  Daily 7 AM – 5 PM
♥ **Location:**  Pike Place Market
⊕ **Visit:** storyville.com

### ADITI CHAI

Run by a mother-and-son duo, Aditi Chai is a true Pike Place Market gem, offering up some of the best chai you'll find in the city. Order the classic Masala Chai—rich, spicy, and a local favorite. It's a quick stop to grab a cup to sip on as you begin your stroll through the market.

◎ **Hours:**  Daily 9 AM – 6 PM
♥ **Location:**  Pike Place Market
♥ **IG:** @aditi_chai

### THE NEST

The best brunch views in town! The Nest is located atop the Thompson Hotel. It's the most female-friendly atmosphere, so dress up and play "city girl". If you're a salmon lover, you're going to love their brunch menu including the Salmon Benedict. Get boozy with mimosas or a martini for breakfast. Why not?

◎ **Brunch:**  Sat–Sun 8 AM–3 PM
◎ **Lunch:**  Mon–Fri 11 AM–3 PM
◎ **Dinner:** Mon–Sun 4 PM–10 PM
♥ **Location:** Thompson Seattle, 110 Stewart St
⊕ **Visit:** thenestseattle.com

### BISCUIT BITCH

Head to Biscuit Bitch where the biscuits are fluffy, the gravy is rich, and the attitude is sassy. Order The "Hot Mess Bitch" with scrambled eggs, cheese, sausage gravy, and garlic grits, along with a hot black coffee. Note: Outdoor seating is limited so plan to stand or take this to go!

♥ **Pro Tip:** This spot is popular, so get there early or be prepared to wait—but trust me, it's worth it. While you wait, walk to Metsker Maps and look for a signed copy of my book, The One-Way Ticket Plan.

⊙ **Hours:** Daily 8 AM – 3 PM

♥ **Location:** Near Pike Place, 1909 1st Ave

⊕ **Visit:** <u>biscuitbitch.com</u>

## THE CRUMPET SHOP

A Pike Place Market staple since 1976, The Crumpet Shop is perfect for a cozy, British-inspired breakfast. They serve freshly baked crumpets topped with everything from simple butter and honey to rich ricotta with preserves. Try the Smoked Salmon with Cream Cheese for savory or the Walnut and Honey Butter for sweet. Pair with a locally roasted coffee or a hot chai latte.

⊙ **Hours:** Mon-Sat: 8 AM - 3 PM | Sun: 9 AM - 3 PM

♥ **Location:** Pike Place, 1503 1st Ave

⊕ **Visit:** <u>thecrumpetshop.com</u>

# LUNCH/DINNER

*Casual*

## MATT'S IN THE MARKET

Did you stroll through the market and think, "hmm I'd like to eat all this,"? Well, you can at Matt's in the Market. Located on the second floor above the market, you'll get views of the puget sound and the iconic Pike Place sign below. Pro Tip:

The lunch menu is a great value if you're on a budget.

♥ **Pro Tip:** Ask for a window seat giving views of the market and fishmongers below plus the iconic glowing Pike Place sign!

⊙ **Hours:** Lunch: Mon-Fri 11:30 AM – 2:30 PM | Dinner: Mon-Fri 5:30 PM – 9:30 PM Happy Hour Mon- Sat 5pm to 6pm (bar stools only)

♥ **Location:** Pike Place Market

⊕ **Visit:** <u>mattsinthemarket.com</u>

## SALUMI

Here is my favorite place to grab sandwiches for a picnic! Family-owned, Salumi is famous for its house-made salami and cured meats. Create your own masterpiece by choosing from their selection of salami, cheeses, onions, and peppers. Or do what I do and order The Porchetta Sandwich—it's a life changer with tender, slow-roasted pork that melts in your mouth.

⊙ **Hours:** 10 AM – 3 PM

♥ **Location:** 404 Occidental Ave S, Pioneer Square

⊕ **Visit:** <u>salumideli.com</u>

## POST ALLEY PIZZA

The most famous thing to order is actually the Post Alley Chopped Cheese Sandwich with ground beef, piparra peppers, lettuce, mozzarella, sharp provolone, and mayo on a roasted garlic hoagie roll. It's gone viral in Seattle. And yea, their pizza is pretty damn good, too. This place is super casual, a great spot for a quick bite in between explorations.

⊙ Hours:  Varies, open late
♥ Location: 1123 Post Ave, Downtown

## ALIBI ROOM

A dark hole in the wall where you can sit in a dimly lit bar, order a cocktail and eat comfort pizza with thin crispy crust! Alibi Room is a favorite for locals looking to escape the crowds and tourists discovering Seattle's hidden gems.

⊙ Hours:  11:30AM-2AM / Mon-Fri 11:30 AM – 6 PM
♥ Location:  Post Alley
⊕ Visit: thealibiroom.com

## Date-Night Approved

(don't forget that you can take yourself on a date, baby)

## UMI SAKE HOUSE

My favorite happy hour spot! Ask to sit at the bar or the sushi bar for a front-row view of the chefs in action. Order a "sushi set" paired with a draft Sapporo beer during happy hour. Even during happy hour, however, I order one big, fancy roll from their regular menu. It's huge, perfect for two people. Not happy hour? Still totally worth a visit.

☞ What to Order: Sushi Set paired with a Sapporo on draft
♥ Pro Tip: If you want a table (rather than bar), make a reservation
⊙ Hours: Daily 4 PM – 2 AM
Happy Hour: Daily, 4 PM–6 PM, and late-night 10:30 PM–close
♥ Location:  Belltown
⊕ Visit: umisakehouse.com

## THE PINK DOOR

This experience will exceed your expectations. Known for its Italian-American menu, lively atmosphere, and nightly entertainment—from trapeze acts to live music—this Seattle staple offers more than just dinner. What looks like a speakeasy on the outside (literally look for the pink door in Post Alley) feels like fine dining with white tablecloths and impeccable service. Walk-ins are possible, but as one of Seattle's most popular spots, reservations are highly recommended. **Pro Tip:** Ask about the catch of the day!

⊙ Hours: Daily 11:30 AM – 10 PM
♥ Location:  1919 Post Alley, Seattle, WA 98101
⊕ Visit: thepinkdoor.net

## WA'Z SEATTLE

Want to experience the magic of Japanese fine dining without the Tokyo flight? Wa'z Seattle transports you with an artfully crafted multi-course kaiseki meal. Kaiseki is a centuries-old Japanese dining tradition, a multi-course journey that emphasizes seasonality, precision, and balance—each plate designed to reflect nature. Think tender wagyu beef paired with rare mushrooms and fresh truffles. This is how celebrities eat. I loved sitting at the bar top as the chef explained each dish. But do keep an open mind to eating exotic ingredients you might not have tried yet. Trust. Ps. My boyfriend took me here for my birthday, it's absolutely a splurge but an unforgettable princess treatment experience.

⊙ **Hours:** Wed- Sunday, lunch and dinner reservation only

♀ **Location:** Belltown, 411 Cedar Street

☞ Make a reservation in super advance at <u>wazseattle.com</u>

## HUNT AND GATHER AT THE COLUMBIA TOWER CLUB

Want to have dinner on the 75th floor of the tallest building in Seattle? Most people don't know that although The Columbia Tower Club is a member-only club, you can snag a reservation there on OpenTable. Think risotto, wedge salads, perfectly grilled halibut - you know, fancy club food. The backdrop is absolutely insane with stunning, panoramic views of the Seattle skyline, Puget Sound, and surrounding mountains. This is better than the Space Needle.

♥ **Pro Tip:** Book a window table at sunset for jaw-dropping views, and try the chef's tasting menu for a true Seattle showcase.

⊙ **Hours:** Monday – Friday, 4 PM – 10 PM

♀ **Location:** 75th Floor, Columbia Tower Club, 701 5th Ave

☞ Book on <u>OpenTable</u>

Ps. Find a tutorial of how to get to the 75th floor on my website.

Pss. This is how good the view from up here is!

## SIX SEVEN AT THE EDGEWATER

Award-winning food, wine, and unbeatable over-water views of Elliott Bay -- this is the most romantic spot in Seattle. Located inside the Edgewater Hotel, Six Seven is consistently recognized and awarded for its exceptional dining experience and wine list which highlights Washington, Oregon, and Northern California wineries. **Pro Tip:** Visit during Happy Hour, Sunday to Thursday from 3 PM to 5 PM,

⊙ **Hours:** Daily, 7 AM – 1PM / 5:30 PM-9 PM

☆ **Happy Hour:** Sunday–Thursday, 3 PM – 5 PM

⚲ **Location:** The Edgewater Hotel, 2411 Alaskan Way

⊕ **Visit:** edgewaterhotel.com



# Where to Drink

## BATHTUB GIN & CO.

For the true craft cocktail snobs and enthusiast who want their drinks prepared like whimsical science experiments, this sexy speakeasy-style bar will not disappoint. Pro Tip: Look for the unmarked door—it's easy to miss!

⊙ **Hours:** Daily 6 PM – 2 AM
⚲ **Location:** Belltown, 2205 2nd Ave #310
⊕ **Visit:** bathtubginseattle.com

## THE NEST AT THOMPSON SEATTLE

For unbeatable views and killer cocktails, The Nest is the rooftop bar you've been dreaming of. Located on top of the Thompson Seattle hotel, get your camera ready for panoramic views of the Puget Sound, downtown Seattle, and the Olympic Mountains. With comfy lounge seating and a vibe that screams "Instagram-worthy," it's the perfect place to sip a cocktail while watching the sunset over the water.

⊙ **Hours:** Mon–Thu, 5 PM – 10 PM; Fri, 3 PM – 11 PM; Sat, 3 PM – 11 PM; Sun, 5 PM – 10 PM

♥ **Location:** Downtown, atop the Thompson Hotel, 110 Stewart St

⊕ **Visit:** thenestseattle.com

## CLOUDBURST BREWING

Cloudburst is easily one of my top 3 breweries in Seattle. Their hazy IPAs are so incredible that out-of-town friends have told me this place "ruined" beer for them—nothing else ever measures up. Just a short walk from Pike Place Market, it's the perfect spot to reset with a drink that sets the gold standard.

⊙ **Hours:** Noon – 10 PM

♥ **Location:** Downtown, 2116 Western Ave

⊕ **Visit:** cloudburstbrew.com

# NIGHTLIFE AND LIVE MUSIC

## TEATRO ZINZANNI

If you want a night out that's completely out of the ordinary, Teatro ZinZanni delivers an unforgettable experience. This dinner theater combines circus, cabaret, and comedy, all while you enjoy a multi-course meal. Expect acrobatics, theatrics, and plenty of audience interaction— it's like stepping into a fantasy world for the evening.

♥ **Pro Tip:** Teatro ZinZanni operates seasonally, typically running shows from Spring/Summer (April to September) and Fall/Winter (October to February). Check dates.

⊕ **Visit:** zinzanni.com/seattle

## DIMITRIOU'S JAZZ ALLEY

For a more laid-back yet sophisticated night, head over to Dimitriou's Jazz Alley, Seattle's premier jazz club. With top-tier jazz artists performing in an intimate setting, this venue is perfect for music lovers looking to enjoy smooth tunes over a drink.

⊙ **Hours:** 6 – 10 PM

♥ **Location:** Belltown, 2033 6th Ave

⊕ **Visit:** jazzalley.com

## THE CROCODILE

A Seattle music institution, The Crocodile is where grunge legends like Nirvana and Pearl Jam once played, and it remains a go-to spot for live music today. Now located in a larger venue in Belltown, The Crocodile hosts everything from indie rock to hip-hop to comedy shows.

♥ **Pro Tip:** Check their calendar for secret shows—big-name artists occasionally pop in for surprise performances.

⊙ **Hours:** 5 PM - 2 AM

♥ **Location:** Belltown, 2505 1st Ave

⊕ **Visit:** thecrocodile.com

# Shopping Downtown

### #1 - PIKE PLACE MARKET (DUH)

✻ Fun Fact: Many flower farmers at Pike Place are of Hmong descent, a tradition that began in the 1980s to support Southeast Asian refugee farmers. You can get beautiful and affordable fresh bouquets here – even on your wedding day! Brides and bridesmaids will come for a fresh, spontaneous bouquet.

### SEATTLE ANTIQUES MARKET

If you love hunting for vintage treasures, the Seattle Antiques Market is a must. Located near the waterfront, this shop is filled with retro furniture, mid-century décor, and collectibles.

⊙ Hours: Daily 10 AM – 6 PM.

📍 Location: 5 minutes walk from Pike Place Market, along the waterfront.

🌐 Visit: seattleantiquesmarket.com

### WESTLAKE CENTER & WESTLAKE PLAZA

Westlake Center is your go-to for an outdoor shopping experience with stores like **Sephora** and **Zara.** With the Seattle Monorail right there, it's a central shopping hub in downtown Seattle.

📍 Location: 10 minutes walk from Pike Place Market

### PACIFIC PLACE

This is a small mall with an AMC movie theater. There's also a Din Tai Fung restaurant. Great for ducking out of the rain for an afternoon.

⊙ Hours: 11 AM – 7 PM, Sun 12pm – 7 PM.

📍 Location: 2 minutes' walk from Westlake Center, on Pine Street.

🌐 Visit: pacificplaceseattle.com

### NORDSTROM FLAGSHIP STORE

Seattle's own Nordstrom Flagship Store is a shopping landmark. Their service is excellent, with personal stylists available to help you find exactly what you're looking for.

⊙ Hours: Monday to Saturday 10 AM – 8 PM, Sunday 11 AM – 7 PM.

📍 Location: 5 minutes' walk from Pike Place Market, near Westlake Center.

🌐 Visit: nordstrom.com

# Beauty & Wellness

## HAIR

### GARY MANUEL SALON

A Capitol Hill favorite, Gary Manuel Salon is the most recommended salon in Seattle (by my friends, at least). It's an Aveda-concept hair salon (incredible products that leave your hair healthy) where they are masters at both color and cut. Ps. Remember that in Seattle, people request crazy colors and shapes. These guys have seen and done it all!

⊙ Hours: 8AM-6PM / closed Sun-Mon
♀ Location: Downtown 528 2nd Ave
⊕ Visit: garymanuel.com

## NAILS

### LEILA KLEIN

Clean, polished, classy nails, this is for the girl that wants to look like a rich bitch. Leila is your manicurist but she's also an esthetician so consider staying for a facial. Get ready for a one-on-one spa experience that feels like hanging with a girlfriend.

⊙ Hours: 7AM-10PM
♀ Location: Belltown
⊕ Visit: @leilaklein10

## SKIN

### PENELOPE AND THE BEAUTY BAR

Located in the luxurious Fairmont Olympic Hotel, Penelope and the Beauty Bar is Seattle's go-to for high-end spa treatments in a chic, Parisian-inspired setting. They offer everything from hydrafacials and detoxifying massages to LED therapy and microcurrent facials, with serene, softly lit rooms and heated treatment tables for peak relaxation.

☞ Try: Ultimate Body Detox
⊙ Hours: Daily, 8 AM – 8 PM
♀ Location: Downtown at the Fairmont Olympic Hotel, 411 University St
⊕ Visit: penelopeandthebeautybar.com

### BELLORA MEDICAL AESTHETICS & SPA

For skin treatments and medical-grade aesthetics, Bellora Medical Aesthetics offers a range of services including facials, chemical peels, and injectables like Botox and dermal fillers. Their expert team focuses on helping clients achieve a natural look with healthy glowing skin and lips!

⊙ **Hours:** Closed Sunday
⊕ **Visit:** <u>belloramedicalaesthetics.com</u>

## BODY

**URBAN YOGA SPA**

A wonderland of pampering! This modern yoga studio offers hot yoga classes to help improve flexibility, increase strength, and detoxify your body -- but also, they have a full-service spa with massages, waxing and manicures! Not to mention a coffee house. This is your one-stop-shop to starting your day in a healthy and happy way.

♥ **Pro Tip:** New students can take advantage of introductory offers, so it's a great opportunity to try a class while you're visiting.

🏷 **Cost:** Drop-in classes around $25
⊙ **Hours:** Mon–Sun, 8 AM – 8 PM
📍 **Location:** Downtown at the Fairmont Olympic Hotel, 411 University St
⊕ **Visit:** <u>urbanyogaspa.com</u>

## LOCAL TIPS FOR DOWNTOWN FOR BELLTOWN

### 01. Take Advantage of Free Museum Days

Several downtown museums, including the **Seattle Art Museum (SAM)** offer free entry on the first Thursday of every month.

### 02. Take the Seattle Center Monorail

If you're heading to Seattle Center (Space Needle, MoPOP, Chihuly Garden), skip the Uber and take the **Seattle Center Monorail.** It's cheap, quick, and will get you from Westlake Center to the heart of Seattle Center in minutes. Plus, it's a bit of local history—it was built for the 1962 World's Fair and it gives you a little tour of the city.

### 3. Skip the "Original" Starbucks Line

The "Original" Starbucks is iconic… but surprise, that Starbucks with the ungodly line across from Pike Place **isn't the real original!** The first Starbucks opened down the road on Western Avenue in 1971, before moving to the Pike Place location in 1976. So while it's historic, it's just another standard Starbucks drink with a really long line. Instead, I recommend you visit **Starbucks Reserve Roastery in Capitol Hill** for a truly unique Starbucks experience.

# Best Ways to Get Around Downtown

## SEATTLE CENTER MONORAIL

The Seattle Center Monorail is a fast, iconic way to zip between downtown Seattle and the Seattle Center.

### Key Stops:

▶ **Westlake Center:** Right in the heart of downtown, this stop connects with buses, light rail, and streetcar options, making it easy to explore downtown or head to Pike Place Market.

▶ **Seattle Center:** At the base of the Space Needle, this stop is steps away from major attractions like MoPOP, Chihuly Garden and Glass, and Climate Pledge Arena.

........................................................

♥ **Pro Tip:** Travels from Westlake Center (5th Avenue and Pine Street) to Seattle Center.

🎟 **Cost:** $3 one-way for adults

◷ **Hours:**
**Monday-Friday:** 7:30 AM - 11 PM,
**Saturday-Sunday:** 8:30 AM - 11 PM

## LINK LIGHT RAIL

The Link Light Rail is the most affordable and straightforward way to get around Seattle and beyond.

### Main Downtown Stops:

▶ **Westlake Station:** Heart of downtown, close to shopping and Pike Place Market.

▶ **Symphony Station:** Near Seattle Art Museum and waterfront access.

▶ **Pioneer Square Station:** Seattle's historic district, full of art galleries and cafés.

▶ **International District/Chinatown Station:** Fantastic for food, markets, and culture.

........................................................

🎟 **Cost:** $3 one-way for adults

◷ **Hours:**
**Monday-Saturday:** 5 AM - 1 AM
**Sunday:** 6 AM - Midnight

**FUN FACT!** After the Great Seattle Fire of 1889, the city was rebuilt one level higher, leaving an underground network of tunnels beneath Pioneer Square. <u>Tour it here</u> ☞

# Mini Downtown / Belltown Itineraries

## ALEXA'S ADVENTURE

⊘ **8am:** Savor Seattle Tour

⊘ **10am:** Visit Storyville for a coffee

⊘ **10:30am:** Stroll to SAM (Seattle Art Museum) or the MoPop Museum

⊘ **12pm:** Have lunch at The Pink Door

⊘ **1:30pm:** Penelope and the Beauty Bar or Banya 5

⊘ **3pm:** Head back to the hotel to freshen up

⊘ **5pm:** Visit Umi Sake House for Happy hour

▸ Walk to BathTub and Gin for a drink afterward

▸ Finish your night at The Crocodile for live music

## THE BEST SEATTLE STUFF

⊘ **8am:** Start at Biscuit Bitch. While you wait (there's always a wait) pop into Metsker Maps - and look for a signed copy of my book, The One-Way Ticket Plan.

⊘ **9am:** Visit the Seattle Aquarium

⊘ **11am:** Explore Pike Place Market

⊘ **12pm:** Lunch at Matt's in the Market or Beecher's

⊘ **1:30pm:** Board an Argosy Harbor Cruise for a scenic tour of Seattle

⊘ **3pm:** Head back to your hotel to relax and freshen up.

⊘ **5:30pm:** Sunset dinner at The Nest

▸ Walk to the Alibi Room for a drink and dessert afterward

♥ **WILD ADVENTURE RECOMMENDATION:**

Ever wanted to be in the circus? Come for a class at Emerald City Trapeze. Located in SODO, just 6 minutes from Pioneer Square, this is a haven for aerial arts, flying trapeze, acrobatics, pole dance, and circus classes. On Fridays, don't miss Date Night with acro yoga! Taught by professional circus performers, these classes are designed for all skill levels – from seasoned athletes to total beginners.

⊕ **Visit:** emeraldcitytrapeze.com

## CHAPTER THREE

# Seattle Center

**DAYS NEEDED:**
1-2 days

*Seattle Center is your newly divorced friend. She still has the mansion on the hill but is ready to enter her era of unadulterated fun.*

Seattle Center and Queen Anne are a perfect pairing for your itinerary. Start at Seattle Center, home to must-see landmarks like the Space Needle, MoPOP, and Climate Pledge Arena—all conveniently close to each other. Then, head into Lower Queen Anne for lively restaurants, bars, and pre- or post-event excitement.

Finish your day with a climb to Upper Queen Anne, where you'll find stunning views, cozy cafes, and a quieter vibe. These neighborhoods flow seamlessly together, offering a mix of iconic sights, vibrant energy, and laid-back charm. Just be ready for the hills and stairs—they're worth it!

**INCLUDES:**
Lower Queen Anne
& Upper Queen Anne

**BEST FOR:**
▸ Iconic landmarks and views
▸ Sports events and concerts at Climate Pledge Arena

# Areas to Know

## SEATTLE CENTER

The centerpiece of Seattle's tourism scene, with the Space Needle, MoPOP, Chihuly Garden and Glass, and Climate Pledge Arena all within a few walkable blocks. This is also where Seattle Center Park hosts festivals and events throughout the year! Check the Seattle Center Events Calendar before you come: seattlecenter.com/events/event-calendar

## LOWER QUEEN ANNE

Aka "Uptown". This neighborhood is packed with dining and nightlife options. It's where you'll find McCaw Hall, home to the Seattle Opera and Pacific Northwest Ballet, plus plenty of spots to grab a pre-show dinner or post-concert drink.

## UPPER QUEEN ANNE

Perched high above, this neighborhood is known for its gorgeous skyline views —Kerry Park is the go-to spot for that iconic Seattle photo. It's also a great place to explore quaint cafes, boutique shops, and some of the city's most beautiful historic homes (and rich housewives).

## PRO TIPS FOR SEATTLE CENTER

▸ **Plan Ahead on Holidays:** Kerry Park has the most spectacular views of Seattle for New Years and holidays... but everyone thinks so. It can get so busy and gridlocked. Get here early, plan to walk up the hill.

▸ **Avoid Driving Up Queen Anne Hill in Snowy Conditions:** Queen Anne's steep roads become slick and treacherous during winter storms. Local news often features brave (or reckless!) souls snowboarding or sledding down these hills, which can be risky for vehicles.

▸ **The Best Parking:** For events and game days, try to park on the street around 1st Ave and Ward.

▸ **Check for Meter-Free Zones:** Parts of Queen Anne have free street parking after 8 PM, so if your plans extend into the evening, look for these areas on the lower slopes of Queen Anne Ave.

♥ **FUN FACT!** Seattle is known as the "Emerald City" due to the lush, evergreen forests and abundant greenery that surround the area and remain vibrant year-round, thanks to the region's mild, wet climate.

# Things to Do

♥ **Pro Tip:** **You can bundle many of these adventures and save money. Check out <u>the bundles here</u>** ☞ 

## VISIT THE SPACE NEEDLE

Built for the 1962 World's Fair, the Space Needle is Seattle's ultimate icon, embodying the city's forward-thinking vibe. Standing at 605 feet, it was the tallest building west of the Mississippi when it first opened. The observation deck features floor-to-ceiling glass windows and a rotating glass floor, offering jaw-dropping 360-degree views of the city, Puget Sound, and beyond. But hey, check the weather. When it's gray and cloudy, you can't see a thing up there! Clear weather days are best.

☞ **What to expect:** The experience starts with a quick elevator ride that zooms up 520 feet in just 41 seconds. Expect some lines, especially during peak times like weekends and holidays. Once at the top, you'll find interactive touchscreens that provide fun facts about Seattle's skyline. The rotating glass floor is not for the faint-hearted, but it's a thrill if you're up for it. There's also a small café for grabbing a latte or snack while you take in the views.

⊙ **Time needed:** Budget around 1-2 hours to fully enjoy the experience.

🎟 **Cost:** $35 adults, but you can combine it with Chihuly Gardens & Glass for $54 for adults

⊙ **Hours:** Sun–Fri, 10 AM – 9 PM; Sat, 9 AM – 9 PM

📍 **Location:** Seattle Center

🌐 **Visit:** <u>spaceneedle.com</u>

📷 Photo by Emy! @__helloemilia

## EXPLORE CHIHULY GARDEN AND GLASS

Opened in 2012, this Seattle Center gem combines the vibrant glass art of Dale Chihuly with Pacific Northwest nature and sleek architecture. The museum's experience unfolds across three main areas: the Galleries showcasing Chihuly's iconic series, the breathtaking Glasshouse with a 100-foot-long suspended sculpture, and the Garden, where vivid glass installations nestle among native plants. Each piece interacts with changing natural light for a surreal, dynamic effect that's different every time you visit.

🎟 **Cost:** $29–$37.50 for adults
Hours: Sun–Tues 10 AM – 5 PM, Wed 10 AM – 6 PM, Thurs 10 AM – 6:30 PM, Fri–Sat 10 AM – 7 PM,
📍 **Location:** Next to the Space Needle
🌐 Visit: chihulygardenandglass.com

## MUSEUM OF POP CULTURE (MOPOP)

Seattle's music scene is legendary, and MoPOP captures it all. This place pays tribute to the city's icons like Nirvana, Jimi Hendrix, and Pearl Jam. Designed by Frank Gehry, the building itself is a twisted, colorful masterpiece. Inside, you'll find the Nirvana and Pearl Jam exhibits that dive deep into the city's grunge roots, plus the Sound Lab, where you can try your hand at guitars and drums. And if you're into sci-fi and horror, their collections have something for you too, with props from classics like Star Wars.

★ **Adventure Pairing:** Follow up with a trip to Easy Street Records or head up the Space Needle next door.
🎟 **Cost:** General admission starts around $30
Hours: Daily, 10 AM – 5 PM
📍 **Location:** 325 5th Ave N
🌐 Visit: mopop.org

## PACIFIC NORTHWEST BALLET

This renowned ballet company is celebrated for its classical favorites like Swan Lake and Romeo & Juliet held at the beautiful McCaw Hall. During the winter season, the PNW Ballet's production of The Nutcracker is a beloved Seattle tradition. Dress up, take yourself to dinner and a show.

♥ **Pro Tip:** Check their calendar for special matinee performances if you want to catch a show before sunset and still have time to explore the nearby Seattle Center attractions.
📍 **Location:** McCaw Hall, 301 Mercer St
🌐 Visit: pnb.org

## PACIFIC SCIENCE CENTER

The Pacific Science Center is a hands-on science museum designed for all ages to explore everything from biology to space. The center offers interactive exhibits like a planetarium, an IMAX theater, and a butterfly!

But this place isn't just for kids. In the evening, adults come for the Laser Dome. This massive 80-foot dome transforms for laser light shows set to rock classics—think Led Zeppelin and Pink Floyd—that sync with mind-bending visuals for a surreal experience. And in Washington, weed is legal, so let's just say that the laser show vibe works well with a little "enhanced" relaxation. Ps. I started coming here as a stoner teenager like 20 years ago.

☛ Cost: General admission starts at $25; laser shows are $15.
♥ Location: Seattle Center
⊕ Visit: pacificsciencecenter.org/events

## SPORTING EVENTS AND CONCERTS AT CLIMATE PLEDGE ARENA

Climate Pledge Arena, home to the Seattle Kraken and the WNBA's Seattle Storm, isn't just any arena—it's a groundbreaking venue in the world of sustainability and green building. Originally the Seattle Center Coliseum, built for the 1962 World's Fair and later renamed KeyArena, this iconic structure was completely redone. Jeff Bezos announced the new name as a commitment to environmental action, aiming for it to be the first net-zero carbon arena in the world. Notably, the venue uses all-electric operations, renewable energy, and even repurposes reclaimed rainwater for the NHL's "greenest ice" .

Beyond hockey and basketball, Climate Pledge Arena hosts the biggest concerts that come to town!

☞ Best Free Parking: Aim for street parking in the Lower Queen Anne area.
⊕ Visit: climatepledgearena.com

## SHOPPING & PAMPERING

There are tons of cute stores alone Queen Anne Ave that make for the perfect stroll and shop session, Start at Queen Anne Book Company, a cozy indie bookstore known for its thoughtfully curated selection.

For retail therapy, don't miss MILLIE, one of the cutest boutiques in the area. And if you want cozy, chic Seattle gear (like sweatshirts and t-shirts) without looking like you raided a tourist shop? Check out my friend's Seattle clothing line— I'd recommend it even if she wasn't my friend.

⊕ Visit: Peacelovelocal.shop

## QUEEN ANNE FARMERS MARKET

If you're in Seattle between June and October, the Queen Anne Farmers Market showcases the best of the Pacific Northwest's seasonal produce. But more importantly, they have tons of food for you to eat *like now*. Come hungry as there are pastries, fresh fruit popsicles, a rotating lineup of food trucks and live music performances!

🎟 **Cost:** Free entry
Hours: Thursdays, 3 PM – 7:30 PM (June–October)
📍 **Location:** West Crockett St & Queen Anne Ave N
⊕ Visit: qafm.org

♥ **FUN FACT!** The Space Needle was built in just 400 days, and that was back in the 60's!

*Fun excercise challenge!*
## QUEEN OF THE HILL: A GREEN SPACE CRAWL

**This is how Emilia and I explored Queen Anne while writing this book!** For the traveler who wants to exercise her way around the city, my Queen of the Hill greenspace adventure is perfect for solo travelers looking to pair some cardio with stunning views.

### 1. Start at Kinnear Park

Start your crawl at Kinnear Park's lower section, where you'll find a gentle trail winding through old-growth trees. The lush forested area is perfect for a warm-up walk or a short jog. Take a moment to enjoy the cool shade before heading up the hill for your first leg of cardio.

☆ Challenge: Jog up the hill to the upper part of the park to get your heart pumping.
📍 Location: Lower Queen Anne, 899 W Olympic Pl

### 2. Make Your Way to Marshall Park

From Kinnear Park, head further up the hill to Marshall Park. It's a smaller green space but a perfect stop to soak in panoramic views of Puget Sound and the Olympic Mountains.

☆ **Challenge:** Walk up the steep incline to get here, and reward yourself with a few deep breaths while enjoying the view.

♥ Location: Upper Queen Anne, 7th Ave W & W Highland Dr

## 3. Explore Parsons Gardens

Adjacent to Marshall Park, Parsons Gardens feels like a little secret garden tucked away from the city. Take a calming walk around the flowers and greenery— and then do like my best friend, Emy: find your favorite tree and give it a hug.

☆ Challenge: Try some walking lunges as you explore the garden paths.

♥ Location: Upper Queen Anne, 650 W Highland Dr

## 4. Finish at Kerry Park

End your Queen of the Hill adventure with a visit to Kerry Park, where you'll find the postcard-perfect view of the Seattle skyline, Space Needle, and, if you're lucky, Mount Rainier in the distance. Plan to reach this spot right at sunset to catch the city bathed in golden light, a perfect reward after a day of exploring.

This small park has become a top spot for photographers and was famously featured in the opening credits of the TV show Frasier!

☆ **Challenge:** Do a set of push-ups or planks while soaking in the stunning view before cooling down with a few stretches.

♥ Location: Upper Queen Anne, 211 W Highland Dr

☉ Suggested Start Time for Sunset:

▶ **For a 7:00 pm summer sunset:** Start your adventure around 4:30 pm. This allows for a leisurely pace and some extra time to explore each spot.

▶ **For a 5:00 pm winter sunset:** Begin around 2:30 pm for the same relaxed pace.

♥ **Total Distance:** Approximately 2 miles (but with so many stairs AND HILLS)

Since you've earned it...

✦ Seattlite Pizza Recommendation:

My Go-To Pizza Delivery in Seattle is Pagliacci's Pizza. Pro Tip: order it well-done. During mushroom season, they often have pies with morels or chanterelles. I also order their gelato which is made with seasonal ingredients!

# Where to Eat

## BREAKFAST AND BRUNCH

### KEXP & VITA CAFE

KEXP, Seattle's beloved indie radio station, is housed inside the KEXP Gathering Space, right next to Seattle Center. You can literally see the DJs spinning tunes live through the studio's glass windows, creating a unique experience where music, coffee, and community blend seamlessly. Grab a seat at VITA Cafe, located inside the same space, and enjoy the sounds while savoring fresh pastries and a signature Seattle coffee.

☞ **Order this:** The Cortado

◔ **Hours** Monday–Friday: 7 AM–6 PM / Sun & Saturday: 8 AM–6 PM

♥ **Location:** 472 1st Ave N

♥ **IG:** @vitaxkexp

### SKYBOWL CAFE

A healthy start to your mornin'! They specialize in smoothie bowls that look like works of art, topped with fresh fruit, granola, and superfood extras. This will give you energy and nourishment before a big day exploring Seattle

Order this: The COCO PARADISE—a smoothie bowl with acai, banana, mango, raw cacao, and almond milk!

◔ **Hours:** 9AM - 6PM ish (closed on Monday)

♥ **Location:** 2120 Queen Anne Ave N

♥ **IG:** @SkybowlCafe

## LUNCH / DINNER

*Casual*

### THE MASONRY

This is my go-to dinner spot before the Kraken game - but it gets busy! If there is room to sit (which there often is), I prefer to sit outside on the patio watching the world go by, or with the bartender at the bar. Alternatively, get a table where you can watch the pizza oven! If The Masonry is too full, order to-go and tell them you'll be sitting next door at Fast Fashion (one of my favorite micro-brew tap rooms). They'll deliver it to you there.

☞ **Order this:** The classic pepperoni is incredible, but so are the meatballs in marinara. I dream of those bad boys.

◔ **Hours:** Sun–Thurs 12 PM–10 PM; Fri–Sat 12 PM–12 AM

## DICK'S DRIVE-IN

A true Seattle classic since 1954! The burgers are simple, affordable, and incredibly tasty—just what you need to refuel during your day of exploring. But what makes Dick's truly special is how they treat their employees: they pay some of the highest wages in the fast food industry, offer excellent benefits, and even provide scholarships to help staff pay for college. It's a feel-good stop that supports both your appetite and the local community.

☞ **Order this:** The Deluxe Burger. Add a side of hand-cut fries and a milkshake.

**Hours:** Daily 10:30AM-2AM

**Location:** 500 Queen Anne Ave N, Lower Queen Anne

IG: @dicksdrivein

## QUEEN ANNE BEER HALL

For a non-fancy night out, Queen Anne Beer Hall is my favorite casual spot with its Bavarian-style brews, giant pretzels, and communal tables that make it easy to meet new people. Check out their trivia nights and live music night.

☞ **Order this:** The Giant Bavarian Pretzel—served with warm cheese sauce and mustard, perfect for sharing with new friends over a stein of beer.

**Hours:** Hours: Mon–Thurs 11 AM–12 AM, Fri–Sat 11 AM–2 AM, Sun 10 AM–12 AM

**Location:** 203 W Thomas St, Lower Queen Anne

IG: @queenannebeerhall

## MOONTREE SUSHI

Sushi lovers, rejoice! Moontree Sushi has been a neighborhood favorite in Queen Anne for nearly a decade! The nigiri is melt-in-your-mouth good, and their specialty rolls are delicious! The quality of the fish is so fresh that I always leave here feeling full in a healthy way (depending on how much sake I drink).

☞ **Order this:** The Salmon Lover Roll

**Hours:** Mon 4–9 PM; Tues–Thurs 11:30 AM–9 PM; Fri–Sat 11:30 AM–10 PM; Sun 12–9 PM
Happy Hour: Weekdays 3–5 PM

**Location:** 216 First Ave W, Lower Queen Anne

IG: @moontreesushiandtapas

## SAL Y LIMÓN

A fantastic choice for vegetarians and meat lovers! This tex-mex style spot serves up vegetarian enchiladas, tamales, and burritos that are to-die for. I'm a meat lover so

I can't resist the Enchiladas Michoacanas. Order a margarita, and you'll feel like you've been transported to a sunny beach in Mexico (even if it's raining in Seattle).

☞ **Another thing to order:** The Baja Fish Tacos
⊙ **Hours:** Fri-Sat 11AM-11PM, Sun-Thurs 11AM-10PM
⚲ **Location:** 2100 Queen Anne Ave

♥ IG: @salylimonseattle

## TAYLOR SHELLFISH OYSTER BAR

Calling all seafood lovers! Taylor Shellfish is known for more than just fresh oysters from the Puget Sound, they also serve Dungeness crab, clam chowder and local delicacies like geoduck (I dare ya to Google that). Sit at the bar and enjoy shucking with a glass of white wine or a crisp beer.

☞ **Order this:** The Shuckers Dozen
⊙ **Hours:** Sun-Thurs 12PM-8PM, Fri-Sat 12PM-9PM
✷ **Happy Hour:** Mon - Frid 3PM- 5PM
⚲ **Location:** 124 Republican St, Lower Queen Anne

♥ IG: @taylorshellfish



## CANLIS

Get your wallet ready as this is the fanciest place in town. Canlis is a Seattle institution known for its breathtaking views and impeccable, celebrity-level service. The tasting menu showcases Pacific Northwest flavors with a fine dining twist. It's a place for celebrating milestones or just treating yourself to a luxurious evening out. Jackets are encouraged here, so dress to impress.

☞ **Order this:** The Canlis Salad—a classic since 1950, with romaine, mint, oregano, and a house-made dressing that's a perfect blend of simplicity and elegance.
⊙ **Hours:** 5PM-midnight (closed Thurs, Sun, Monday)
⚲ **Location:** 2576 Aurora Ave N, Queen Anne

♥ IG: @canlisrestaurant

## HOW TO COOK A WOLF

Ethan Stowell's How to Cook a Wolf in Queen Anne combines Italian-inspired small plates with Northwest ingredients, all in a rustic, intimate setting. Known for its seasonal menus, the restaurant offers everything from handmade pastas to inventive, shareable plates, alongside a carefully curated wine list. Perfect for date nights or small gatherings.


- **Dinner:** Mon–Thurs 4 PM–10 PM; Fri–Sat 4 PM–11 PM; Sun 4 PM–10 PM
- **Weekend Brunch:** Sat–Sun 10 AM–2 PM

♀ Location:  2208 Queen Anne Ave N, Seattle, WA 98109

♥ IG: @hctawolf

## ROCHAMBEAU

Another great solo girl spot when you want a Negroni and some friendly local company. Also a great date night spot when you want an intimate setting with a stranger - but you also want to be able to make eye contact with the bartender in case of stranger danger. You are taken care of in all ways here, especially with your cocktails and bites. From seafood to steak, their small menu is often changing but never disappoints.

⊙ **Hours:** Wed–Thurs 5–10 PM, Fri–Sat 5–10:30 PM, Sun 5–9 PM, closed Mon–Tues

♀ Location: 2209 Queen Anne Ave N

♥ IG: @rochambeau_seattle

# DRINKS AND COCKTAILS

## BAR MIRIAM

This cozy, Parisian-inspired wine bar is the go-to spot for a glass of wine or a sexy cocktail. The bartenders are friendly and love to share their knowledge, making it an ideal spot for solo travelers who want some local advice. Pair your drink with a small plate of charcuterie or cheese, and you'll be in heaven.

☞ **Order this:**  The French 75—gin, lemon juice, and champagne for a bubbly, refreshing twist.

⊙ Hours: Mon-Sun 4PM-10PM (open til midnight Fri & Sat)

♀ Location: 1531 Queen Anne Ave N

♥ IG: @BarMiriam.seattle

## FAST FASHION

One of my favorite breweries in the Pacific Northwest; they never miss. FF has a micro-brew taproom and is a hidden gem in Lower Queen Anne. It's not the sexiest tap room but it's very convenient when you want a good beer without the theatrics. If you're hungry, you can place an order at The Masonry next door—they'll even deliver it right to your table at FF.

⊙ Hours: Mon-Sun 4PM-10PM

♀ Location: 20 Roy St, Lower Queen Anne

♥ IG: @FastFashionBeer

## CHAPTER FOUR

# South Lake Union

**DAYS NEEDED:**
Half a day

*Capitol Hill is Seattle's artsy, educated, eccentric sibling with a secret underground double life.*

There are two reasons to visit South Lake Union.

1. **You work at Amazon or are visiting someone who works at Amazon.** This is where Amazon headquarters is, in addition to the housing and watering holes for all the tech people.

2. **The lake!** Lake Union is an outdoor lover's dream! And just south of the lake is where adventures begin!

Imagine a neighborhood that rolls from kayaking on Lake Union in the morning to cocktails with a techie crowd in the evening—that's South Lake Union. Once an industrial shipping hub, South Lake Union has transformed in recent decades, thanks in large part to Amazon and other tech giants that made it their headquarters. Today, this neighborhood is packed with sleek offices, high-rise apartments, and green spaces, all connected by the South Lake Union Streetcar. But what really gives SLU its charm is the lake itself. You'll see seaplanes taking off, kayakers gliding along, and an unbeatable view of the skyline from the water.

This chapter is going to be quick, okay?

### ♥ FUN FACT!

Lake Union is famous for its floating homes and houseboats, including the one featured in the movie Sleepless in Seattle.

# Areas to Know

## LAKE UNION PARK

The heart of the neighborhood where you can rent kayaks or eat lunch with a view. It's also home to the Museum of History & Industry (MOHAI)!

## AMAZON SPHERES & NEARBY DINING

The famous glass Spheres are surrounded by trendy restaurants and coffee shops, ideal for people-watching (or tech-spotting).

## SOUTH LAKE UNION STREETCAR ROUTE

Connecting you to Downtown, Belltown, and the International District, the SLU Streetcar is your ticket to navigating Seattle...slowly. Locals don't use this for quick transfers, but its a scenic way to get around.

Most likely, you'll visit South Lake Union just for the day, unless you're moving here then welcome!

## HOW TO GET AROUND

**South Lake Union is one of Seattle's most walkable neighborhoods.** But to explore efficiently, and to breeze in and out of this neighborhood, take the South Lake Union Street Car.

**The South Lake Union Streetcar** is one of the easiest ways to get around South Lake Union, especially for quick hops between its main areas. Running every 10-15 minutes, the streetcar connects downtown to South Lake Union and provides a stress-free option for exploring the area. **Here's a quick guide:**

▶ **Route:** Starts at Westlake in downtown Seattle and travels through South Lake Union, ending at Fairview Ave N & Ward St.

✏ **Cost:** $2.25 per ride

⊙ **Hours:** Mon–Thurs 6 AM–9 PM; Fri–Sat 6 AM–11 PM; Sun 10 AM–7 PM

### Key Stops to Know:

▶ **Westlake Hub:** Ideal starting point for connections to light rail, buses, and the monorail.

▶ **7th & Westlake:** Near Amazon Go, Whole Foods, and other eateries.

▶ **Terry & Thomas:** Close to coffee spots and the Museum of History & Industry (MOHAI).

▶ **Mercer Street:** Great access point for Lake Union Park.

▶ **Fairview Ave N & Ward St:** The final stop for a scenic lakeside walk or waterfront dining

# Best Things to Do in South Lake Union

## VISIT BANYA 5

Banya 5 in South Lake Union is a Russian-style bathhouse with a mix of hot and cold therapy! Cycle between a 200-degree sauna, a eucalyptus steam room, and a 104-degree hot pool, followed by a 55-degree cold plunge for full-body rejuvenation. Pair it with one of their massages—like the Swedish or Russian Honey Scrub Massage—for the ultimate relaxation.

⊙ Hours: Daily, 11 AM – 10 PM

⊙ Location: South Lake Union, 217 9th Ave N

⊕ Visit: banya5.com

## KAYAK ON THE LAKE

Seaplanes will be taking off over your head and landing next to you on the water! If you want a true Seattle experience, renting a kayak is my go-to way to see and experience the city from the water! Better yet, this is a budget-friendly adventure!

Two Rental Options:

1. **MossBay** open Sat & Sun 11AM-6PM

⊙ Location: Lake Union Park

⊕ Visit: mossbay.co

2. **Northwest Outdoor Center** (NWOC) open Wed–Sun, 11 AM – 6 PM

⊘ Cost: Single kayak or SUP at $23/hour, double kayak at $30/hour, triple kayak at $40/hour

⊙ Location: East lake (drive or Uber there) - 2100 Westlake Ave N, Suite 1

⊕ Visit: nwoc.com

## HOT TUB BOATS

Your boat is literally a hot tub that floats on the water! Steer your hot tub boat over to the community of houseboats (literally houses that float) and see how Seattlites live. Not all hot tub boats are made the same, however. I prefer the fully electric Lux Hot Tub Boats that you steer with a joystick, but there is also the option to go wood-powered with a company simply called Hot Tub Boats. Both have headquarters on East Lake...just east of the lake. Gosh, Seattle is an oddly shaped city.

⊙ **Hours::** 8AM-11PM (how fun would a sunset cruise be?!)

✒ **Cost:** $400 - $450 for 2 hours (fits up to 6 people)

⊕ **Visit:** luxhottubboats.com or hottubboats.com

## SAILING SEATTLE

Sailing Seattle offers a front-row seat to the magic of Lake Union whether you're sailing past those iconic houseboats (yes, the Sleepless in Seattle ones), watching seaplanes land right next to you, or looking for marine animals. And they've got a selection of sailing sessions to choose from: the classic Lake Union Cruise takes you around all the must-see spots, the Sunset Sail makes a perfect date night, or go all-out with a Private Charter if you're with a group and want the boat to yourselves.

♥ **Pro Tip:** Bring some snacks and your favorite wine—it's completely BYOB.

✒ **Cost:** $45 - $65 per person, depending on the tour.

⊕ **Visit:** sailingseattle.com

♥ **FUN FACT!** In Seattle, the South Lake Union streetcar has a cheeky nickname—the "S.L.U.T." or "South Lake Union Trolley"!

## VISIT MUSEUM OF HISTORY & INDUSTRY (MOHAI)

Adventure pairing alert! When you come to the lake, pop into this museum covering everything from Seattle's origins as a port city to its rise in tech and aerospace, highlighting influential figures like Bill Boeing and celebrating cultural moments in Seattle's history, including the grunge era. Interactive exhibits make it a hit with all ages, and you'll leave with a true appreciation of Seattle's pioneering spirit.

✒ **Cost:** $22 for adults

⊙ **Hours:** Daily 10 AM – 5 PM, open until 8 PM on First Thursdays (free days).

⊕ **Visit:** mohai.org

## SCENIC FLIGHTS FROM SOUTH LAKE UNION

Take to the skies with a scenic flight from Seattle Seaplanes. In just 20 minutes, you'll fly over 31 miles of Seattle's landmarks, including the Space Needle, University of Washington, and Gasworks Park. Seaplanes have been a unique part of Seattle's culture for decades, offering locals and visitors an exciting way to experience the city's waterways and skyline from above. Perfect for visitors and locals alike, this flight offers unbeatable aerial views of the city.

♥ **Pro Tip:** Try to snag the co-pilot seat for the ultimate view!
🎫 **Cost:** $136 per person.
🌐 **Visit:** seattleseaplanes.com

## VISIT THE SPHERES

Amazon's Spheres are a nature-lover's dream right in the middle of the city. These futuristic domes house over 40,000 plants from all over the world, creating a lush indoor garden. Built as part of Amazon's innovative workspace, The Spheres represent a fusion of nature and technology, aimed at inspiring creativity in both visitors and employees. The mix of innovation and nature makes it a must-see in Seattle.

♥ **Pro Tip:** Public access is only available twice a month with confirmation of a reservation, so book in advance...but reservation spots are only made available 15 days in advance, so pay attention to the schedule. If you can't get in, visit Understory, the interactive exhibit at the base of The Spheres.

🎫 **Cost:** Free with a reservation.
🌐 **Visit:** seattlespheres.com

♥ **Find a Seattle Sister to explore with!**
Post in your community, Girls in Seattle, and find a friend!

facebook.com/groups/girlsinseattle

## SOUTH LAKE UNION SATURDAY MARKET

This lively, seasonal market offers food trucks, handmade goods, and local produce in the heart of SLU. Running May through September, it's the perfect way to spend a sunny Saturday. The market features a rotating selection of vendors, ensuring there's always something new to try, from craft beers to locally-made jewelry.

♥ **Pro Tip:** Arrive early to beat the lunch rush at the food trucks! When: Saturdays, 11 AM – 4 PM, May through September.
🌐 **Visit:** slumarket.com

☞ **Where to Grab Picnic Supplies:**
**Metropolitan Market**
For all your gourmet picnic needs, head to Metropolitan Market in South Lake Union.

🌐 **Visit** metropolitan-market.com

# Where to Eat & Drink in South Lake Union

## COFFEE, BREAKFAST AND BRUNCH

### PORTAGE BAY CAFÉ

Portage Bay Café has earned its reputation as a brunch haven in Seattle, thanks to a farm-to-table ethos and the beloved breakfast bar — featuring berries, whipped cream, and other toppings—where you can customize your pancakes, waffles, or French toast to your heart's content. I also recommend trying one (or three) of their seasonal mimosas!

☞ **Order this:** Go for the Classic French Toast.

♥ **Pro Tip:** Weekends get busy, so plan to arrive early to avoid the wait.

☉ **Hours:** Daily 8 AM – 2 PM

♥ **IG:** @portagebaycafe

## LUNCH/DINNER

### I LOVE SUSHI

The first time I ever had nigiri was here, and it was unforgettable—the fish was so fresh, those first bites are still vivid! For some of Seattle's best sushi and fantastic lake views, this spot is a must. The menu offers everything from classic nigiri to creative rolls, plus an extensive sake list and tasty lunch specials.

☞ **Order this:** Salmon Nigiri

♥ **Pro Tip:** Call ahead for reservations, especially on weekends—it fills up fast!

☉ **Hours:** Mon–Sat: Lunch 11:30 AM–2:30 PM, Dinner 5 PM–9 PM (closed Sundays)

📍 **Location:** 1001 Fairview Ave N

♥ **IG:** @ilovesushiseattle

### KATI VEGAN THAI

South Lake Union's Kati Vegan Thai is the kind of place where you take a die-hard meat lover and convert them into a veggie fan, at least for tonight. They specialize in vegan spins on traditional Thai dishes that still pack all the flavors of the originals. And here's the kicker: they're committed to using authentic Thai ingredients, so you still get the classic comfort

Thai food you crave. The cozy outdoor patio is a nice touch, perfect for people-watching or catching up with friends.☺

Hours: 11:30AM – 3PM / 4:30PM — 9PM

📍Location: 1190 Thomas St

♥ IG: @kativeganthai

## BA BAR SOUTH

Ba Bar is your go-to for Vietnamese street food with a killer happy hour. The bar here is a hidden gem for mingling. South Lake Union's tech crowd rolls through after work, so if you're conveniently alone at the bar looking super cute and you lock eyes with a hot Seattle dude/lady...I mean, that could be fun, right? Oh and the food. Their Bun Cha tastes just like I used to eat when I lived in Hanoi!

♥ Pro Tip: Head here late-night for their "Midnight Menu"— they stay open until 2 AM on weekends!

🕙 Hours: Monday-Friday: 10 AM – 11 PM | Saturday-Sunday: 10 AM – 2 AM

📍Location: 500 Terry Ave N

♥ IG: @babarseattle



# Drinks & Cocktails

## FLATSTICK PUB

Flatstick Pub is a date night goldmine if you're ready to break the ice and see how your date handles a little friendly competition. With mini-golf, Duffleboard (a quirky hybrid of mini-golf and shuffleboard), and plenty of spots to sit and chat, it's easy to shake off any first-date awkwardness. Plus, seeing how they handle a win (or a loss) can be a solid glimpse into their character—a true test!

**What to Order:** Grab a few local IPAs on tap and share the pepperoni pizza.

♥ Pro Tip: Start with a game to loosen up, then find a cozy spot to keep chatting over drinks. It's casual but tells you a lot about their vibe.

🕙 Hours: Daily, 11 AM – 11 PM (open til 1am Fri & Sat)

📍Location: 609 Westlake Ave N

♥ IG: @flatstickpubslu

## MBAR

For one of Seattle's best rooftop views, head to Mbar, located just on the edge of South Lake Union. This chic rooftop bar offers sweeping views of the city skyline, Space Needle, and

Lake Union. With a Middle Eastern-inspired menu and a fantastic selection of craft cocktails, it's the perfect spot to unwind while taking in the view. The ambiance is chic but laid-back, making it ideal for anything from casual drinks to a special night out.

⊙ **Hours:** Mon-Sat: 4:30 PM – 8:30 PM (9:30PM Fri & Sat)

♥ **Location:** 609 Westlake Ave N

♥ IG: **@mbarsea**

## ALTITUDE SKY LOUNGE

Perched atop the Residence Inn by Marriott, Altitude Sky Lounge offers stunning, 360-degree views of Seattle's skyline, including the Space Needle, Lake Union, and Puget Sound. This rooftop bar has a chic, upscale atmosphere but is still welcoming for casual outings, making it ideal for both date nights and solo adventures with a book. With fire pits and cozy seating, it's an excellent spot to watch the sunset or take in the city lights.

♥ **Pro Tip:** Arrive early to snag a prime seat by the fire pits—this place fills up fast around sunset!

⊙ **Hours:** Daily: 3 PM – 11 PM (til midnight Fri & Sat)

♥ **Location:** Astra Hotel Seattle, 300 Terry Ave N Atop

♥ IG: **@altitudeskyloungeseattle**

## PRO-TIP FOR SLU

☞ **Visit the REI Store:**
The most epic REI with a climbing wall! So hey, if you've ever been interested in buying a true backpacker's backpack (for going to Asia with the rest of my guide-books) then pop into REI and have a staff member help you get fitted for a back-pack. Yes, you must be fitted for these. Don't want to use it now? They can ship it to you back home for you.

♥ Hey sister, I bring this book to life on TikTok **@SoloGirlsTravelGuide** – you'll find tutorials, guides and pep talks there.

## CHAPTER FIVE

# Capitol Hill

**DAYS NEEDED:**
1-2 days

*Capitol Hill is Seattle's artsy, educated, eccentric sibling with a secret underground double life.*

It's the neighborhood with a loud opinion on everything! By day, it's vintage shops, green spaces, and coffee everywhere you look. But after dark, get ready for the real Capitol Hill—home to Seattle's best speakeasies, karaoke bars, and dance clubs.

But Capitol Hill wasn't always so eclectic. In the early 1900s, it was known as "Millionaire's Row," home to Seattle's elite who built stately mansions along 14th Avenue, many of which still stand today as a nod to the neighborhood's polished past. You can still stroll through parts of Capitol Hill and spot these historic homes, a reminder of a more tailored era before the dive bars and disco balls moved in.

But as Seattle's culture shifted, Capitol Hill transformed, attracting artists, activists, and students, and bringing in a wave of colorful murals, indie theaters, and LGBTQ+ pride. Today, this mix of history and grit gives Capitol Hill its distinct character—it's a place that honors its roots but thrives on fresh ideas and bold expression.

After a night out, you'll need brunch and Capitol Hill's got it, with plenty of spots for mimosas, hash browns, and those classic "I'll never drink again" hangover meals. It's also a breeze to get here—buses, Ubers, or a quick Lime bike ride from wherever you are in Seattle. Bonus: I'm going to show you a couple of my favorite spots in a nearby quieter neighborhood called The Central District for more can't-miss eats.

**BEST FOR:**

▸ Nightlife and karaoke
▸ Greenspaces & mansion strolls
▸ Coffee connoisseurs and brunch lovers

♥ **PRO TIP!** If you get drunk at crowded bars and leave your phone on the table, someone might steal it. FYI so be mindful. See anti-theft bags at <u>Alexa-West.com/Travel-Shop</u>

# Areas to Know

## BROADWAY

Capitol Hill's main street where history meets the present. Here you'll find landmarks like the Jimi Hendrix statue honoring Seattle's music legend, alongside eateries and local shops that reflect the neighborhood's eclectic spirit.

## PIKE/PINE CORRIDOR

The beating heart of Capitol Hill's nightlife, known for its historic buildings that house popular bars, live music venues, and restaurants.

## VOLUNTEER PARK

One of Capitol Hill's green gems, Volunteer Park is home to a historic conservatory, peaceful trails, and the 1906 Water Tower. Climb to the top of the tower for one of the best free views of Seattle.

## CAL ANDERSON PARK

Seattle's first park specifically designed as an inclusive community space, Cal Anderson is known for outdoor events, casual sports, and festivals. However, this park gets sketchy after dark.

## MILLIONAIRE'S ROW

Located on 14th Avenue E between E Prospect St and E Roy St, this stately avenue reflects Capitol Hill's early 20th-century roots. Once (and still) home to some of Seattle's elite, Millionaire's Row features grand historic homes, fascinating for architectural history buffs.

**♥ PRO TIP FOR CAPITOL HILL:**

Stop by Boon Boona's for a cup of coffee and to pick up some of my favorite bags of beans to go for yourself or as a Seattle Souvenir / gift.

**♥ IG: @boonboonacoffee**

☞ **For more on Capitol Hill History, YouTube "What Happened to Seattle's Millionaire's Row?"**

# Top Things to Do in Capitol Hill

## KARAOKE & NIGHTLIFE

Capitol Hill is Seattle's unofficial karaoke capital. From Japanese-style private singing rooms at Rock Box (@rockboxseattle) to belting it out for a crowd at Hula Hula (@hulahulabarseattle), Capitol Hill's karaoke scene has you covered. If you're after something with character, head to The Crescent Lounge (@crescent.lounge) for free karaoke every night, drag shows, and an old-school vibe that's always entertaining.

♥ Pro Tip: For a true dive-bar karaoke experience, visit Baranof, where the bartenders serve sass alongside the drinks, and the karaoke is refreshingly no-frills.

## JOIN A DANCE CLASS AT CENTURY BALLROOM

So you're socially awkward and maybe more than a little afraid of public dancing—perfect! Century Ballroom is here to make sure you have a night you'll laugh about later. With everything from Salsa and Bachata to Swing and Waltz, each night feels like a giant, inclusive party where no one cares if you mess up. Don't have a partner? Neither do half the people there! It's all about going with the flow, laughing at your mistakes, and connecting with a room full of strangers who are just as nervous and/or enthusiastic as you.

♥ Pro Tip: Show up early for the intro lesson—it's basically "awkwardness warm-up," and you'll leave with new friends before the real dancing starts.

🕐 Hours: 8 PM – 1 AM
🎟 Cost: $10–$20
📍 Location: Central Capitol Hill
🌐 Visit: centuryballroom.com

## WANDER VOLUNTEER PARK

Volunteer Park in Capitol Hill is an ideal spot for walks, picnics, and taking in scenic views from the 1906 Water Tower, which offers some of the best free panoramas of Seattle. Explore the park's paths and the Volunteer Park Conservatory for unique tropical plants and cacti in a historic greenhouse.

♥ Pro Tip: Visit the Dahlia Garden

in late summer for vibrant blooms.
⊙ Hours: Park open daily, 6 AM–10 PM; Conservatory open Tues–Sun, 10 AM–4 PM (closed Mondays).

## CAL ANDERSON PARK

In the heart of Capitol Hill, Cal Anderson Park is where locals gather for picnics, sports, and casual hangouts. With lawns, sports courts, and a reflecting pool, it's a lively, welcoming place perfect for people-watching and summer events.

♥ Pro Tip: Summer brings street performers and community events to the park.
⊙ Hours: Daily 4 AM–11:30 PM .

## SEATTLE ASIAN ART MUSEUM

Located in Volunteer Park, the Seattle Asian Art Museum is an elegant Art Deco landmark showcasing Asian art from ancient to modern. Exhibits rotate regularly, so there's always something new.

♥ Pro Tip: Climb the nearby Water Tower afterward for amazing views.
☞ Cost: $14.99 for adults; free for kids under 14
⊙ Hours: Wed–Sun, 10 AM–5 PM; free on the first Thursday of the month
⊕ Visit: seattleartmuseum.org

## WANDER THE ARBORETUM

Just outside Capitol Hill, the Washington Park Arboretum offers trails through gardens, wetlands, and wooded areas. Walk Azalea Way for floral views or take Foster Island Trail for wildlife sightings. Kayaks can be rented nearby to paddle through serene waterways.

♥ Pro Tip: The Seattle Japanese Garden offers a quiet escape nearby for a small fee.
⊙ Hours: Open daily, dawn to dusk
☞ Kayak Rentals: Waterfront Activities Center

### BLACKBERRY ALERT!

Emilia and I were out for a walk around 8 a.m. when we paused to pick blackberries along the road (they grow everywhere)! Suddenly, a man approached us, saying, "I'm sorry to ask, but I keep seeing people at these bushes. What are you doing?" We happily explained the magic of **blackberry season! Between late July and September,** keep an eye out for wild blackberries. **Here's the trick:** if they're ripe, they'll pull off the bush easily, and the inside will have a white circle. A quick tip, though—skip the low-hanging berries where dogs pee!

# Where to Eat in Capitol Hill

## BREAKFAST, BRUNCH AND COFFEE

### STARBUCKS RESERVE ROASTERY

You can't come to Seattle without visiting one of the world's fanciest Starbucks. The Starbucks Reserve Roastery on Capitol Hill is like Disneyland for coffee lovers. With exclusive drinks, small-batch roasts, and a peek into how coffee is produced, this is an educational Starbucks experience!

♥ **Pro Tip:** Try the Coffee Flight, where you can sample different brew methods.
⊙ **Hours:** Daily, 6:30 AM – 11 PM
📍 **Location:** 1124 Pike St
🌐 **Visit:** starbucksreserve.com
♥ **IG:** @starbucksreserve_seattle

### VOLUNTEER PARK CAFE & PANTRY

Start your day with a peaceful stroll through Volunteer Park, taking in the views and historic features. Then, head over to Volunteer Park Cafe for coffee and a delicious pastry or brunch in this charming, sunlit spot. This beloved neighborhood spot is a Capitol Hill staple for breakfast, brunch, and baked goods. They serve freshly baked pastries, breakfast classics, and even have their own herb garden and backyard chickens for the freshest ingredients.

⊙ **Hours:** Wed–Sun, 8 AM – 5 PM; closed Mon–Tues
📍 **Location:** 1501 17th Ave E
♥ **IG:** @cafeandpantry

### ODDFELLOWS CAFÉ + BAR

This isn't just a café, it's a Capitol Hill institution. With its worn-in, rustic charm and lofty ceilings, Oddfellows feels like the cozy home of your coolest friend who's always up for brunch. The vibe is laid-back and artsy, making it perfect for people-watching while you sip your cappuccino.

♥ **Pro Tip:** Don't sleep in—by 10 AM, the line's out the door.
⊙ **Hours:** Mon–Fri 8 AM – 9 PM; Sat–Sun 8 AM – 3 PM
📍 **Location:** 1525 10th Ave
♥ **IG:** @oddfellowscafe

## THE FRENCH GUYS BAKERY

Tucked away on East Olive Way, The French Guys Bakery feels like a slice of Paris in the middle of Seattle. Known for its perfect croissants, this place is the place to go if you want to start your morning with flaky pastry bliss. The interior is tiny but cozy, and the smell of fresh-baked goods is irresistible. ☞ **Order this:** The almond croissant—seriously, it'll ruin all other croissants for you.

♥ **Pro Tip:** Get there early because once they sell out, they're gone.

☉ **Hours:** Tues–Sun 8 AM – 2 PM (Closed Mon)

♀ **Location:** 321 NE 103rd St

♥ **IG:** @thefrenchguysseattle

## GLO'S DINER

Serving classic diner fare with Capitol Hill charm, Glo's is where you go when you want no-fuss, all-satisfaction breakfast. It's been a neighborhood staple since forever, and it's one of those places where regulars know exactly what they're getting. The space is small and simple, but the flavors are big.

☞ **Order this:** Their Eggs Benedict.

♥ **Pro Tip:** : Be ready to wait for a table on weekends. ☉

**Hours:** Sat–Sun 8 AM – 3 PM

♀**Location:** 928 E. Barbara Bailey Way

⊕ **Visit:** glosseattle.com

## NEKO CAT CAFÉ

If you're a cat person, Neko Cat Café is your dream come true. Where else can you sip on a chai latte while petting adoptable cats lounging around you? The cozy interior is designed for ultimate relaxation—both for humans and cats. It's the ultimate feel-good spot for a quiet coffee or tea session with new feline friends.

☞ **Order this:** Their seasonal lattes are always a win, and pair it with a locally baked pastry. Pro Tip: Reservations are highly recommended, especially weekends.

☉ **Hours:** Mon–Sun 11 AM – 8 PM

♀ **Location:** 519 E Pine St

♥ **IG:** @neko.cat.cafe

## MIMOSAS CABARET DRAG BRUNCH

For the most fabulous brunch experience in Seattle, Mimosas Cabaret is the place to be. Featuring over-the-top drag performances alongside bottomless mimosas, this brunch show is pure entertainment. Expect a lively crowd, killer performances, and plenty of champagne to go around.

☞ **Order this:** Go for the classic brunch combo.

♥ **Pro Tip:** Make reservations in advance!

⊙ **Hours:** Sundays, shows at 12 PM & 2 PM
♥ **Location:** 1518 11th Ave
♥ **IG:** @mimosascabaret

## BONITO CAFÉ Y MERCADITO

A hidden gem with a Latin twist, Bonito Café y Mercadito serves up rich coffee, Salvadoran pupusas, and other Latin favorites. It's a great spot for brunch or a casual breakfast, with a welcoming atmosphere and delicious homemade treats.

♥ **Pro Tip:** Grab some fresh pupusas — sold outside on Sundays by local Salvadoran vendors.
⊙ **Hours:** Mon–Sat 8 AM – 6 PM; Sun 8 AM – 4 PM
♥ **Location:** 1045 S Jackson St, Seattle, WA 98104

## LUNCH, DINNER & DESSERT

### Casual

## WOODSHOP BBQ (CENTRAL DISTRICT)

Craving BBQ? Head to Woodshop BBQ for some of the best smoked meats in Seattle. Try their chicken wings with homemade ranch. Their brisket! The pork ribs. All of it is melt in your mouth perfection.

☞ **Order this:** Pulled Pork Mac n Cheese which is big enough to share.
⊙ **Hours:** Tues-Sun 11 AM – 8 PM

♥ **Location:** 2513 S Jackson St
♥ **IG:** @woodshopbbq

## RUMBA

A menu filled with Caribbean-inspired dishes that bring a taste of tropical paradise to the Pacific Northwest. Start with plantain chips and fresh ceviche or guacamole. My go to is the Cuban sandwich but they also have jerk chicken sliders that are to die for! Afterwards, head to Inside Passage, their speakeasy bar.

☞ **Order this:** The Spam Sliders & a rum punch!
⊙ **Hours:** Fri-Sun 4 PM–1 AM; Mon-Thurs 5 PM–1 AM
♥ **Location:** 1112 Pike St
♥ **IG:** @rumbaseattle

## BIANG BIANG NOODLES

This tiny hole-in-the-wall is all about the hand-pulled noodles. It's perfect for a quick, solo lunch or casual dinner when you're craving something hearty and spicy. The portions are huge and it's easy on the wallet.

☞ **Order this:** Spicy Lamb Biang Biang Noodles.
⊙ **Hours:** Mon - Thurs: 5 PM – 1 AM / Fri - Sun: 4 PM – 1 AM
♥ **Location:** 601 E Pike St
♥ **IG:** @biangbiangnoodles_sea

## CARMELO'S TACOS

No matter if you're hungry for lunch or need some drunk food late at night, every bite at Carmelo's es rico. Family-owned, cash-only. Like spicy? Top with their homemade Manzano Salsa!

☞ Order this: I typically go for the Birria Tacos or the Al Pastor Tacos with homemade tortillas!

♥ Pro Tip: Carmelo's is cash only!

⊙ Hours: Monday-Saturday: 11 AM – 10 PM | Sunday: 11 AM – 8 PM

⚲ Location: 110 Summit Ave E

♥ IG: @carmelostacos

## *Date-Night Approved*

## POQUITOS

Sultry atmosphere, familiar Mexican comfort food, huge margaritas. This is a low-pressure first-date spot that still feels classy and sexy. Get a little dressed up, if you wish. I recommend ordering a bunch of things to share including the street tacos. Located right in the heart of Capitol Hill, you two can plan to walk to nearby Foreign National for a speakeasy cocktail.

⊙ Hours: Mon–Thurs 12 PM – 10 PM; Fri 12 PM – 12 AM; Sat 11 AM – 12 AM; Sun 11 AM – 10 PM

⚲ Location: 1000 E Pike St

♥ IG: @vivapoquitos

## NUE RESTAURANT

Nue is a quirky, globally-inspired spot on Capitol Hill that feels like a mini trip around the world. With dishes from places like South Africa, Thailand, and Jamaica, it's perfect for adventurous eaters and a great choice for casual date nights. The eclectic, mismatched décor adds to the fun, making it a great place to break the ice without any awkwardness.

☞ Order this: The Szechuan Chicken Wings.

⊙ Hours: Mon–Wed 11 AM – 10 PM; Thurs–Fri 11 AM – 11 PM; Sat 10 AM – 11 PM; Sun 10 AM – 10 PM

⚲ Location: 1519 14th Ave (between Pike & Pine)

♥ IG: @nueseattle

## *Late Night Eats*

## BIG MARIO'S PIZZA

When my boyfriend and I want to snuggle in the corner of a dark pizza place and have a beer, this is where we come. New York-style pizza by the slice, served until late. Perfect after a night of bar hopping. You'll walk in and see pizza by the slice. Point and choose which you want crisped up for you.

♥ Pro Tip: I accidentally ordered vegan pizza here once as it looks like the real deal!

⊙ **Hours:** Monday-Thursday: 11 AM – 2 AM | Friday-Saturday: 11 AM – 3 AM | Sunday: 11 AM – 2 AM

♥ **Location:** 1009 E Pike St

♥ **IG:** @bigmariospizza

## MOLLY MOON

Locally owned and operated, Molly Moon's is a true Seattle gem. Founded by Seattleite Molly Moon Neitzel in 2008, this beloved ice cream shop prides itself on using organic, locally sourced ingredients from nearby farms. Beyond serving delicious scoops, Molly Moon's is big on community engagement—supporting social causes like paid family leave for employees and offering free ice cream to kids in need.

⊙ **Hours:** Monday-Sunday: 12 PM – 10 PM (open till 11PM on Fri & Sat).

♥ **Location:** 917 E Pine St

♥ **IG:** @mollymoonicecream

## DICK'S DRIVE-IN

Seattle's best drunk food destination, Dick's Drive-In has been the late-night spot for decades. After a night out in Capitol Hill, there's nothing better than a greasy Deluxe burger and fries under the glow of their retro neon sign. The vibe? Pure 1950s Americana with a drive-in feel and plenty of outdoor space for Seattle's night owls.

📷 Photo by Emy! @__helloemilia

Ps. Dicks is Seattle's drunk food as it's open so late!

⊙ **Hours:** Daily, 10:30 AM – 2 AM

♥ **Location:** 115 Broadway E

♥ **IG:** @dicksdrivein

# Where to Drink in Capitol Hill

## A/STIR

Oh my goodness, you must check their calendar for events that overflow with music, cocktails and friendship. Like the Wednesday Day Cider Jam Sessions where they "party like a jazz club" with open mic! Outside the events, this place makes the most deliciously inventive cocktail experiments in Seattle!

♥ **Pro Tip:** Ask for a cocktail that pairs with the pork belly bao buns.
☉ **Hours:** Tues, Wed, Thurs, Sun 5–10 PM; Fri 5 PM–2 AM; Sat 3 PM–2 AM; Closed Mon
⚲ **Location:** 818 E Pike St
⊕ **Visit:** astirseattle.com

## INSIDE PASSAGE

This isn't your average tiki bar—Inside Passage is a whimsical deep-sea adventure tucked away inside Rumba restaurant. The drinks here are as outrageous as the setting, with towering cocktails that double as Instagram-worthy spectacles. If you're into rum, punchy flavors, and a bit of flair, this rare find is your tropical oasis in the middle of Seattle.

☞ **Order this:** The Kraken Bowl is a must for groups—served in a giant octopus bowl.
☉ **Hours:** Monday-Saturday: 5PM - 11:30PM | Closed Mon
⚲ **Location:** Inside Rumba
⊕ **Visit:** insidepassageseattle.com

## FOREIGN NATIONAL

Speakeasy alert! Tucked behind Stateside restaurant, this dimly-lit, moody cocktail lounge feels like a secret getaway from the city. If you're into strong, Asian-inspired cocktails that taste as adventurous as they look, this is your spot. No reservations here, so get there early or be ready for a short wait. It's totally worth it.

☞ **Order this:** The Banana Daiquiri is legendary
☉ **Hours:** Mon-Sat 6PM - 12 AM
⚲ **Location:** 300 E Pike St
♥ **IG:** @foreign.national

## STOUP BREWING CAPITOL HILL

Incredible beer and an impressively large warehouse-style space! Want to throw a small private event? This is the place to reserve a table, bring some pizza and a cake, and celebrate. Known for its inventive small-batch brews and it's inclusive community vibe, you'll get a real sense of the neighborhood just by sitting here and people watching. The indoor-outdoor setup is perfect for Seattle's unpredictable weather! This is also the spot I come to laptop work with a beer!

⊙ **Hours:** 12–10 PM Sun–Thu, 12–11 PM Fri–Sat
♥ **Location:** 1158 Broadway
⊕ **Visit:** stoupbrewing.com

## CHUCK'S HOP SHOP (CENTRAL DISTRICT)

For beer nerds who like variety, Chuck's Hop Shop is a wonderland of endless options. With over 50 rotating taps and the biggest selection of canned beers from around the world, Chuck's has a reputation for being one of the best places in the city to grab a pint or stock up for home. The laid-back picnic table setup and rotating food trucks make this a routine stop for local Seattleites.

★ **Adventure Pairing:** Visit Woodshop BBQ and Chucks on the same trip!
♥ **Pro Tip:** Order popcorn.
⊙ **Hours:** Monday-Sunday: 11 AM – 10 PM (11 PM on Fri & Sat)
♥ **Location:** Central District, you'll need a car!
⊕ **Visit:** chuckshopshop.com

## NIGHTLIFE AND LIVE MUSIC IN CAPITOL HILL

Capitol Hill is buzzing every night of the week, from dive bar karaoke to underground live music venues. If you're looking for a place to let loose and have fun, this neighborhood has you covered, no matter your vibe.

## HULA HULA

I don't even like Karaoke but I do like hanging out here and watching my friends do Karaoke. Hula Hula sets the tone for that quintessential drunk girls night out! The decor is all palm fronds, neon lights, and kitschy tiki accents, setting the stage for a lively, no-judgment karaoke experience! Karaoke starts every night at 9 PM. Expect tropical drinks served in whacky mugs and girls in line for the bathroom complimenting your hair.

⊙ **Hours:** Mon-Sun 4 PM – 2 AM
♥ **Location:** 1501 E Olive Wy
⊕ **Visit:** hulahula.org

## BARANOF

During the day, Baranof is your classic greasy spoon diner, but at night on the weekends, it transforms into one of the most quintessential karaoke spots in the city. On Friday and Saturday nights, karaoke kicks off around 9 PM, drawing a quirky mix of regulars and newcomers belting out '80s rock and guilty-pleasure ballads. They've got pull tabs, pool, darts, and karaoke every night. Open til 2am, this is Seattle's diviest dive bar.

📍Location: 8549 Greenwood Ave N
♥ IG: @baranofseattle

## THE CRESCENT LOUNGE

Crescent Lounge identifies as "Seattle's oldest gay/dive/come as you are/karaoke bar"! Free karaoke every night, drag shows, and a mischievous atmosphere make it a chaotic Capitol Hill classic. Whether you're here to sing or just to watch, it's always a good time!

☞ Order this: A cheap beer and a shot—it's that kind of place.
⊙ Hours: Mon - Sun: 2 PM – 2 AM
📍Location: 1413 E Olive Wy
♥ IG: @crescent.lounge

## ROCK BOX

If you find a crew of people at Karaoke that want to keep singing, take them here. Rock Box is Capitol Hill's favorite Japanese-style karaoke bar where you sing in private rooms. Check in at the front desk, and if you've made a reservation, they'll escort you to your private room. Rooms vary in size, fitting anywhere from 2 to 15 people. Each room has comfy seating, disco lights, and a touchscreen karaoke system with a massive song library. Order Japanese-inspired cocktails and sake, plus a small selection of food like takoyaki and edamame to your room by using the service button! Very Japanese.

♥ Pro Tip: Book your room in advance, especially on weekends. They fill up quickly!
⊙ Hours: Daily, 4 PM – 2 AM
📍Location: 1603 Nagle Pl
♥ IG: @rockboxseattle

## CHOP SUEY

A true staple of Capitol Hill's live music scene, Chop Suey hosts everything from indie bands to electronic dance nights. This intimate venue is perfect for catching up-and-coming artists or dancing to underground beats with a crowd that's all about the music.

♥ Pro Tip: Check out their weekly "Dance Yourself Clean" night for indie beats and good vibes.
⊙ Hours: Wed–Thurs 7 PM–2 AM; Fri–Sat 9 PM–2 AM; Sun 10 PM–2 AM; Mon 9 PM–2 AM; Closed Tues
📍Location: 1325 E Madison St
🌐 Visit: chopsuey.com

## NEUMOS

One of the most iconic live music venues in Seattle, Neumos is the place to see your favorite indie or alternative bands up close and personal. Neumos has been graced by major names like Billie Eilish, Lorde, and Macklemore, who performed surprise sets before launching larger tours. With great acoustics and an energetic crowd, it's a fantastic spot for live music fans who want an unforgettable concert experience.

♥ **Pro Tip:** Stop by Barboza downstairs for smaller, more intimate shows.
◷ **Hours:** 4PM - 2AM
♥ **Location:** 925 E Pike St
⊕ **Visit:** neumos.com

☞ **Want to travel safer, cheaper and smarter?**

The One-Way Ticket Plan: Find and Fund Your Purpose While Traveling the World

https://alexa-west.com/the-one-way-ticket-plan

## ★TOP PICK:
## CAPITOL HILL COMEDY / BAR

Come solo or bring a friend and get ready to laugh til you cry. Comedy / Bar has a fun lineup of stand-up, themed shows, and if you've ever considered a career in comedy – Open Mic Night. The events typically start anywhere between 7-10pm, so grab a bite before you come but know that you can order dinner or snacks from the bar, like burgers, salads, nachos. Pair the laughs with a tasty dinner from their bar menu, and you've got a perfect night out.

♥ **Pro Tip:** Venue is small so arrive a bit early to grab a prime spot near the stage and settle in with a drink.
◷ **Hours:** Show times vary, typically 7PM-10PM
✐ **Cost:** $10-$25 (depending on the event)
Address: 210 Broadway E
⊕ **Visit:** comedyslashbar.com

# Beauty & Wellness in Capitol Hill

Capitol Hill is full of spots to treat yourself, whether you're looking for a quick pampering session or a full day of relaxation. Here are the top beauty and wellness destinations that will have you looking and feeling your best.

## HAIR

### SUGAR & SHEARS SALON AND ORGANIC SPA

They handle all kinds of hair: on your head, your legs, your mustache! Pop in for a cut and a blow out before a fun night out. And maybe a Brazilian wax. Gotta stay hopeful, ya know?

⊙ Hours: Mon 2–8 PM; Tues–Fri 10 AM–8 PM; Sat 10 AM–6 PM; Closed Sun

⊕ Visit: sugarandshearsseattle.com

## NAILS

### NINA'S NAILS AND SPA

For an affordable, high-quality mani-pedi, Nina's Nails and Spa is the place to go. They've got those big comfy massage chairs for a spa pedicure, and they work fast!

♥ Pro Tip: Walk-ins are welcome, but it's best to make a reservation for weekends.

⊙ Hours: Closed Sundays

⊕ Visit: facebook.com/NinaNailsSpa

## ♥ HEALING BONUS!

### SPIRITUAL MUSHROOM CEREMONY

Ever wanted to try psilocybin as therapy? Twice I have attended a magical mushroom ceremony on Vashon Island where I spent the night in the most magical space! Women-only and guided by a doula, this is a transformative experience.

☞ DM me or email me for details.

# Shops & Markets Not to Miss

Capitol Hill's main shopping stretch is along **Broadway Avenue**, especially around **East Pine** and **East Pike Streets**, where you'll find an eclectic mix of boutiques. **Walk along 10th Ave** where you'll find everything from funky fashion at **Trendy Wendy** to unique thrift finds at **The New York X Change**. Or visit **M2M Mart**, a big Korean market (I go there for Korean snacks and candies). The thrift stores to hit up are: **Revival Shop, Lifelong Thrift, Out of the Closet.**

### CAPITOL HILL FARMERS MARKET

A year-round weekly celebration of Seattle's finest local flavors and crafts, popping up every Sunday from 11 AM to 3 PM at the intersection of Broadway and Pine. You'll find 40 stalls and tables heaped with the season's best—sweet summer berries, crisp fall apples, and fresh-cut flowers even on Seattle's grayest days. With occasional live music, friendly vendors, and lots of cheese, this market is a quintessential Capitol Hill experience

♥ **Pro Tip:** Come here to buy Seattle coffee beans to take home as a souvenir.

◷ **Hours:** Every Sunday, year-round | 11 AM – 3 PM

♥ **Location:** Broadway and Pine, next to Seattle Central College

⊕ **Visit:** seattlefarmersmarkets.org

### ELLIOTT BAY BOOK COMPANY

This bookstore is alive in a way most bookstores dream of being. The staff picks are legendary, with handwritten notes and recommendations that make book-browsing feel like an adventure. If you're a book lover, this is your happy place. Keep an eye out for signed copies of The One-Way Ticket Plan: Find and Fund Your Purpose While Traveling the World.

♥ **Pro Tip:** Hit up their events calendar and see what authors are doing readings!

◷ **Hours:** 10AM-10PM

♥ **Location:** 1521 10th Ave

♥ **IG:** @elliottbaybookco

## MELROSE MARKET

Melrose Market is a hidden gem on Capitol Hill that brings together some of Seattle's top local artisans, gourmet food vendors, and specialty shops in one intimate space. Whether you're picking up picnic supplies before heading to Volunteer Park or looking for a relaxed dining experience, Melrose Market captures the best of Capitol Hill's artisanal food scene.

♥ **Pro Tip:** Inside you'll find a restaurant called Sitka & Spruce that delivers farm-to-table dining in a rustic setting.
⊙ **Hours:** 6AM-11PM
📍**Location:** 1527 Melrose Ave
🌐**Visit:** melrosemarketseattle.com

## LATE NIGHT VINTAGE MARKET

You could hang out here for hours, wandering, shopping, exploring, pretending to be a totally different person. This very much reminds me of an asian market where you have multiple vendors down multiple rows. It's thrilling, honestly.
⊙ **Hours:** 3PM - Midnight
📍 **Location:** 517 E Pike St
🌐 **Visit:** facebook.com/latenightvintagemarket

## LOCAL PRO TIPS FOR CAPITOL HILL

### 01. Make Reservations for Brunch on Weekends
Especially on Broadway. If you can't get a reservation, expect a line - and make the most of it! Maybe you'll make a friend while you're waiting!

### 02. Book Early for Hotels
Capitol Hill has limited hotel options - like barely any. On Alexa-West.com/Seattle-Hotels, I have Airbnb options for you, too.

### 03. Catch a Sunset at Louisa Boren Park
Instead of the more crowded Volunteer Park viewpoint, head to Louisa Boren Park for a quieter, equally stunning view of downtown Seattle and the Space Needle. It's a hidden gem for sunset views, and fewer people know about it.

### 04. Stick to Broadway at Night
For nighttime strolls, Broadway Avenue is the safest and most well-lit street. It's also lined with restaurants and bars, so you're never far from people and activity.

### 05. Parking Times and Tips
Meters generally operate until 8 PM, with free parking on Sundays and major holidays.

### 06. Remember to check for dates of Capitol Hill Block Party (follow @capitolhillblockparty)

# Capitol Hill Itineraries

## SUNNY DAY PICNIC EDITION

**8am:** Breakfast at Oddfellows Café + Bar

**9:30 am:** Stroll and relax at Volunteer Park, and visit the Asian Art Museum

**12 pm:** Pop in to Volunteer Park Cafe & Pantry for lunch and a coffee.

**1 pm:** Back to the hotel to freshen up.

**3 pm:** Stop by Nina's Nails for a pedicure

**4 pm:** Stroll the boutique shops

**5 pm:** Have an early dinner at Nue

**6 pm:** Drinks at Foreign National

**7pm:** Get an ice cream at Molly Moon and stroll home

## RAINY DAY ALTERNATIVE

**9 am:** Breakfast at Oddfellows Café + Bar

**10 am:** Find your 'Book of the Week' at Elliott Bay Book Company

**11 am:** Walk to Cal Anderson Park to read and people watch

**12 pm:** Have lunch at Biang Biang Noodles

**1 pm:** Back to the hotel to rest and freshen up

**4 pm:** Get a blow out and trim at Sugar & Shears Salon And Organic Spa

**5:30 pm:** Grab a drink at a/ stir (looking hot)

**6:30 pm:** Dinner at Poquitos (sit at the bar).

**8 pm:** Catch a show at Capitol Hill Comedy / Bar

**10 pm:** Late night tacos at Carmello's

**Want help planning your trip?**

Call me for an itinerary check or hire me to plan the whole thing.

Visit Alexa-West.com/Services ☞ 

# SOUTH SEATTLE



## CHAPTER SIX

# International District

**DAYS NEEDED:**
Half a day

*The International District is like your witchy, world-traveling aunt—full of stories, superstitions and medicinal herbs.*

If you're a foodie, the ID is absolutely worth a visit.

Seattle's International District, or the "ID," is a vibrant and historic neighborhood that showcases the city's deep Asian-American roots, dating back to the late 1800s when Chinese immigrants first settled here. Over time, Japanese, Filipino, and Vietnamese communities added their own layers of culture, transforming this area into a richly diverse neighborhood.

After living in Asia myself for nearly a decade, this area holds a special place in my heart and stomach. It's where I go when I'm craving Asian food, when I need a niche ingredient for a worldly recipe or when I want a cheap massage.

But let's be real: the area's got its sketchy moments. I'd advise you to visit during the day and head out before 9 PM.

**BEST FOR:**
Authentic Asian food & grocery and pre-game food and drinks near the stadiums (Lumen Field and T-Mobile Park)

# Areas to Know

## CHINATOWN

Full of iconic Chinese-American landmarks, bustling dim sum spots, and Hing Hay Park, the lively public square where you'll see old grandpas playing chess or badminton. Chinatown is just a quick walk to Lumen Field, so if you're going to a Sounders or Seahawks game, pre-game here.

## LITTLE SAIGON

Don't come. Drug addicts everywhere. It's a total shock and such a shame because there are so many well-deserving Vietnamese businesses that are suffering because the city has allowed this little pocket to become lawless and sad. Rant over.

## UWAJIMAYA

More than just an Asian market, Uwajimaya is a cultural monument. Come for fresh seafood, unique snacks, kitchen gadgets, and even Japanese housewares. There's also food to grab and go.

### History...

Uwajimaya has been a cornerstone of Seattle's International District since 1928, when Japanese immigrant, Fujimatsu Moriguchi, founded the business as a small storefront selling traditional Asian food and gifts to Japanese immigrants. Moriguchi started by selling fish cakes and other Japanese staples to workers in the local community and expanded his offerings over the years, building a loyal customer base. During World War II, the Moriguchi family was interned in the Minidoka War Relocation Center, like many Japanese-Americans, but they reopened the business in Seattle after the war. By the 1960s, Uwajimaya had evolved into a full grocery store and, eventually, the large supermarket and cultural center it is today.

## KING STREET STATION

A historic train station dating back to 1906, King Street Station is the ID's gateway to Seattle and beyond. With its iconic clock tower and beautifully restored interior, it's not only a transport hub but also an architectural gem worth seeing. This station connects you to Amtrak, making it easy to explore neighboring cities. Visit Tacoma for the day!

## LUMEN FIELD

Home of Seattle Seahawks football and Seattle Sounders soccer. The ID is a popular pre-game destination for fans looking to grab food or drinks before heading to the stadium (I typically hit up DoughZone before a game).

## HOW TO GET AROUND THE ID

## LIGHT RAIL

The link will take you to International District/Chinatown Station. This is the best option if you're coming from downtown, Capitol Hill, or the airport.

☞ **Don't take the bus here:** In this particular area, the buses have a lot of drama with crazy riders.

☞ **Once here, walk:** Seattle's International District spans roughly 10 blocks by 6 blocks, covering an area bounded by S Jackson Street to the north, Rainier Avenue S to the east, S Dearborn Street to the south, and 4th Avenue S to the west.

## LOCAL TIPS FOR THE ID

▸ **Take Advantage of Cheap Parking Near Uwajimaya:** Uwajimaya offers validated parking for shoppers. Park here if you're exploring the ID, especially if you're planning a grocery or souvenir stop.

▸ **Be Mindful of Timing for Safety:** The ID is best explored during the day or early evening. While the area is lively, especially around restaurants and events, some parts can be quieter and feel less safe late at night.

▸ **Attend Weekend Markets or Festivals:** For a unique experience, visit during one of the neighborhood's festivals like Lunar New Year.

♥ **FYI:** Locals come to the ID to get Chinese traditional herbs and teas from traditional apothecaries like **New An Dong.** Just bring a photo of what you're looking for in case of language barriers.

## FUN RAIN FACT:

Seattle is not the rainiest city in the US! Cities like New York and Houston actually receive more total rainfall annually. Seattle, however, has more days with light precipitation, thanks to its consistent drizzles.

# Best Things to Do

## WANDER UWAJIMAYA & KINOKUNIYA

Coming here feels like you're traveling abroad! The first time I ever made sushi in college, I came here to collect all the exotic ingredients needed. They have everything Asian. Come hungry because they also have prepared sushi to-go. There's also food stalls, like a mini hawker center. Beyond food you'll find Kinokuniya Bookstore, a haven for manga fans and stationery enthusiasts!

⊙ **Hours:** Mon-Sun 8 AM – 9 PM
📍 **Location:** 600 5th Ave S

## SEATTLE PINBALL MUSEUM

Step into the past at the Seattle Pinball Museum. This unusual hangout is packed with vintage pinball machines from different decades, and the best part? You get unlimited play with your entry ticket. It's a nostalgic dive into arcade culture.

🎟 **Cost:** $23 per adult for unlimited play
⊙ **Hours:** Wed-Sun 12 PM – 6 PM
📍 **Location:** 508 Maynard Ave S

## CHEAP MASSAGES

The ID is also famous for its affordable massage parlors. If you've been on your feet exploring all day, you're going to want to stop for a quick foot massage or full-body at Magical Massage. It's the cleanest, least sketchy cheap massage in the area. Don't expect luxury, but do expect them to get those kinks out.

🎟 **Cost:** $30-$75 depending on the service
⊙ **Hours:** Mon-Sun 10 AM – 9 PM
📍 **Location:** 651 S Jackson St

### Bonus!

## JOIN A LOCAL CLEAN UP

When I travel, I join beach clean ups to meet other travelers while doing good (Goodcations I call them). The same works here. Explore the heart of Seattle's International District with a guided tour organized by the Chinatown-International District Business Improvement Area (CIDBIA)...while you pick up trash. This immersive experience gives you a behind-the-scenes look at the neighborhood's rich history and even takes you into the sketchy areas (there's safety in numbers). This is such a popular event that spots really do fill up fast! Register for your clean up ASAP.

✒ **Cost:** Free with RSVP

♥ **Pro Tip:** Wear comfortable shoes and bring a water bottle—there's a lot to explore, and you won't want to miss a step!

⊕ **Visit:** For tour dates and registration, visit cidbia.org

♥ **Another Playlist for You**

The One-Way Ticket Playlist belongs in this chapter. It's full of hopes and dreams and whimsical things.

Find it here ☞ 

# Where to Eat

Eating in the International District is nothing short of a culinary adventure. With options ranging from hole-in-the-wall noodle spots to legendary sushi joints, the ID offers some of the best food in Seattle.

## COFFEE AND BREAKFAST

### FUJI BAKERY

A small, takeout-only gem specializing in Japanese-inspired pastries and bread. Go for the Japanese Curry Beef Bun—a savory, flaky pastry filled with 100% Angus beef and a rich curry sauce. Be sure to ask for it warmed up for maximum yumminess. Another standout is the Matcha Malasada (a pillowy donut filled with matcha cream); it's a Hawaiian-inspired treat with a Japanese twist that's subtly sweet. Beyond these specialties, you'll also find an array of classic pastries, from buttery croissants to fruit danishes.

☞ **Order This:** Japanese Curry Beef Bun, Matcha Malasada
⊙ **Hours:** Daily, 7 AM – 5 PM
♥ **Location:** 526 S King St, Seattle

## HOOD FAMOUS CAFE + BAR

Start your morning with a unique blend of Filipino fla vors at Hood Famous Cafe + Bar. Known for its ube lattes (purple yam) and Filipino pastries, this place brings a refreshing twist to Seattle's coffee scene. Hood Famous started as a small bakery specializing in ube cheesecakes and quickly grew into a beloved local brand.Their breakfast offerings are a fusion of traditional Filipino tastes and classic cafe items—think ensaymada (Filipino sweet rolls), ube donuts, and Spanish lattes. The cozy, welcoming space in the heart of the International District makes it a great spot to start your day.

☞ Order This: Ube latte and en-saymada, or grab an ube cheese-cake slice for a morning treat.
⊙ Hours: Wed-Sun, 8 AM – 3 PM
♥ Location: 504 5th Ave S, Suite 107, Seattle, WA 98104

## TP TEA

Did you know that Bubble tea was invented in Taiwan? Tradi-tionally, Bubble Tea is milk tea with tapioca balls that require a thick straw that you poke through the plastic top of the drink. If you've never experi-enced it, it's strange. But it's ad-dicting.

♥ Pro Tip: Get a Bubble Tea be-fore waiting in line elsewhere.
☞ Order This: The classic bubble tea, low sugar, low ice.
⊙ Hours: Daily, 11 AM – 8 PM
♥ Location: 668 S Weller St

## LUNCH & DINNER

## DOUGH ZONE

Soup dumpling heaven! Dough Zone is your go-to for mouth-watering xiao long bao (soup dumplings) and other Chinese comfort foods like dan dan noodles. When you sit down, you'll be given a white piece of paper and a pencil; this is the menu. For two people, my boyfriend and I typically order cucumber salad, xiao long bao (soup dumplings), and one dan dan noodle each. Solo, I'd get the dumplings and either the noodles or cucumbers! Heads up: It's always packed before games, but trust me, it's worth the wait. Check out their menu online before you go, it has pic-tures!

⊙ Hours: Daily 11 AM – 10 PM
⊕ Visit: doughzonedumplinghouse.com

## MANEKI

A Seattle icon and historical landmark, Maneki opened in 1904 and is one of the oldest

Japanese restaurants in the U.S. After Japanese internment in WWII, Maneki reopened and continued to serve its community, becoming a cherished institution. With cozy tatami rooms, it's like stepping into a little piece of Tokyo. Reservations are a must!

☞ **Order This:** The chirashi bowl!
◷ **Hours:** Tues-Sat, 5 PM – 9 PM | Closed Sun & Mon
📍**Location:** 304 6th Ave S
🌐**Visit:** manekiseattle.com

## KAMONEGI

Kamonegi is a little gem that focuses on traditional handmade soba noodles, often flavored with regional, seasonal ingredients like matcha or yuzu. Owned by Chef Mutsuko Soma, Kamonegi has won numerous awards and gained a devoted following for its unique spin on Japanese comfort food. It's small and intimate, perfect for a quiet, memorable date night.

☞ **Order This:** Cold soba with prawn tempura
◷ **Hours:** Tuesday-Saturday, 5 PM – 9 PM | Closed Sun & Mon
📍**Location:** 1054 N 39th St
🌐**Visit:** kamonegiseattle.com

## HENRY'S TAIWAN

Ya'll I lived in Taiwan for a year and have been searching for that perfect bowl of beef noodle soup, Taiwan's national dish. And I finally found it at Henry's Taiwan. The noodles are handmade and thick, the beef falls apart! I'm hungry thinking about it.

☞ **Order This:** Beef noodle soup.
◷ **Hours:** Mon-Sun 11 AM – 9 PM
♥ **IG:** @henrystaiwankitchen

## PHNOM PENH NOODLE HOUSE

Phnom Penh Noodle House is a beloved Cambodian spot that has a powerful comeback story: after closing in 2018, the restaurant was reopened by the owner's three daughters, reviving their family legacy. The menu combines rich Cambodian flavors with a Pacific Northwest twist. Here, breakfast includes dishes filled with lemongrass, lime, and plenty of herbs, reflecting Southeast Asian culture. They even have a durian milkshake. Be sure you know what you're getting yourself into before you order it...

☞ **Order This:** Amok Trei (white fish in a red curry)
◷ **Hours:** Mon-Sat, 9 AM – 8 PM | Closed Sun
📍**Location:** 716 S King St

### E-JAE PAK MOR

Forget the green curry and pad thai. At my favorite Thai restaurant in the city, I want you to order Khao Soi (a northern thai dish with chicken, noodles and a rich broth) and the mango sticky rice. If you've been to Thailand and are missing these flavors, I bet you're going to cry when you taste this. It tastes just like Thailand, and the staff there will speak to you in Thai! Aroy mak mai?

☞ Order This: Khao Soi
⊙ Hours: Mon-Sat, 11 AM – 9 PM
♥ Location: 504 5th Ave S Unit 118
♥ IG: @ejaepakmor

### THE BEST PHO SPOT

This is the best pho I've had in the USA. But it's my go-to spot. And I don't want to openly share it with the world so here's the deal, I'll trade you: Leave me a review for this book on Amazon, send me a screen shot @SoloGirlsTravelGuide on Instagram or TikTok and I'll tell you my pho secret.



# Beauty & Wellness

### MAGICAL MASSAGE

Need a quick and affordable massage? Magical Massage offers everything from foot rubs to full-body treatments at unbeatable prices.

☞ Price Range: Starting at $20
⊙ Hours: Mon-Sun 10 AM – 9 PM
♥ Location: 651 S Jackson St

### HO'S HERBS & MASSAGE CENTER

Dr. Ho is a master of holistic medicine using traditional Chinese herbs, patches and ointments to help treat injuries, ease discomfort, and improve overall wellness. From sore muscles to chronic ailments, Dr. Ho's remedies are rooted in centuries-old techniques that focus on natural healing. Ho's Herbs & Massage Center is a trusted spot for traditional Chinese medicine in the International District. But here's the catch, you've got to call him (like on the phone) to discuss.

☞ What to try: Consultations for tailored herbal remedies or traditional massage therapy.
⊙ Hours: Mon-Sat, 10 AM – 6 PM
♥ Location: 519 S King St
☎ Phone: 206-652-0696

## CHAPTER SEVEN

# West Seattle

**DAYS NEEDED:**
1 full day

*West Seattle is that friend who throws the best beach bonfires and always looks effortlessly beautiful and put together—in that perfectly Seattle kind of way.*

I call it **The Beauty Capital of Seattle.** West Seattle is where I come for nails, hair, lashes, and, with Alki Beach right there, a little inner soul rejuvenation. But beyond the beauty havens and the easygoing vibe (think Newport Beach, but with more flannel), West Seattle is also quite historical.

West Seattle is literally where Seattle began! **The first settlers** landed on Alki Beach in 1851, and after one frigid winter on the exposed cape, they decided to pick up and move to what we now call downtown. But West Seattle kept its own identity, evolving into a thriving community with a relaxed, grounded charm. Connected to the rest of the city by the West Seattle Bridge and the West Seattle Ferry, this peninsula feels just far enough removed – like you've got out of town for the day. It's a totally different vibe here and the ceremonious crossing of the ferry feels like you're traveling between different worlds (and I'd say, you most certainly are).

West Seattle is a neighborhood I adore—a place where locals and visitors alike can unwind, beautify, and experience Seattle from a totally different perspective.

# Areas to Know

## WEST SEATTLE BRIDGE

The vital link connecting West Seattle to the rest of Seattle, typically a 10–15 minute drive from downtown when traffic is light. Recently reopened, this bridge makes access easy.

## WEST SEATTLE FERRY DOCK

For a scenic commute hop on the West Seattle Water Taxi from Pier 50 downtown. The ferry drops you at Seacrest Park in under 15 minutes. Your ultimate destination will be Alki Beach. So you must either walk 30 minutes, scooter 10, or hop on the free shuttle which I'll tell you more about soon.

## ALKI BEACH & MAIN STRIP

Alki Beach is where the action happens—stretching along Alki Avenue with its sandy beaches, beachside cafes, seafood shacks, and rental spots for bikes and kayaks. Whether sunbathing, grabbing a bite, or biking along the water, Alki's beachy strip gives you that vacation-day feeling.

## THE JUNCTION

Known as "The Junction," this is West Seattle's heartbeat. California Avenue's collection of shops, cafes, and top-notch restaurants bring together locals and visitors, making it a lively spot for people-watching, local eats, and casual shopping. Farmer's markets and community events add a small-town charm that makes The Junction feel like the true center of West Seattle.

## WEST SEATTLE NEIGHBORHOODS

You might park back here but besides that, you won't venture into the residential areas of West Seattle. However, if you're looking to move to the Seattle, consider this area!

## WHITE CENTER (not technically West Seattle but close by):

Just south of West Seattle, White Center offers some of the best Mexican food in the area and a diverse selection of international eateries and dive bars. Consider that an extracurricular adventure to this book.

# Best Things to Do

## ALKI BEACH

Alki Beach is the ultimate Seattle beach experience with sandy shores, driftwood logs, and unbeatable views of Puget Sound and the city skyline. It's a hot spot for paddleboarding, kayaking, and beach volleyball, and the beachfront promenade is perfect for long strolls or bike rides. Grab some fish and chips, dip your toes in the water, and enjoy the laid-back beach vibes.

♥ **Pro Tip:** Bring a blanket for sunset—Alki offers one of the best views in town.

☉ **Hours:** Open daily, sunrise to sunset

⚲ **Location:** 1702 Alki Ave SW

## WEST SEATTLE FARMERS MARKET

If you're in West Seattle on a Sunday, don't miss the West Seattle Farmers Market. Open year-round, this market brings together local farmers, bakers, and artisans offering fresh produce, handmade goods, and delicious street food. It's the perfect spot to grab brunch and explore unique, locally-made finds.

♥ **Pro Tip:** Try a fresh-baked pastry from one of the local vendors!

☉ **Hours:** Sundays, 10 AM – 2 PM (year-round)

⚲ **Location:** California Ave SW & SW Alaska St

## VIEWPOINTS AND PARKS

The views of the water and the city from West Seattle are unmatched. In this section, I'll guide you to the must-see viewpoints. Bring your camera and consider a park-hop as an adventurous way to get your work out in.

## BEAUTY AND WELLNESS

Welcome to the beauty capital of Seattle, where West Seattle's tight-knit beauty scene is like a vortex of wellness. You enter all stressy and messy and leave glowing from the inside out. This peninsula is packed with clusters of locally-owned spas, salons, and skincare havens—all obsessed with what they do. The beauty pros here are true experts, mixing years of experience with the latest trends and techniques. Come for a facial, hair refresh, or an all-out makeover; leave with a little extra confidence, courtesy of West Seattle's best. This chapter's beauty guide is extensive...

# Where to Eat

## COFFEE, BREAKFAST, BRUNCH

### BAKERY NOUVEAU

The croissants—especially the twice-baked almond—are the stuff of Seattle legend. And while the kouign-amann (often described as a "caramelized croissant") might look unassuming, I can't get enough of these. And you guys, they have macaroons of all flavors! It's no surprise that the shop gets busy (especially on weekends). It's worth the line. Pick up a pastry to-go or grab a seat by the window and order a more hearty breakfast sandwich on a croissant. Eat slow. Enjoy this.

⊙ Hours: 7AM-5PM (closed Tue)
♀ Location: West Seattle Junction
⊕ Visit: bakerynouveau.com

### HARRY'S BEACH HOUSE / Brunch

With a breezy beach vibe, Harry's Beach House sits right across from Alki Beach and makes a perfect week-end brunch destination. Get the Farm Stand Brunch Bowl filled with PNW seasonal ingredients or the quiche of the day!

♥ Pro Tip: Try to snag a window seat for prime beach views.
⊙ Hours: Brunch is Saturday & Sunday 9AM - 2PM (also open for lunch and dinner)
♀ Location: Alki Beach
⊕ Visit: harrysbeachhouse.com

### TASTE OF MUMBAI / Indian Brunch

Taste of Mumbai transforms brunch into a savory, spice-filled experience inspired by Indian street food. Instead of classic American pancakes, brunch here centers on bold flavors: think spiced potatoes, lentils, naan wraps, and chutneys. If you don't know what to order, ask for guidance! And don't miss their masala chai. Ps. They also have a daily lunch buffet from 11am-3pm!

⊙ Hours: Thurs–Sat 9 AM–2 AM, Sun 9 AM–11 PM, Mon–Tues 10 AM–10 PM, Wed 10 AM–12
♀ Location: West Seattle Junction
⊕ Visit: tasteofmumbaiwa.com

### BONUS!

If you have a car, go to Luna Park Cafe for breakfast!

## *Casual*

## MARINATION MA KAI

The first restaurant you'll see when you get off the ferry is Marination Ma Kai, a beloved Seattle gem that has picnic tables, umbrellas and views of the city! Instant gratification! The menu is Hawaiian-Korean fusion! Try the essence of Marination Ma Kai by ordering the Taco Two-Pack where you can choose your protein – and I recommend the Hawaiian-style braised pulled pork and the Spicy Pork inspired by Korean bulgogi. For your walk, get a tropical drink to go.

⊙ **Hours:** 11AM-8PM (closed Mon-Tues).
**Location:** Alki Beach
⊕ **Visit:** marinationmobile.com

## SUNFISH

Many people say that this little family-owned fish shack is where you find the best fish and chips in Seattle. Sunfish serves up crispy, golden fish and chips - I like it with the Halibut which comes with fries. Order a side of clam chowder or calamari.

⊙ **Hours:** 11AM-8PM (closed Mon-Tues).
**Location:** Alki Beach

## OH'S SANDWICHES

Picnic alert. Come grab a sandwich before you head to the beach. At Oh's, they claim to make the best banh mi in the city. Many locals would agree that Oh's Banh Mi has the crispiest baguette, the juiciest roasted pork and the perfect ratio between veggies and pate. It's simple, affordable, and ridiculously tasty. Ps. They have more Vietnamese sandwiches beyond Bahn Mi. Go explore (with your mouth).

⊙ **Hours:** 10AM-4:30PM
**Location:** West Seattle Junction
♥ **IG:** @ohssandwiches

## ALKI PHO AND BAR

Seattle's Vietnamese food scene is the closest you'll get to authentic Vietnamese food without actually flying to Vietnam. This is your chance to try some really delicious Pho! Not in the soup mood? Order a vermicelli bowl with grilled pork. And don't skip the spring rolls which come with the creamiest peanut sauce in town. Just want to socialize and drink? The bar here is the (unsuspecting) local hangout!

⊙ **Hours:** 11AM-9PM
**Location:** Alki Beach
⊕ **Visit:** alkiphoandbar.com

## CACTUS ALKI BEACH

Start with chips, guac and a big margarita. Then order anything with brisket: the tacos, the burrito or the nachos. Cactus also knows how to use PNW seafood to make delicious, seasonal seafood enchiladas! Where to sit? The outdoor patio is lovely on sunny days. During colder weather, sit at the bar inside and chat with some locals.

⊙ **Hours:** 11AM-9PM
**Location:** Alki Beach
⊕ **Visit:** cactusrestaurants.com

## SUPREME

Sometimes I'll just get a random craving to sit in a dark bar with a random sports game on the TV, while I sit in a swivel chair and eat some cheesy pizza on a paper plate. When I get this craving, I come here to Supreme. Ps. Sports fans, this is a great place to watch the games!

⊙ **Hours:** 3pm-1am (2am Fri & Sat)
**Location:** The Junction
♥ **IG:** @supremebarseattle

*Date-Night Approved*

## DRIFTWOOD

This sophisticated, upscale restaurant is all about fresh seafood and small plates. They refer to their menu as "hyper-seasonal" meaning their ingredients are constantly changing depending on what's in season. This is basically the Pacific Northwest on a plate. No visit here will ever be the same.

⊙ **Hours:** Thurs-Mon 5PM-9PM
**Location:** Alki Beach
⊕ **Visit:** driftwoodseattle.com

## IL NIDO

Il Nido is a farm-to-table Italian restaurant in a beautifully restored historic building. The menu is inspired by regional Italian dishes with local Pacific Northwest ingredients—think handmade pastas and seasonal dishes that are simple yet extraordinary. Candle-lit and intimate, Il Nido is ideal for a cozy, romantic night. If you're celebrating or just want a quiet escape, this place sets the perfect mood.

⊙ **Hours:** 4PM-9PM (Closed Sun-Mon)
**Location:** Alki Beach
⊕ **Visit:** ilnidoseattle.com

## LA RUSTICA

Remember that Lady and the Tramp spaghetti moment? This place reminds me of that. Quaint, charming, dimly lit, plates full of homemade pasta in rich sauce...but you may have to wait. This place is in demand.

Make a reservation and be patient. Good gnocchi comes to those who wait. Located near Beach Drive, it's a little off the beaten path but well worth the trip!

⊙Hours: Open daily for dinner
♀Location: Beach Drive SW
⊕Visit: larustica.com

## MATADOR WEST SEATTLE

Matador is elevated Tex Mex with plenty of dishes to share. With its dark, moody interior, Matador is ideal for an intimate date night with intentional conversation and spicy margaritas. Solo? I love this place for you! Come sit at the welcoming bar, make up a fake name, and bullshit with the bartenders.

⊙ Hours: 11AM-12AM (2AM on Fri & Sat)
♀Location: West Seattle Junction
⊕Visit: matadorrestaurants.com



# Parks & Viewpoints

Follow this section, park by park in succession, and you've got a "Park Hop". Remember, West Seattle is the only area where I "okay" Lime Scooters but just remember they are still dangerous as hell if you're not wearing a helmet. Ride at your own risk, baby.

## PARK HOP STARTS HERE!

### 01. SEACREST PARK

When you get off the ferry, you're at Seacrest Park where you'll find the award-winning restaurant called **Marination Ma Kai.** Enjoy waterfront views of the Seattle skyline with ferries crossing Elliott Bay, plus kayak and paddleboard rentals nearby. Consider getting a slushie and walking to your next park.

⊙Best time to visit: Afternoon to evening, when ferries are most active.

⇢Next Stop: Jack Block Park Viewpoint
▸ Distance: 0.8 miles
⊙Time: ~15 minutes walking or ~5 minutes biking

## 02. JACK BLOCK PARK VIEW POINT

Get sweeping views of Seattle's skyline and Elliott Bay, with frequent sightings of ferries, cargo ships, and on clear days, Mt. Rainier. There are a couple benches here for you to sit and ponder upon.

⊙ **Best time to visit:** Sunrise or sunset.

♀ **Location:** Get off the boat and head left - away from Alki. 20-minute walk or a 6-minute bike.

⇢ **Next Stop:** Hamilton Viewpoint Park
▸ **Distance:** 1.2 miles
⊙ **Time:** ~25 minutes walking or ~7 minutes biking

## 03. HAMILTON VIEWPOINT PARK

Is this the best park in Seattle? I think you might think so. This 16.9-acre public park offers the most all-encompassing view of downtown Seattle, Elliott Bay, and the Cascades in the distance. This spot is quieter than other viewpoints and is a favorite of photographers and locals alike.

⊙ **Best time to visit:** Besides the usual, New Years for the fireworks!

♀ **Location:** The very northern tip of the peninsula

⇢ **Next Stop:** Rhenals Cove
▸ **Distance:** 1.5 miles
⊙ **Time:** ~30 minutes

## 04. RHENALS COVE

A hidden gem just downhill from Hamilton Viewpoint, Rhenalds Cove offers a quieter waterfront experience where you can sometimes spot seals lounging on the rocks or swimming nearby.

⊙ **Best time to visit:** Early morning or late afternoon when seals are most active near the shore.
♀ **Location:** Heading towards Alki Beach

⇢ **Next Stop:** Charles Richey Sr. Viewpoint
▸ **Distance:** 1.4 miles
⊙ **Time:** ~30 minutes

## 05. CHARLES RICHEY SR VIEWPOINT

Located along Alki Beach, this expansive viewpoint offers stunning views across Puget Sound with the Olympic Mountains as a backdrop.

⊙ **Best time to visit:** Sunset
♀ **Location:** South of Alki Beach

◄► **Next Stop:** Schmitz Preserve Park
► **Distance:** 1 mile
⊙ **Time:** ~20 minutes

## 06. SCHMITZ PRESERVE PARK

Step into an old-growth forest with towering trees and a lush canopy, offering a tranquil nature experience in the city. The trails are short and natural, making it a perfect quick retreat.

⊙ **Best time to visit:** Mid-morning for great light through the trees.
♀ **Location:** Inland

◄► **Next Stop:** Alki Beach Park
► **Distance:** 0.6 miles
⊙ **Time:** ~12 minutes

## 07. ALKI BEACH PARK

Alki Beach Park is the heart of West Seattle's beach scene, lined with sandy shores, volleyball courts, and a lively promenade with plenty of dining options. After exploring the viewpoints and Schmitz Preserve, this is the perfect place to relax, grab a meal, and enjoy the beach atmosphere.

⊙ **Best time to visit:** Any time
♀ **Location:** Beachfront!

## WHEN TO START THE PARK HOP?

**Driving over to West Seattle?** Plan it so that you start with a sunrise at Jack Block. Plan it so that you finish and get to Alki Beach in time for sunset.

**Catching the West Seattle Water Taxi?** Here are some tips to make the most of it.

⊙ **Earliest Ferry Times:**

► **Weekdays:** The first ferry leaves Pier 50 at 5:55 AM—perfect for a sunrise view over Elliott Bay in the summer.
► **Weekends and Holidays:** The first ferry departs at 8:30 AM, giving a relaxed start to your morning on Alki Beach.

► **Seasonal Considerations:**
In summer, early ferries let you see Seattle's skyline glow in the sunrise—a memorable start to any day of park-hopping or beach walking.

In winter, arriving in West Seattle this early means it's still dark; be cautious when traveling alone, and consider bringing a personal safety alarm for added security.

You can find a reliable one on my site at Alexa-West.com/Safety

# Beauty & Wellness in West Seattle

Say it with me: appointments! These are boutique beauty salons plus they are popular - so prioritize planning your West Seattle day and build your itinerary here first. It's worth it, I promise.

## HAIR

### LA LUNA HAIR STUDIO

The ultimate West Seattle salon for a hair transformation! After months of grow-out, Lisa at La Luna gave me a total Princess Diaries makeover with perfect blonde highlights and fresh bangs—she's truly the "bangs queen." Her cozy, private studio is right across from the beach, so after your appointment, have a bite to eat while watching the water.

⊙ **Hours:** Tues–Fri 10 AM–7 PM; Sat 9 AM–4 PM; Closed Sun–Mon
📍 **Location:** 2609 58th Ave SW
♥ **IG:** @lalunaonalkisalon

## NAILS

### ADMIRAL NAIL SALON

There are only two pedicure chairs here, meaning, you're not one of 200 toes your nail tech is rushing through! Just the opposite at Admiral Nail Salon! You get to have girl time with Christina, the incredibly talented and lovely owner... who is very busy so make your appointments well in advance!

⊙ **Hours:** 10AM-6PM; (closed Sun)
📍 **Location:** 4219 SW Admiral Way
☎ **Phone:** 206-938-0795

### YAMADA NAIL ATELIER

When you want stiletto-shaped acrylics with glitter, art and Harijuku-style gems, this is the place you visit! You can also just get a classic manicure or a french manicure and leave loving your nails. In West Seattle fashion, this is a tiny treasure of a salon so book your appointments!

⊙ **Hours:** 10AM-7PM; (closed Sun)
📍 **Location:** 2523 41st Ave SW
🌐 **Visit:** yamadanail.com

## BROWS

### UKIYO BEAUTY & INK

If you've wanted brows but have been nervous that they'd end up fake looking, I have the solution to your anxiety. Julie at Ukiyo Beauty and Ink is a master in nano brows. This is micoblading with tiny hair-like strokes that look so natural. She also does brow lamination and tinting, consider pairing it with an eyelash tint and lift to walk out of her salon as a new woman.

⊙Hours: 9AM-8PM (closed Mon)
♥ Location: 3280 California Ave SW
♥ IG: @ukiyobeautyink

## LASHES

### SKYLASH STUDIO

Forget the heavy lashes that hide your pretty eyes! The queen of lashes is here! Hanim is a genius designer of lash looks. I adore her ethereal, whimsical yet natural-looking fluttery lashes that feel effortlessly natural. Don't know what you want? She's the girl to ask. Ps. Hanim is a certified peer counselor!

⊙ Hours: Mon-Thurs 10AM-9PM, Fri-Sun 10AM-5PM
♥Location: 3280 California Ave SW B1
♥ IG: @skylashstudio3280

## SKIN

### AESTHETIX BEAUTY

When you want to look 20 years younger you visit Aesthetix Beauty for their chemical peels, microneedling, and microdermabrasion. Woman-owned, Georgia Jenkins is an esthetician raised in her mother's beauty salon. According to Georgia, she is "Esthetician born and bred". Beauty is what she does best.

⊙ Hours: 9AM-5:30PM (closed Sat-Sun)
♥ Location: 3280 California Ave SW B1
⊕Visit:
aesthetixbeautyseattle.com

## BOTOX & LIPS

### FOREVER YOUNG AESTHETICS

The kind of doctor who can look at your face and (gently) tell you how to balance your look. Whether that's with filler or botox to define your chin or open eyes – this is the man Seattlites trust for natural results that make you more you.

⊙Hours: Fri-Sun 8AM-5PM
♥Location: 3813A California Ave SW
♥ IG: @foreveryoungseattle

## HEAD SPA

### AURORA BEAUTY

Please don't leave Seattle without trying a Head Spa. Aurora Beauty offers this luxurious Japanese-style head spa experience that leaves you feeling refreshed from scalp to soul. It's one of my favorite treatments to get around the world, and here in West Seattle.

⊙ **Hours:** 9:30AM-7:30PM (closed Tues)
♀ **Location:** 4208 SW Oregon St Suite A
♥ IG: @aurorabeautyseattle



## HEAD TO TOE DAY SPA

Come for a massage in a cozy, welcoming space. They specialize in therapeutic massage, with options like deep tissue, hot stone, and Swedish for deep relaxation. Bonus: I recommend upgrading your appointment and adding on the use of the Steam Room (especially on a cold Seattle day).

⊙ **Hours:** Mon, Wed, Thurs, Fri 9 AM–7:30 PM; Tues 9 AM–5 PM; Sat 9 AM–5 PM; Sun 11 AM–6 PM
♀ **Location:** 2328 California Ave SW
♥ IG: @headtotoedayspaws



## BARRE3

Barre3 brings strength, flexibility, and mindfulness to every class, with full-body workouts designed to boost both physical and mental wellness. Their classes blend ballet barre, yoga, and Pilates for a balanced non-boring workout.

⊙ **Hours:** Mon–Thurs 5:45 AM–8 PM; Fri 5:45 AM–6:30 PM; Sat 7:15 AM–12 PM; Sun 8:30 AM–5 PM
♀ **Location:** 3218 California Ave SW
♥ IG: @barre3westseattle

## INNER ALCHEMY

A visit to Inner Alchemy offers a soulful, transformative experience for those seeking spiritual wellness and awakenings. Maari is a gifted woman who offers a range of therapeutical sessions, medication workshops, sound healings, shamanic reiki sessions, and energy healings. You can trust her to hold space and guide you towards peace and healing.

⊙ **Hours:** Fri-Sun 12PM-5 PM
♀ **Location:** 3043 California Ave SW
⊕ **Visit:** inneralchemytt.com

# How to Get to West Seattle

## DRIVE

The West Seattle Bridge connects downtown to West Seattle in just 20 minutes.

## BUS

To get from **downtown Seattle to West Seattle by bus, King County Metro's RapidRide C Line** is the most direct option, running frequently from downtown to the West Seattle Junction. Other routes, like Route 21 and Route 50, also connect downtown with Alki Beach and other West Seattle spots.

The C Line operates daily with peak-time departures every 10-15 minutes, providing a quick, traffic-friendly route. **Check King County Metro's Trip Planner** for times and stops based on your specific location

☞ tripplanner.kingcounty.gov

## WATER TAXI TO WEST SEATTLE

The King County Water Taxi offers one of the quickest and most scenic ways to get to West Seattle from downtown. Here's how it works:

☞ **From Seattle:** Where to Board: The water taxi departs from Pier 50 in downtown Seattle, located near Pioneer Square.

☞ **Where It Drops You:** The ferry arrives at Seacrest Dock in West Seattle, close to Alki Beach. From there, it's a 5-minute walk to Seacrest Park and the start of the Alki trail.

**NOTE:** The walk to Alki Beach is 35-minute stroll along the water. Or keep an eye out for the free shuttles, Routes 773 & 775, which connect to Alki and West Seattle Junction. They look like Airport Shuttles.

**Duration:** The crossing takes about 15 minutes, providing fantastic views of the Seattle skyline and Elliott Bay along the way.

**First and Last Trips:**
▶**Weekdays:** First departure at 5:55 AM; last return from West Seattle at 7:05 PM.
▶**Weekends:** First trip at 8:30 AM; last return at 7:00 PM.

**Cost** $5.75 per ride ($5 with ORCA card)

# Getting Around West Seattle

## WALKING

West Seattle, particularly around Alki, is pretty flat which makes it a dream for walking! And this area is very safe.

## LIKE BIKE AND SCOOTER

Because West Seattle is flatter than other parts of the city, I approve of you riding a scooter (sober). Download the Lime app and connect it to your card.

## FREE SHUTTLE

The shuttles make it easy to take the ferry over and then explore, running between 5:55am and stopping around 7pm. When you get off the ferry at Seacrest Park, keep an eye out for the one you want.

▸ **Route 773:** Alaska Junction, Seacrest Park
▸ **Route 775:** Admiral Junction, Alki, Seacrest Park

I'll have more on West Seattle, including transportation, at Alexa-West.com

## SOME TECHINICAL SEATTLE LINGO TO LEARN

▸**The Sound:** Refers to Puget Sound, the vast body of water bordering Seattle to the west. It's home to ferries, islands, stunning coastal views and marine life galore, including the biggest octopus in the world (the Giant Pacific Octopus).

▸ **I-5, I-90, and 520:** Major highways that run through or around Seattle. I-5 runs north-south, I-90 goes east-west, and the 520 bridge crosses Lake Washington (with tolls!).

▸ **The Bridge:** Usually refers to the 520 floating bridge, one of two bridges connecting Seattle to the Eastside suburbs like Bellevue and Redmond.

▸ **Amazonia:** Sometimes used to refer to the South Lake Union neighborhood, where Amazon's headquarters dominate the area.

## CHAPTER EIGHT

# Beacon Hill

**DAYS NEEDED:**
1 full day

*Beacon Hill is that friend who hosts elegant dinner parties in her pristine garden with wine and cheese – then kicks everyone out to head to bed and read a book by 10 PM.*

Historically, Beacon Hill has always been a literal beacon. Early Seattleites would navigate by the bright lights of the "beacon" atop the hill. Today, the neighborhood of North Beacon Hill still feels like Seattle's best kept secret when it comes to telling the tourists – and I'm here to let you in on it all.

In the early 1900's, North Beacon Hill was known as the "Garlic Gulch" home to one of the biggest Italian Immigrant populations in the country. While that community has since dispersed, Beacon Hill still holds true to its legacy and has evolved into a melting pot of Asian, Mexican, and other cultures. Today, you'll find markets and eateries offering everything from authentic tamales to fresh dim sum.

The true reason to come to Beacon Hill? For an easy breezy day away from the chaos of the city. Stroll, eat. Stroll and eat again.

Beacon Hill is the safe solo girl haven you didn't know you needed—a place where comfort and independence go hand-in-hand. Up here, it's all about lush parks, scenic overlooks, and a neighborly feel with cafes, bakeries, and murals. Unlike downtown's nightlife, Beacon Hill offers a mellow but steadily evolving scene, however with fancy new champagne bars and pickleball courts popping up, it's definitely got an "up-and-coming" vibe. Here, you can wander with ease. Treat yourself to a solo dinner date or a night of cocktails with a dude you met off Bumble.

However, once you walk down to Rainier Ave or move towards the South of Beacon Hill, things start to get a bit sketchy. So stick to the north, the places I'm guiding you, and you'll be in heaven.

☞ **SPOT IT CHALLENGE:** See if you can spot the **PacMed Building!** This iconic Art Deco fortress was built in 1932 as Seattle's main hospital and even served as Amazon's first headquarters from 1999 to 2010. Can you catch a glimpse of this historic landmark from wherever you are in the city?

# Areas to Know

## NORTH BEACON HILL

The best of Beacon Hill is in the north. Here you'll find safe residential neighborhoods surrounded by the best restaurants, beautiful old buildings, gorgeous murals and artwork, parks and two light rail stations!

## JEFFERSON PARK

Jefferson Park is Beacon Hill's largest green space. There's tennis courts, benches with views, pavilions, and a big cement loop for walking or for kids practicing roller blading. It's such a lovely community vibe.

## BEACON AVENUE

This main thoroughfare captures the multicultural essence of Beacon Hill, lined with Salvadoran pupuserías, Vietnamese pho spots, and Korean BBQ joints. It's the soul of the neighborhood's food scene, offering locals and visitors a taste of the area's diversity through comforting, authentic bites.

## BEACON HILL PARK

This small, community-focused park offers basketball courts, a playground, and green spaces perfect for families. It's less bustling than Jefferson Park, but its simplicity makes it a neighborhood favorite for locals to gather and relax.

## RAINIER AVENUE

Once you go down the hill, things get a little sketchy. More homelessness and addiction down here, especially at that QFC. However, some new beautiful apartments with a large outdoor shopping area are coming and I presume this will make the area feel a bit more safe soon.

## BEACON HILL PLAYFIELD

Pickleball courts! There are 4 courts with two nets. Next to a basketball court, some picnic tables and a playground. It's where the community comes to walk dogs their or just unwind in the fresh air.

## BONUS! SODO

Just a quick jaunt over the I-5 overpass, SoDo (short for "South of Downtown") is Seattle's industrial and commercial hub, but it's also full of stores, breweries, and even some edgy art spaces. Though not technically part of Beacon Hill, it's so close that many Beacon Hill residents swing down for errands or a change of scenery.

# Best Things to Do

## BAR HOP & EAT

Solo girls, remember that we have a 4-drink maximum for safety so we're gonna make them count. Put on something cute and follow this routine. Start at **Bar Del Corso** at 4:30pm for happy hour drinks and dinner. If Bar Del Corso is busy, go to **The Oak.** After, have a digestif at this champagne bar, **The Coupe and Flute.** Then, have a glass of wine at the quaint and intimate **Little Thing Wine.** Next, Perihelion for dessert! Take a booze break here. If the weather is nice, sit outside with a fire. Finally, cozy into the bar at the back of The Oak. This whole walk is between 3 well-lit, safe blocks.

## JEFFERSON PARK

One of Seattle's oldest parks, Jefferson Park dates back to 1912 and spans over 50 acres on Beacon Hill's highest point, offering some of the best views in town. With its open green spaces, you can take a morning jog or read a book with your coffee. The park also features a golf course, playgrounds, and winding trails!

## WALK THE BEACON FOOD FOREST

This community-led permaculture project is designed to provide fresh produce for the neighborhood, fostering sustainable practices and food accessibility. The food forest has sections where visitors can harvest produce for free and learn about gardening, permaculture, and local plant varieties. Go have a walk in the spring.

## SEATTLE BOULDERING PROJECT

Founded in 2011, the Seattle Bouldering Project (SBP) has grown into one of the country's largest indoor climbing gyms, attracting climbers of all skill levels. Here, you can tackle everything from easy-to-handle walls for beginners to advanced climbs with challenging overhangs. SBP has become a local favorite not only for bouldering but also for its wellness-focused amenities, including yoga classes, a cozy café, and even a community lounge. The gym is a perfect spot for solo adventurers looking to meet new friends, as the friendly SBP community is full of climbers willing to share tips and encouragement.

⊙ **Hours:** Mon–Fri 6 AM – 11 PM; Sat–Sun 8 AM – 10 PM
📍 **Location:** 900 Poplar Pl S

## ☞ HOW TO GET TO BEACON HILL

### THE LIGHT RAIL
Get off at Beacon Hill Station and you're right on Beacon Ave!

## ☞ HOW TO GET AROUND BEACON HILL

### WALK
If you were to get off the Light Rail at Beacon Hill Station, you could walk along Beacon Ave for 15 leisurely minutes until you hit Jefferson Park – and you've just walked the most interesting route! This neighborhood is ultra walkable.



# Where to Eat

## COFFEE, BREAKFAST AND BRUNCH

### FRESH FLOURS
The most beautiful pastries like seasonal fruit tarts, macaroons, and shortbread cookies! You'll often see people taking a box of treats to-go in the morning. Coffees are fabulous, too, of course. Seating inside is limited, but there are chairs and seating outside. If you cannot find seating, take your coffee to-go, cross Beacon Ave towards Perihelion and explore the neighborhood behind. I love walking through this safe little cove.

⊙ **Hours:** Mon – Fri 6 AM – 5 PM / Sat – Sun 7 AM – 5 PM
♥ IG: @freshfloursbakery

### FABLE ALL DAY
The fancy coffee shop in town, but still locally-owned with a boutique feel. I like to order an iced lavender oat milk latte (is that basic?) and when it's nice, I sit outside in the courtyard or at a little table on the street to watch people. Oh, and there's freshly made cookies.

⊙**Hours:** Sunday & Monday: 7 AM – 5 PM, Tuesday – Saturday: 7 AM – 9 PM

♥ IG: @fableallday

## LUNCH/DINNER

*Casual*

### PERIHELION BREWERY

It's a brewery, but I rarely order a beer here. I'm here for their incredible food and female-friendly atmosphere. In the fall, especially, this place is so dreamy with tables outside that have fire in the middle! The whole neighborhood comes out to gather. Lots of dogs! The burgers, sandwiches (the Reuben is great), salads - it's all such a treat with such high-quality ingredients. And you guys, this is the place for dessert! Cakes, fruit pies, ice cream! I could eat here every day.

⊙**Hours:** Tues – Thurs 4 PM – 10 PM / Fri – Sun 12 PM – 10 PM (kitchen closes at 9:30 PM)

♥ IG: @perihelionbeer

### MILK DRUNK

The best damn spicy chicken sandwich in the city is called The Nashville. They also make a mean veggie burger called The Porto and some less spicy options, too. Take your chicken burger and eat outside (there is also seating inside). When you're done, loop back inside for an ice cream. This place turns me into a child. A sophisticated one, though, because they create flavors like Fig Leaf Coconut swirled with Black Plum Ginger . You can always just got for a classic cone but go crazy with toppings like fruity pebbles or chocolate sprinkles.

⊙**Hours:** Tues – Sun: 12 PM – 9 PM / Closed Mondays

♥ IG: @themilkdrunk

### STEVIES FAMOUS PIZZA

Hidden inside Clock Out Lounge – known for live music and trivia – is Stevie's Famous Pizza! This place is such a dive-bar so plan to pair your pizza with a local beer. I'd recommend this for a super causal date night, a solo bite to eat or with a group of new friends. Maybe ask in Girls in Seattle, who wants to join for trivia night or a show. Check their events on Instagram

⊙**Hours:** Sun – Thurs: 12 PM – 9 PM / Fri & Sat: 12 PM – 10 PM

♥ IG: @steviesfamous @clockoutlounge

### THE OAK

In the summertime, all the tables outside the oak, lining the sidewalk and tucked into a little alley are full of people getting off work and meeting their friends for a drink. But my favorite spot? The dark bar in the back! Like, really dark in a way that everyone looks hotter. Order dinner and a drink and hang out long enough to meet some strangers. If you're in the mood, get the Oak Bacon Cheeseburger with tater tots and ranch. Ps. Sunday Brunch is 9am to 3pm.

☉Hours: Mon – Thurs: 4 PM – 12 AM, Fri – Sat: 4 PM – 1 AM, Sun: 9 AM – 12 AM
★ Happy Hour: 4PM – 6PM
♥ IG: @oak_seattle

## LOWE'S HOTDOG

In front of Lowe's hardware store is this incredible food truck called Rainy City Hot Dogs. They make a mean Seattle Dog with a perfectly crisp bun, melty cream cheese and sautéed onions. They've also got adventurous combinations like the PB&J Dog! They've also got flame-broiled burgers, fries and Louisiana hot links! There is a little picnic table bench to eat. If you're single, afterwards, go wander around Lowe's looking lost. Maybe a handy man will help you...

☉ Hours: 10AM – 5PM, closed on Sundays
♥ Location: At the entrance of Lowe's on Rainier Avenue South (so drive, don't walk)
♥ IG: @raincityhotdogs

## THE CHINESE FOOD INSIDE RED APPLE GROCERY

Hear me out! There is an independently-owned Chinese food restaurant inside the Red Apple Grocery store. They have a daily special for $11 where you get to pick chow mein and rice plus two sides like teriyaki chicken or beef and broccoli. And it's comical how much they pack it high! Take it as a picnic to Jefferson Park. Expect fast food though, ya know. It's still grocery store Chinese at the end of the day, and I love it.

☉Hours: Lunch through Dinner
♥ Location: Inside the Red Apple Grocery Store at 2701 Beacon Ave S

## Date-Night Approved

### BAR DEL CORSO

This place keeps winning awards so get here early (or late) to get a table or a seat at the bar. Bar del Corso is a beloved Italian eatery on Beacon Hill known for wood-fired pizzas, an array of small plates inspired with seasonal PNW ingredients and a well-curated wine list. Bar del Corso also offers a cozy, heated patio for year-round dining.

⊙ **Hours:** Tues – Sat: 4:00 PM – 9:00 PM, Closed Sun-Mon

♥ IG: @bardelcorsoseattle

## MUSANG

"Intimate Filipino dishes inspired by our childhood memories," Musang is a family-owned Filipino restaurant serving elevated comfort filipino dishes like Pancit lomi, short rib kare kare, and grilled corn bibingka. Never had filipino food? You'll fall in love with it here. Oh and this place is female-owned! Melissa Miranda is an award-winning chef who pours everything into this restaurant, and you can taste it.

⊙ **Hours:** 5:00 PM – 10:00 PM, closed on Tues

♥ IG: @musangseattle

## DRINKS AND COCKTAILS

### THE COUPE AND FLUTE

Babe, you deserve a caviar and champagne happy hour ("Cavi-hour)! Deals on the best caviar, champagne flights and pours! The decor is whimsical, the bartenders feel like characters out of a storybook - just delightfully colorful and wise. But there is no bad time to visit The Coupe and Flute. Visit for brunch with tempura battered cream puffs, french onion soup, and smoked cod bagel!

⊙ **Hours:** Tues – Thurs: 4:00 PM – 10:00 PM, Fri: 4:00 PM – 11:00 PM, Sat: 9:00 AM – 11:00 PM, Sun: 9:00 AM – 10:00 PM, Closed Monday

♥ IG: @thecoupeandfluteseattle

### LITTLE THING WINE

Wine and bottle shop with very limited seating -- in the best way possible, making it easy for you to connect with strangers. Don't worry. There's also standing room, but sitting at this little bar feels like you're at a friend's house for a glass of wine and gossip. Sip and learn and listen.

⊙ **Hours:** Tues-Thurs 3PM-8PM, Fri-Sun 3pm-9pm

♥ IG: @littlething.wine

### THE OAK

I've mentioned this place above but just want to reiterate how lovely and divey it is. The Oak is my favorite place to sit at a dark bar and drink a cocktail as the mysterious girl in the corner. *(info above).*

## CHAPTER NINE

# Georgetown

**DAYS NEEDED:**
1 full day

 *Georgetown is that friend who is always up for a beer and a heart-to-heart no matter the day or the time.*

Easily one of my top 3 favorite neighborhoods in the city! This is a quick chapter for my foodie friends, brewery hoppers and vintage shoppers. Georgetown is a tiny little patch of restaurants, breweries, bars and shops that you could saunter around all night.

Georgetown is and always has been a beer haven. Back in the late 1800s, this area grew as a hub of industry with the establishment of Rainier Brewing Company in 1884. The main road became lined with small restaurants and saloons in red brick buildings. Today, not much has changed. You'll still find pubs, saloons and breweries tucked inside these brick buildings like little divey speakeasies.

But as with most cool neighborhoods, Georgetown has attracted some incredible restaurants to feed the beer drinkers. Come have a taste.

# Areas to Know

## AIRPORT WAY (MAIN ROAD)

The main strip through Georgetown, Airport Way, is lined with Georgetown's best pubs, eateries, and art spaces. You'll want to take your time walking this street and exploring its strange, eclectic places.

▶ **North End: Georgetown Brewing** — A Seattle institution, this brewery marks top of the Georgetown Patch. Start here and walk south for a Georgetown crawl along Airport Way.

▶ **Central: Georgetown Trailer Park Mall** — I'll talk about the shopping later but you can consider this the "center" of Georgetown, geographically - and on weekends, it's the center of Georgetown with its vintage mall!

▶ **South End: Great Notion Brewing** — A Portland brewery, once you've hit Great Notion, there's nothing further to explore. At least, not in this chapter.



# Where to Eat

## COFFEE, BREAKFAST AND BRUNCH

### VOI CÀ PHÊ

A traditional yet inventive Vietnamese coffee shop run by a family that used to own a cafe in Saigon! You can order classics like Vietnamese coffee pour over with condensed milk (Cà Phê Sữa Đá), or try something new like their Pho Latte with oat milk! Hungry? The banh mi here is *chef's kiss*. Try it with the homemade sausage patty or the pho spiced beef. Pro Tip: If you're not super hungry, order the mini Banh Mi as a snack! There's no indoor seating so plan to sit outside or take your banh mi for a walk.

⏱ Hours: 8AM – PM (closed Sun)
♥ IG: @voicapheseattle

### POST PIKE

Breakfast bagel alert! They've got lox, they've got bacon, they've got an abundant selection of schmears! They have a morning happy hour from 10am-11am where you get discounts on their bagel sandwich, schmears and drip coffee. For Lunch, they also have classic sandwiches...on bagels.

⊙ **Hours:** 10AM–10PM (open til midnight Fri & Sat)
♥ IG: @postpikebar

## JULES MAE SALOON

The problem with brunch spots is that they can be pretentious with a 2-hour wait and portions for a bird. Not here. This is the brunch spot you visit when you're hung-over and need sustenance ASAP! If the Waffles and Berries doesn't fix ya', the Stuffed Hash Browns will. If there's two of you, order the Chicken and Waffles with grits and mimosas made to share. Brunch goes 'til 1pm. And when you're ready to get back on the bull, Happy Hour is from 3-6pm. Ps. This place is female-owned! If you see Rache, say hey!

⊙ **Hours:** 11AM–2AM
♥ IG: @jules_maes_saloon

★ **Adventure Pairing:** Remember you can always pick up food to go and eat at one of the breweries or Full Throttle.



*Casual*
**(FROM NORTH TO SOUTH)**

## DON BURI STATION

I crave the chirashi bowl from Don Buri Station. What I love most about this place is that it's so casual. You'll often see people eating here alone, grabbing a quick bowl of sushi and miso soup before heading out to meet their friends. The prices are reasonable, there's plenty of seating and the service is quick, just order-at-the-counter.

⊙ **Hours:** Fri-Sat 11:30 AM–2 PM, 4:30–9 PM; Sun-Thurs 11:30 AM–2 PM, 4:30–8:30 PM
♥ IG: @donburistationseattle

## STAR BRASS WORKS LOUNGE

On a night out in Georgetown, I always end up at Star Brass (even if I've already had dinner). I crave their Tavern Burger, their salty tater tots, and their ranch. Most recently I've fallen in love with their onion rings served with a delightful horseradish sauce. Star Brass is that kind of place. The bar is dark and cozy. Sit at the bar because the bartenders here are the coolest to talk to and always have local advice!

⊙ Hours: 11AM–12AM (2am on Sat & Sun)
♥ IG: @starbrasslounge

## CALOZZI'S CHEESESTEAKS

If you don't like junk food you won't like this place, but if you like cheese whiz from a can, proceed. Order the pepper steak with whiz. Eat it at the picnic table or take it to one of the breweries. Full disclosure: this is an order-at-the-window Philly cheesesteak shop across from a weed-grow operation. It looks super sketchy which is how you know it's going to be good. It's safe but it's not walkable from Airport Way, so best if you have a car!

⊙ Hours: 11AM–4PM (5PM on Sat-Sun)
♥ IG: @calozzischeesesteaks

## Date-Night Approved

## CIUDAD

Looking for a date spot that feels a little off the radar? Ciudad in Georgetown is your place! It's got that hidden, speakeasy vibe—low-key and cozy, but still buzzing with energy. The food? Mediterranean-inspired tapas that are all about sharing, so you can try a bit of everything together. Start with their flatbread and dips and don't miss the lamb and beef köfte. And remember, if you're taking yourself on a date. sit at the bar for a show!

⊙ Hours: 11:30AM–9PM (10pm Fri-Sat)
♥ IG: @ciudadseattle

## GEORGETOWN LIQUOR COMPANY

When I first looked at the menu, I said out loud, "Hey I thought this place was vegan"! When you see the roast beef sandwich, the BBQ pulled pork, the street tacos - you'd never think this is a 100% plant-based restaurant! You won't even miss the meat. Ps. Consider the fact that this place was recommended to me by Boston Jon from the bottle shop; that says a lot.

⊙ Hours: 11AM–10PM
♥ IG: @glcseattle

## GEORGETOWN PIZZA & ARCADE

Full of pinball machines and old arcade games – this is the perfect date spot to see how playful or competitive they truly are. At night, this dark bar is lit up with neon lights, making for a surreal experience. Expect groups of kids, once in a while, though. If you'd like to avoid that, just come after 7. The pizza is delish and they have gluten-free options!

⊙Hours: 4PM–11PM (12AM on Sat & Sun)
♥ IG: @gpa.seattle

## BOP BOX

Beautiful and delicious Korean food! Bright pink pickled radish, perfectly boiled eggs, fragrant Kimchi fried rice! And it's all as good as it looks. I lived in South Korea for two years and I can tell you that every bite here is spot on with the flavors - but I love that the dishes are elevated and playful. Get the daily Banchan Bento to try a bit of everything.

⊙Hours: Tues–Sat 11 AM–3 PM, 4–8 PM; Closed Sun & Mon
♥ IG: @eatbopbox

## ☞ HOW TO GET AROUND GEORGETOWN

### WALK

It takes just 18 minutes to walk from Georgetown Brewing to Great Notion Brewing (remember those are my North End and South End markers).



# Where to Drink

**Note:** If a bar isn't on this list, don't go to it. There are a couple places I want you to avoid but I don't want to get sued so I can't explain it here. The bars on this list are run by great people who will take care of you.

## FULL THROTTLE BOTTLES
### Safe Girl Spot ♥

A collection of friends and locals. The place where you walk in as a stranger and if you mingle at the bar, you'll quickly find yourself in a conversation about dinosaurs or aliens with new friends. The owner, Boston Jon, will go out of his way to make sure you're happy and taken care of. They have the most expertly curated selection of beers and ciders on tap – like this is the place I visit when I want to try the newest, freshest, best beers. Also they have reasonably-priced bottles of wine with no corkage fee!

Ps. Show them you have this book or your Flamingo sticker so they know you're one of my girls! Get yours at Alexa-West.com/Travel-Shop

⊙ Hours:  Fri-Sat 12–10 PM, Sun 12–7 PM, Mon Closed, Tues-Thurs 12–9 PM
♥ IG: @fullthrottlebottles



## GEORGETOWN BREWING

When I want to sit outside in the sun surrounded by fellow beer nerds, I come here. Georgetown Brewing is iconic, known for its Manny's Pale Ale. Spacious and buzzing with energy, this is a great place to come solo or with friends.

⊙Hours: 10AM – 8PM
♥ IG: @georgetownbrewingco

## MIRAGE

The best beer in Seattle, according to me. Mirage is also award-winning, most recently winning 1st Place Pale Ale award at the 2024 Fresh Hop Ale Festival. The brewery is housed in an old warehouse with a little wrap-around bar. It's quite literally an unfinished work in progress that makes you feel like you're drinking in someone's garage; someone who happens to make incredible beer.

⊙ Hours:  Open weekends (check their Instagram for updated hours)
♥ IG: @miragebeer

## JULES MAE SALOON

A historic hangout serving pub grub with a back room for live music, pinball, Ping-Pong and air hockey. They also have trivia nights on Mondays and sometimes, live music (check their IG)! Ideal for a solo girl who wants to have some wholesome fun...with alcohol or not.

⊙Hours: 11AM–2PM
♥ IG: @jules_maes_saloon

## GREAT NOTION BREWING

Great Notion is a must for beer drinkers who like fruity, juicy IPAs. On a sunny day, this is the perfect place to sit on their patio in a big deck chair in the sun, drinking your cold beer or playing a game of Jenga with a friend. Their motto is "Keep beer fun" and they certainly have succeeded.

⊙Hours:  12PM–8PM (10PM Sat & Sun)
♥ IG: @greatnotionwashington

♥ **PARTY ALERT!** The Dead Baby Downhill Race, a bike race and street party, takes over Georgetown the first Saturday of August.

# Shopping

## GEORGETOWN TRAILER PARK MALL

A weirdly wonderful outdoor shopping space with an eclectic mix of vintage, handmade, and artisan goods, Georgetown Trailer Park Mall is a must-visit for anyone looking to find one-of-a-kind treasures. Each trailer hosts a different vendor, offering everything from retro clothing to unique artwork. It's not really a mall though, more like a parking lot with a collection of whimsical vendors.

⊙ Hours: Sat and Sun, 11 AM - 6 PM

⊕ Visit: @georgetowntrailerparkofficial

## THE BARN OWL VINTAGE GOODS

The ultimate stop for vintage lovers—whether you're on the hunt for vintage records, classic denim, or mid-century gems. Finally, you've found a vintage store that does not underwhelm with quality or quantity. You will want everything. Just moved to Seattle? Come initiate yourself by purchasing some vintage flannel.

♥ Pro Tip: Follow them on Instagram and see the new pieces they are posting!

⊙ Hours: Fri-Sat 11AM-7PM, Sun 11AM-6PM, Mon Closed, Tues-Thurs 12PM-7PM

♥ IG: @barn.owl.vintage

## FRAN'S CHOCOLATE

Founded in 1982 by Fran Bigelow, Fran's Chocolates is a Seattle icon celebrated for its luxurious, handcrafted confections. Inspired by a transformative trip to Paris, Fran brought European-style artistry to the Pacific Northwest. Indulge in their world-famous salted caramels, truffles, and more. Pro Tip: Fran's Chocolates are the perfect iconic Seattle souvenir to take home – just keep them cool so they don't melt!

⊙ Hours: Mon – Sat, 10 AM – 5 PM

♥ IG: @franschocolates

## ☞ HOW TO GET TO GEORGETOWN

### ...from Downtown

▸ By Car: Head south on I-5 and take the Corson Ave S exit (Exit 162). Georgetown is just a 10-15 minute drive from downtown, depending on traffic.

▸ By Uber: A 10-15 minute Uber ride from downtown Seattle to Georgetown costs around $12-18, depending on traffic.

▸ By Public Transit: Catch the Metro bus route 60 or 124, both of which will get you to Georgetown in about 20 minutes.

# NORTH SEATTLE



## CHAPTER TEN

# Fremont & Greenlake

**DAYS NEEDED:**
2 days

*Fremont's that friend who's always ready to dance at a drum circle or host a backyard party with no notice—your dogs are invited. Bonus: she has the best thrift shop finds.*

If you're into outdoor, artsy vibes, this is for you.

Fremont, once an industrial neighborhood, embraced its eccentric side in the 1970s and has since been known as the "Center of the Universe". You'll find its famous Troll lurking under the Aurora Bridge, quirky art pieces around every corner, and an undeniable sense of creative, offbeat energy. It's a neighborhood where families, artists, and musicians live side by side. It's a safe albeit strange community.

North of Fremont is Greenlake – and for ease of exploring, I'm going to encourage you to pair these neighboring adventures together.

Green Lake has always been Seattle's favorite outdoor haven. The lake itself formed over 50,000 years ago during the last Ice Age, and today, it's the city's most beloved running loop, drawing Seattleites from every neighborhood for walks, runs, and sunny picnics. The 2.8-mile path around the lake is perfect for a morning jog or afternoon lollylag, surrounded by lush trees, resident ducks, and sunbathing turtles. Greenlake Village, on the west side of the lake, is full of coffee shops, restaurants and wellness boutiques.

These two areas offer similar artsy, outdoorsy vibes – best explored when the sun is out!

Start in Fremont with a coffee at a boho café, browse the local boutiques, and snap a selfie with the Troll, with plenty of friendly faces along the way. Then, wander over to Green Lake for an afternoon by the water, whether you're renting a paddleboard, relaxing with a book, or grabbing a fresh juice from a local stand.

Fremont and Green Lake are welcoming neighborhoods that let you explore freely, shop, people-watch, and even get active, all in the span of a day – while feeling super safe.

### BEST FOR:
Outdoor activities & lake views
Quirky art and indie shopping
Spas and wellness

# Areas to Know

## GREENLAKE PARK
Green Lake has been a beloved Seattle community hub since the early 1900s! The 2.8-mile trail around the lake is popular for walking, paddleboarding, fishing, running, and biking.

## GREEN LAKE VILLAGE
Just across from the lake is this hub for fitness and wellness, offering everything from yoga studios to paddleboarding on the lake. It embodies the idea of "community" so well it almost feels staged.

## TANGLETOWN
Just a stone's throw away from the lake is Tangletown, a residential pocket with winding streets lined with charming cafes and local eateries. Here, you'll find gems like Zoka Coffee. The slower pace makes Tangletown a refreshing stop to vortex to sip a coffee and pause.

## GAS WORKS PARK
*(pictured left)*
Built on an old gas plant, this park offers one of the best

views of Seattle's skyline over Lake Union. Ideal for picnics, kite-flying, and sunsets, Gas Works is also a favorite for summer gatherings and the July 4th fireworks.

## FREMONT DOWNTOWN

The main hub around Fremont Avenue and 36th Street is packed with indie cafes, shops, and eccentric landmarks like the Fremont Rocket and the Lenin statue. On weekends, the Fremont Sunday Market adds even more color, with stalls selling everything from crafts to street food.

## FREMONT AVENUE

This lively street is where locals gather at cafes, shops, and restaurants like The Whale Wins. With sidewalk tables, indie shops, and people-watching aplenty, it's Fremont's heart, offering a true taste of its artsy charm.

## STONE WAY NORTH

Just east of Fremont's main drag, Stone Way connects to Wallingford and offers a more laid-back vibe with coffeehouses, vegan spots, and climbing gyms. It's a quieter stroll but full of hidden gems for those exploring the Fremont-Wallingford area.

## WALLINGFORD

A quaint residential neighborhood that has its charms but not a priority in your itinerary.

## WOODLAND PARK

Home to the renowned Woodland Park Zoo, this area offers a chance to see everything from snow leopards to penguins, making it a top stop for animal lovers. Beyond the zoo, Woodland Park also features trails, picnic areas, and popular pickleball courts!

## AURORA AVENUE & AURORA BRIDGE

Aurora Avenue (aka Highway 99) offers a direct route from Fremont through Wallingford to Queen Anne and downtown without the heavy congestion of I-5. It's practical if you're navigating by car and need an efficient route. Aurora Avenue is lined with old-school diners, budget motels, and also, hookers, particularly closer to the bridge. The Aurora Bridge is home to the famous Fremont Troll.

**PRO TIP!** Visit Book Larder for the best selection of new and used cookbooks!

# Best Things to Do

## VISIT THE FREMONT TROLL

No visit to Fremont is complete without meeting its most famous resident, the Fremont Troll. This larger-than-life sculpture lives under the Aurora Bridge, clutching a real Volkswagen Beetle in one hand. It's a great spot for a unique photo op and an iconic piece of Seattle's funky art scene.

♥ **Pro Tip:** Visit early in the day to avoid crowds and get the best lighting for photos. It's an easy walk from the main part of Fremont.

🎟 **Cost:** Free.

⊙ **Hours:** Open 24/7.

## EXPLORE THE FREMONT SUNDAY MARKET

Every Sunday, Fremont hosts one of Seattle's best open-air markets. From antiques and vintage clothing to local crafts and food trucks, this eclectic market captures the creative, bohemian spirit of the neighborhood. Whether you're in the mood to shop or just enjoy some great food, the Fremont Sunday Market has something for everyone.

♥ **Pro Tip:** Come hungry! The market is known for its diverse food vendors, with everything from wood-fired pizza to gourmet donuts.

🎟 **Cost:** Free to enter, but you'll likely want to shop or eat.

**Hours:** Sundays 10 AM – 4 PM.

♥ **IG:** @fremontsundaymarket

## WALK OR BIKE THE BURKE-GILMAN TRAIL

Fremont sits right along the scenic Burke-Gilman Trail, a popular route for both walkers and cyclists. This flat, multi-use trail runs alongside Lake Union, offering beautiful water views, greenery, and an easy way to explore the neighborhood and beyond.

♥ **Pro Tip:** If you don't have your own bike, consider renting one from a local shop or using one of the city's bike-sharing services.

🎟 **Cost:** Free.

⊙ **Hours:** Open 24/7

## CLIMB TO THE TOP OF GAS WORKS PARK

For stunning views of Seattle's skyline and Lake Union, head to Gas Works Park. This unique park is built on the site of a former gas plant, and its industrial structures give it a one-of-a-kind look. It's a favorite spot for picnics, kite flying, and watching the sunset.

♥ **Pro Tip:** Climb the grassy hill for the best panoramic views of the city. On a clear day, you can even spot Mt. Rainier in the distance.

💵 **Cost:** Free.

🕐 **Hours:** Open daily from 6 AM – 10 PM.

## CATCH A SHOW AT ABBEY ARTS

Live music, improv nights, workshops and story slams! If you're a fan of the performing arts and small venues, head to Abbey Arts in Fremont. Located in a beautifully restored 1914 building, this venue offers exceptional acoustics and a welcoming community-feel. Don't be afraid to come solo. Check their schedule!

💵 **Cost:** $10-$25.

🌐 **Visit:** <u>fremontabbey.org</u>

☞ **SEATTLE DRESS CODE:**

The best shoes for Seattle are Blundstone boots. Expensive but a worthy investment you can wear in the fall, winter and spring!



# Where to Eat & Drink

## COFFEE, BREAKFAST AND BRUNCH

📍 *Greenlake*

### RETREAT

Healthy way to start the day! Retreat's smoothie menu is full of spinach and hemp seed concoctions to give you a healthy boost of energy! Consider ordering a Wellness Latte like the Mushroom Matcha or the Activated Charcoal. Take your drink and sit in a deck chair outside. Sitting across from the lake you can watch the locals start to hit the path with their dogs! So many dogs!

🕐 **Hours:** Daily 7AM-9PM

🌐 **Visit:** <u>retreat-greenlake.com</u>

### ZOKA COFFEE ROASTER

My go-to cafe when I need to do some work on my laptop with caffeine and treats. A big space with plenty of tables, nooks, comfy chairs and outlets! They've also got pastries, bagels and sandwiches – plus plenty of vegan and gluten-free options.

⊙ **Hours:** 6AM – 6PM

⊕ **Visit:** zokacoffee.com

### THE DISH CAFE

When you're in the mood for a no-fuss, classic breakfast or lunch, The Dish Cafe is the perfect go-to spot in Greenlake. This cafe serves up all the comfort food favorites—pancakes, omelets, hash browns, and hearty sandwiches. The portions are hearty so come hungry or plan to take some food home!

⊙ **Hours:** 7AM–1:45PM (Opens 8AM Sat-Sun / Closed Mon)

⊕ **Visit:** dishcafe.net

### ♀ *Fremont*

### SEATTLE BISCUIT COMPANY

See that little shoebox on the side of the road? That is where Seattle's most famous biscuits and gravy are hiding. But what I recommend most is a biscuit sandwich piled high with goodies. I get the Ché with egg, Beecher's Flagship cheese, bacon, ham, Walla Walla sweet onion mustard, apple butter, and pickle. Eat here or order online and pick-up to go.

⊙ **Hours:** Daily 8 AM – 1 PM (2pm on Sat & Sun)

⊕ **Visit:** seattlebiscuitcompany.com

### OLD SALT FISH AND BAGEL

Old Salt smokes their own fish, making this spot perfect for a classic lox bagel or a house-made smoked fish spread. Not in the mood for fish? Get something spicy! Try the White Sesame Bagel with their unique Calabrian Chili Spread. Bonus: you can even buy their smoked salmon, black cod, and spreads by the pound for an at-home brunch feast!

⊙ **Hours:** Wed–Fri 8 AM–1 PM, Sat–Sun 8 AM–2 PM, Closed Mon–Tues

⊕ **Visit:** oldsaltseattle.com

### LUNCH/DINNER

### *Casual*

### ♀ *Greenlake*

### THE LATONA PUB

The Latona Pub is a cozy neighborhood bar with a stellar selection of local craft beers, huge salads, big sandwiches, and other fresh-yet-filling dishes. The laid back setting makes it a casual place to sit at the bar alone, enjoy some fresh Seattle fare and possibly make a friend or two with minimal effort. Ps. This pub often features live music on weekends. It's a great spot to unwind after a day at the lake.

⊙ **Hours:** Wed-Sun 12PM-11PM
⊕ **Visit:** latonapub.com

## KISAKU SUSHI

Come, sit at the bar and order the Omakase experience (a set-menu with chef's choice dishes). Beautifully plated, every dish deserves a photo-op before it's devoured. Want just a quick bite at lunch? Their menu is take-out only at lunch, which is why it's so cheap! Order a Sushi Combination that comes with a classic roll, nigiri and of course, miso soup.

☞ **What to Order:** Opt for the Omakase (chef's choice)
♥ **Pro Tip:** Make a reservation if you want a seat at the sushi bar.
⊙ **Hours:** Lunch 11:30AM-2PM / Dinner: 5PM-8PM
⊕ **Visit:** kisaku.com

♀ *Fremont*

## PASEO

The best Caribbean sandwiches around! Don't miss the Carribean Roast with juicy pork or the Pork Belly Sandwich! They also have veggie options with Tofu Delight and Onion Obsession! Order a side of Tostones to go. Warning: You will need lots of napkins and you will not look dainty trying to fit this in your mouth.

⊙ **Hours:** Daily 11 AM – 9 PM
⊕ **Visit:** paseo.com

## EL LEGENDARIO

I swear this is the most underrated Mexican food in the city! This family-owned Mexican spot is as authentic as it gets! When there is a Mexican holiday, you can typically expect them making celebratory dishes (like Pozole on Mexican Independence Day – which is not cinco de mayo, btw). Perfect for a casual meal that feels like a home-cooked experience. The quesabirria tacos are a must-try. Oh and the margaritas, huge.

⊙ **Hours:** Tues–Sat 12–10 PM, Sun 12–9 PM, Closed Mon
♥ **IG:** @ellegendarioseattle

## LOCAL TIDE

Λ seafood lover's paradise, Local Tide serves up Pacific Northwest seafood classics with a modern twist. The clam chowder is creamy and flavorful, while the crab roll is a fresh take on a classic sandwich. Perfect for a casual bite with a taste of Seattle's coastal vibe.

⊙Hours: 11 AM – 8PM (closed Mon)
⊕ Visit: localtide.com

## MINI BAR SEATTLE

Get ready for Korean fusion that will spoil you with Korean BBQ tacos, ramen, kimbap and dumplings! It's a spot that mixes the cozy vibe of a bar with a wild, creative menu. Before or after, stop by Fremont Brewing, just across the street.

⊙Hours: Tues, Thurs, Fri 5:30 PM–12 AM; Sat 2:30 PM–12 AM; Sun 2:30–9:30 PM; Wed 5:30–10 PM; Closed Mon
♥ IG: @minibarseattle

## BONGOS

Imagine a backyard beach party. There's bonfires, deck chairs and a sand pit. A total hangout space where you can order a beer or cocktail and eat slowly...and you'll want to savor every bite here. Bongos is known for Caribbean bowls and sandwiches with jerk chicken, spicy shrimp, and pulled pork, paired with man go slaw and seasoned rice! This is a great spot to visit during or after a walk around the lake.

⊙Hours: Tues-Sun, 11AM–9PM
⊕ Visit: bongosseattle.com


### Greenlake

### NELL'S

This is fine dining at its best, complete with a sommelier! With a cooking style that blends classic training from top kitchens in New York City and France, chef and owner Phil Mihalski brings a passion for freshness and simplicity to every dish. Known for his global culinary curiosity (Fun Fact: I once ate bugs and frogs with him in Cambodia!), Phil draws inspiration from his travels, then returns to Seattle to source the best seasonal mushrooms, herbs, and proteins from the Pacific Northwest. Wine snob? Nell's has quite possibly the best French wine list in the entire city.

⊙ Hours: Mon–Sun 5–8 PM, Fri & Sat until 8:30 PM
⊕ Visit: nellsrestaurant.com

### Fremont

### RESPITE WINE BAR + BOTTLE SHOP
**Female-owned!**

For a casual, low-commitment date spot, come to RESPITE where you can have a glass of wine and share a cheese board without the pressure of a full meal. The ambiance is warm and inviting, with rustic wood accents, candle-lit tables, and comfortable seating that makes it easy to relax and see where the evening goes.

⊙ **Hours:** Wed–Fri 4–9 PM, Sat 3–9 PM, Closed Sun–Tues
⊕ **Visit:** <u>respitebottleshop.com</u>

## THE WHALE WINS

With a focus on small plates designed for sharing, The Whale Wins is perfect for a cozy date night with a European-inspired menu. This romantic Fremont gem features wood-fired dishes made with ingredients from local beaches, gardens, and farms, bringing the best of Seattle's flavors to the table. Expect excellent service and a curated wine list to elevate your evening.

⊙ **Hours:** Mon, Fri 12–9 PM; Tues, Wed, Thurs 4–9 PM; Sat, Sun 10 AM–9 PM
⊕ **Visit:** <u>thewhalewins.com</u>

## KIN LEN THAI NIGHT BITES

I can confirm that this is some of the best Thai food in the city. For a fun, adventurous date night, Kin Len brings the energy of Bangkok street food to Seattle. Expect delicious Thai small plates perfect for sharing, as Thai food is meant to be!

☞ **What to Order:** Boat Noodles or Battered Chicken Red Curry
⊙ **Hours:** Daily 11:30AM–10PM
⊕ **Visit:** <u>kin-len.com</u>

## FREMONT MISCHIEF DISTILLERY & RESTAURANT

For a one-of-a-kind date night, head to Fremont Mischief, where the industrial-chic vibe and waterfront views set the stage. Known for their craft spirits made in-house, you can enjoy tastings of their famous rye whiskey, gin, and vodka—each distilled with unique flavors from local grains. Start with a flight of whiskey to kick things off, then dive into a meal featuring standout dishes like smoked salmon dip, Dungeness crab cakes, or their Mischief burger topped with housemade bacon jam.

⊙ **Hours:** Thurs–Sat 4–10 PM, Sun 1–7 PM, Closed Mon–Wed
⊕ **Visit:** <u>mischief-on-canal.com</u>

### BONUS!
## AROY MAKE THAI FOOD

I have been searching for the best Khao Man Gai in Seattle, and I found it here! Order the combo Khao Man Gai Tod + Gai Yang.

⚲ **Location:** 15 minutes north of Greenlake
⊙ **Hours:** 11AM- 8:30PM
♥ **IG:** @AroyMak_thaifood

📍 *Fremont*

### KOROCHKA TAVERN
**(Wallingford, technically)**

If beer's not your thing, Korochka Tavern has you covered with its lineup of Old World-inspired cocktails and infused vodkas that bring a taste of Eastern Europe right to Seattle. This cozy, wood-accented spot is perfect for sipping on a crisp Moscow Mule or a custom vodka infusion while enjoying hearty bites like pierogis or smoked fish. With its warm, laid-back atmosphere, it's easy to settle in and relax. Na zdorovye!

🕐 **Hours:** Tues–Sat 4 PM–12 AM, Sun & Mon 4–10 PM
🌐 Visit: korochkatavern.net

### FREMONT BREWING

This woman-owned gem is more than just a brewery—it's a full-on social scene! Known for killer craft beer, but don't sleep on their surprisingly good wine selection and refreshing ciders. With cozy nooks and big communal tables, it's the kind of place where strangers become friends (or more, wink-wink). Cold? There's a fire pit to keep things warm.

🕐 **Hours:** Daily, 11 AM – 9 PM
🌐 Visit: fremontbrewing.com

### TRIANGLE SPIRITS

Start here if you have a hangover. Order their famous Bloody Mary, in addition to the most delicious Chicken and Waffles in the north! Here in the evening? Happy hour is from 3-5pm. Sit at the bar and order some the Truffle Popcorn or in the summer, sit outside under the twinkle lights.

🕐 **Hours:** Mon–Thurs 2 PM–12 AM, Fri 2 PM–1 AM, Sat 1 PM–1 AM, Sun 11 AM–10 PM
🌐 **Visit:** trianglefremont.com



# Beauty & Wellness

📍 *Greenlake*

### RS HEAD SPA

Like getting your hair washed at the salon but 10x better. RS Head Spa offers luxurious scalp treatments that focus on deep relaxation and hair health. During this hour-long experience, your head is massaged, your scalp is purified and your hair is washed with Olaplex (the high quality stuff) as this ring of gentle warm water trickles over your head. The treatment is finished with a neck massage and a blow-out. I love the idea of popping into RS Head Spa after the gym or work – before you hit happy hour. You will leave relaxed and with silky hair. Bonus: They offer a 2-hour package that includes the head spa plus a swedish massage with hot stones for less than $150!

♥ **Girls in Seattle**
**Happy Hour: Spa Edition**
Tuesday & Thursday between 11 AM - 3 PM, use Code **"GIRLSINSEATTLE"** for 10% off.

⊙ Hours: 10AM – 9:30PM
⊕ Visit: rsheadspa.com

## FLOAT SEATTLE

Float therapy is the ultimate way to relax, and Float Seattle provides sensory deprivation tanks for a truly meditative experience. Inside the float tank, you'll float effortlessly in saltwater, which helps reduce stress, ease muscle tension, and calm your mind. Perfect for anyone looking to disconnect and achieve a deep state of relaxation. It can be a little freaky at first so watch a YouTube video to know what to expect.

⊙ Hours:  Mon, Fri–Sun 7 AM–10 PM; Tues, Wed, Thurs 10 AM–10 PM
⊕ Visit: floatseattle.com

## SPAVIA DAY SPA

For the ultimate day of pampering, Spavia in Greenlake offers it all – including massages, facials, body wraps, and more. They also do lash lifts, spray tans and waxing. Literally, it's a one-stop-shop for a Seattle makeover. Ps. If you live here, consider getting their massage membership!

⊙ Hours: 10 AM – 8 PM, Closes 6pm Sat - Sun)
⊕ Visit:  spaviadayspa.com

**♀ FREMONT**

## MAVEN YOGA

Maven Yoga offers a peaceful, inclusive space for yogis of all levels with a range of classes from Vinyasa and Yin to Restorative, allowing you to find the perfect fit for your body and goals. Newbies can get unlimited classes for their first two weeks for cheap! Even if you're here just for a long weekend, it's worth it! And if you're looking to make a few new friends in Seattle, this is a great place to start!

⊙ Hours: Daily starting as early as 6AM 'til 8:30PM
⊕ Visit: maven-yoga.com

# Shopping

## FREMONT FARMERS MARKET

☞ **What to Find:** Fresh produce, artisan crafts, vintage finds, and street food. Great for local treasures and unique bites.

⊙ **Hours:** Sundays, 10 AM – 4 PM (operates year-round, rain or shine)

♥ IG: @fremontsundaymarket

## FREMONT VINTAGE MALL

☞ **What to Find:** Retro clothing, antiques, quirky decor, and one-of-a-kind vintage pieces. Perfect for treasure hunting.

⊙ **Hours:** Daily, 11 AM – 7 PM

♥ IG: @fremontvintagemall

## THEO CHOCOLATE FACTORY

☞ **What to Find:** Handcrafted chocolate bars, free samples, and factory tours that dive into sustainable chocolate-making.

⊙ **Hours:** Daily, 10 AM – 6 PM (closed Mon)

♥ IG: @theochocolate

## PCC COMMUNITY MARKETS / FREMONT CO-OP

☞ **What to Find:** Organic produce, local goods, and eco-friendly products, perfect for stocking up on wholesome essentials.

⊙ **Hours:** Daily, 6 AM – 11 PM

♥ IG: @pccmarkets

# MINI ITINERARIES FOR FREMONT + GREENLAKE

## SUNNY DAY ITINERARY

⊙ **8 am:** Grab a green smoothie or wellness latte at **Retreat** and sit outside.

⊙ **9 am:** Walk the **Greenlake loop**; bring a pickleball paddle if you're up for a game afterwards.

⊙ **11:30 am:** Have lunch at **Latona Pub.**

⊙ **12:30 pm:** Relax with a one-hour head spa and one-hour massage at **RS Head Spa.**

⊙ **3 pm:** Head home to freshen up after your blowout.

⊙ **6:30 pm:** Take yourself on a date to **RESPITE Wine Bar + Bottle Shop** in Fremont for wine and cheese.

⊙ **8 pm:** Live music and dinner at **Fremont Mischief Distillery & Restaurant** to end the night.

## COLD DAY ITINERARY

⊙ **8am:** Warm up with a yoga or meditation class at **Maven Yoga** in Fremont.

⊙ **9am:** Bundle and walk to see the **Fremont Troll** (it will be less crowded at this time and weather).

⊙ **9:45 am:** Have breakfast at **Old Salt Fish and Bagel**

⊙ **11:00 am:** Take an Uber to **FLOAT Seattle** to fully unwind.

⊙ **12:30 pm:** Head home to shower and refresh for the day

⊙ **2 pm:** Back out for a late light lunch at **Local Tide.**

⊙ **3:30 pm:** Head to **Fremont Vintage Mall** for some indoor vintage shopping.

⊙ **4:30 pm:** Stop by **Fremont Brewing** to cozy up with a drink by the fire.

⊙ **6 pm:** Walk across the street to dinner at **Mini Bar Seattle** for Korean fusion and a drink (or two).

⊙ **8 pm:** Catch a Show at **Abbey Arts**

## CHAPTER ELEVEN

# U-District

**DAYS NEEDED:**
1 day

*The U-District is your curious little sister at college who likes second-hand shopping, boba and cheap, drunk nights out.*

Ya'll, I went to school here at UW and let me tell you…I have some very mischievous adventures for you.

Welcome to the vibrant University District, affectionately known as the U-District! Anchored by the University of Washington, this youthful, eclectic neighborhood is alive with student energy, coffee shops, and an ever-growing food scene (lots of incredible Asian options).

The location is incredible, too. You can hop on the Light Rail and be in Capitol Hill or Downtown within 10 minutes. You can jump in an Uber and explore Fremont or Greenlake in 10 minutes. Or you can hang out here. Jump in a kayak and explore the waters. Wander campus and marvel at the architecture. Or stroll down to the U-Village.

While I am no longer a young college student, I still find myself visiting the U-District often as it has all my favorite things: cheap Asian food, the best indie bookstores, affordable spas and the best second-hand shopping! I also love that, as a solo traveler, you'll be in good company with plenty of solo students. Ps. Not all of them are 19-year old undergrads, you've got some more established folks, too.

Oh, and if you're in the mood for a bit more greenery, there is a neighborhood that connects to the U-District called Ravenna which offers a charming, low-key strip of restaurants and cafes perfect for those looking to escape the hustle and bustle.

## BEST FOR:

▶ Being close to the University (duh)
▶ Cheap eats and dive bars
▶ Book lovers and cafe culture enthusiasts

## DAYS NEEDED:

1 day is fine, honestly. A day-visit, even. But if you go to school here, you'll find there are many thrilling (and cheap) things to experience in the U-District!

# Areas to Know

## UNIVERSITY OF WASHINGTON CAMPUS

A must-see! Stroll through the stunning cherry blossoms in the Quad (if visiting in spring), take in views of Mt. Rainier from Red Square, or visit the beautiful Suzzallo Library, often referred to as a "Harry Potter library" for its grandeur.

## THE AVE (UNIVERSITY WAY NE)

This is where the magic happens. When I was a student at UW, I'd walk to this area for everything: restaurants, cafes, bookstores, farmers markets, bars and of course, grocery shopping at Safeway. The "Ave" is technically one street but the lively neighborhood spills over a couple more blocks.

## UNIVERSITY VILLAGE

This is where the fancy people come to shop at Lululemon and the huge Apple Store. This upscale outdoor shopping center is one of my all-time favorite places for a classic shop-and-stroll, especially on a sunny day! They've got everything from Starbucks to hair salons! You can easily spend a few hours shopping, enjoying a meal, or grabbing a coffee while people-watching

## RAVENNA

Located just north the U-Village is Ravenna. The heart of Ravenna is Ravenna Brewing where there are often food trucks and locals gathered with their dogs!

## THE BOBA BUCKET LIST

(by a girl who used to live in Taiwan, where bubble tea was invented in the 1980s)

01. BobaLust
02. Café Happy
03. UW Seattle Best Tea
04. OH! Bear Cafe & TeaHouse
05. Ding Tea Seattle
06. Boba Up
07. MACU TEA - UW
08. Timeless Tea Dessert Cafe
09. Don't Yell at Me
10. Boba Gem Tea House

♥ **FUN FACT!** The U-Disctrict has the most boba per block in all of Seattle.

# Top 5 Things to Do

## WALK THE UNIVERSITY OF WASHINGTON CAMPUS

Start with a walk around Red Square, explore the beautiful Suzzallo Library (affectionately known as the "Harry Potter library"), and if you're here in spring, catch the breathtaking cherry blossoms in the Quad. With its grand architecture and lush gardens, the campus is a mix of elegance and energy.

Fun Fact: Suzzallo Library was named after UW President Henry Suzzallo and opened in 1926, making it a historic gem.

♥ Pro Tip: Early mornings are best for crowd-free photos of campus landmarks.

## SHOP & EAT ALONG THE AVE (UNIVERSITY WAY NE)

Grungy and international, the Ave is the U-District's main strip, perfect for college kids and cafe lovers. This street is packed with international (and affordable) restaurants, thrift stores, and indie bookstores.

## VISIT THE BURKE MUSEUM OF NATURAL HISTORY AND CULTURE

Right on the UW campus, the Burke Museum offers a fascinating dive into Pacific Northwest history, Native American cultures, and natural sciences. From dinosaur fossils to Indigenous artwork, the Burke is a must-see for culture and science enthusiasts alike.

♥ Pro Tip: Stop by the paleontology lab to watch scientists work on real fossils up close.

🎟 Cost: $22 for adults
Visit: burkemuseum.org

## SHOP THE U-DISTRICT FARMERS MARKET

Every Saturday, the U-District Farmers Market fills University Way NE with fresh produce, artisanal goods, and handmade crafts from local vendors.

♥ Pro Tip: Cash recommended for purchases.

🕐 Hours: Saturdays 9 AM–2 PM

## KAYAKING ON LAKE WASHINGTON

Looking for a little outdoor adventure? Just east of the U-District, Lake Washington offers a perfect spot for kayaking. Rent a kayak or paddleboard and enjoy a peaceful trip along the water, with beautiful views of the surrounding landscape. It's an active, yet relaxing way to experience Seattle's natural beauty.

🏷 **Cost:** Rentals average around $20–$30 per hour.
☞ Check out rental spots like Agua Verde Paddle Club for an easy launch.

**Bonus!**

## VISIT SCARECROW VIDEO

One of the only surviving video stores in the USA. So beloved that the community raised $600k to help this store stay open. It's a legend. Go browse the movies.



# Where to Eat

## BREAKFAST & COFFEE

### PORTAGE BAY CAFÉ

A local favorite for breakfast and brunch, Portage Bay Café offers farm-to-table meals with organic, sustainable ingredients. Their famous breakfast bar lets you top your pancakes, waffles, or French toast with fresh fruit, whipped cream, and real maple syrup. Perfect for leisurely mornings or brunch meet-ups, this spot is known for its fresh, healthy, and hearty meals.

🕐 **Hours:** Daily 8 AM – 1 PM (2 PM Sat & Sun)
📍 **Location:** U-District
🌐 **Visit:** portagebaycafe.com

### CAFE SOLSTICE

The caffeine at Cafe Solstice is what got me through University. This is my go-to work-marathon cafe—the kind of place where you can settle in all day with another coffee, a pastry, and a big ice water to stay hydrated.

Whether you're working on a thesis or just stopping by for a to-go coffee, Solstice's atmosphere and welcoming energy make it easy to stay productive (and well-fed).

🕐 **Hours:** Daily 6:30 AM – 5 PM (opens 7am Sat & Sun)
📍 **Location:** U-District
🌐 **Visit:** cafesolsticeseattle.com

## LUNCH & DINNER

### THAI TOM

If you're craving authentic Thai food, Thai Tom is a legendary hole-in-the-wall spot in the U-District. This tiny restaurant is the best place to sit and watch as the chefs prepare stir-fries, curries, and noodles right before your eyes! That is, if you can get a seat. No seat? Order takeaway and head to campus for a picnic. Ps. The Pad See Ew or the Swimming Rama (peanut curry with spinach) are crowd favorites.

🕐 **Hours:** Mon-Sat 11:30 AM – 9 PM (opens 12pm on Sunday)
📍 **Location:** U-District
🌐 **Visit:** thaitomseattle.com

### RACHEL'S GINGER BEER

Here's the inside scoop: there's a secret Nashville-style hot chicken spot tucked away in the back of this Ginger Beer spot that serves up spicy, crispy chicken sandwiches. Trust me, this combo of ginger beer and hot chicken is the best one-two punch you didn't know you needed!

🕐 **Hours:** Daily 11 AM – 9 PM
📍 **Location:** U-Village
🌐 **Visit:** rachelsgingerbeer.com

### MORSEL

Morsel is a breakfast-lover's dream, known for its mouthwatering biscuit sandwiches that are made fresh daily. With its small but cozy interior, it's the go-to spot for locals seeking a satisfying breakfast or lunch. Whether you're a fan of savory or sweet, Morsel's menu has something for everyone, from fried chicken biscuits to house-made jam.

🕐 **Hours:** Wed-Sun 8 AM – 3 PM
📍 **Location:** U-District
🌐 **Visit:** morselseattle.com

### DELFINO'S CHICAGO STYLE PIZZA

Delfino's brings the heart of Chicago to Ravenna with its authentic deep-dish pizzas. Perfect for a hearty meal after exploring the neighborhood, Delfino's offers thick, cheesy slices of pie that are sure to fill you up. With a laid-back family vibe, it's a great place to gather with friends or take home leftovers for later.

⊘ **Hours:** Mon, Tues, Wed, Thurs 11 AM–9 PM; Fri, Sat 11 AM–10 PM; Sun 12–8:30 PM

⚲ **Location:** Ravenna

⊕ **Visit:** delfinospizza.com

## RAVENNA BREWING

My boyfriend is a beer nerd and he chose to bring me here on our first date; that says a lot, right? This neighborhood brewery has it all: food trucks, both indoor and outdoor seating, and IPAs that impresses the Seattle beer snobs. **Pro Tip:** Check their events calendar for trivia nights or live music.

⊘ **Hours:** Mon, Tues, Thurs 2–10 PM; Fri 12–10 PM; Sat 11 AM–10 PM; Sun 12–10 PM

⚲ **Location:** Ravenna

⊕ **Visit:** ravennabrewing.com



# Beauty & Wellness

### SKIN

## SKIN SYNTHESIS CLINIC & SPA

Specializing in advanced skincare treatments, Skin Synthesis Clinic offers facials, chemical peels, microneedling, and more to help you achieve radiant, glowing skin. Their personalized treatments are designed to target specific skin concerns like acne, fine lines, and hyperpigmentation, making it a favorite for those serious about their skincare routine. For glowing skin, try the HydraFacial!

⊘ **Hours:** 10am-6pm (closed Sunday)

⊕ **Visit:** skinsynthesis.com

### BODY

## THE YOGA SHALA

The Yoga Shala offers an array of yoga classes and yoga teacher training in a calming space designed for mindfulness and wellness. Whether you're a seasoned yogi or a beginner, their classes cater to all levels and focus on both mental and physical well-being.

⊘ **Hours:** Mornings and evenings

⊕ **Visit:** theyogashalaseattle.com

# Nightlife

If you're in the mood for trivia, live music, or just want to grab a drink, these spots are perfect for a night out.

## COLLEGE INN PUB -

A favorite hangout for students and locals alike, College Inn Pub has a relaxed, old-school vibe with wood-paneled interiors. The pub is known for its great trivia nights and is always packed with UW students looking to blow off steam. Whether you're grabbing a beer or shooting pool, it's a cozy spot to catch up with friends. Order the fish and chips or their house-made chili.

♥ **Pro Tip:** Trivia night happens every Tuesday at 8 PM, so get there early for a table!

☉ **Hours:** Daily 4 PM – 11:30 PM (closed Sunday)

♥ **Location:** U-District

☞ **Student Factor:** High—packed with UW students.

♥ IG: @thecollegeinnpub

## BIG TIME BREWERY

Seattle's original brewpub, Big Time Brewery is always buzzing with students enjoying craft beer and classic pub food. It's a casual spot for meeting up with friends or grabbing a late-night pizza, with long communal tables that make it perfect for groups. The lively atmosphere makes it a hub for U-District nightlife.

☉ **Hours:** 11:30AM-11PM

♥ **Location:** U-District

☞ **Student Factor:** Very High—expect a student crowd.

♥ IG: @bigtimebrewery

## THE KRAKEN BAR & LOUNGE

Pinball machines, live music, open mic night and gosh darn delicious bar food that you crave --The Kraken Bar is the kind of place where the drinks are cheap, the music is loud, and the crowd is always ready to party. Check them out on Instagram to see what events are happening!

☉ **Hours:** 3PM-midnight

♥ **Location:** U-District

☞ **Student Factor:** High—popular with students, especially for live music.

♥ IG: @the.kraken.seattle

## CHAPTER TWELVE

# Ballard

*Seattle's cool, laid-back aunt who now spends her days perfecting her sourdough recipe while wearing expensive gold hoops she got in Spain.*

Story time. I was originally not planning to cover Ballard in this travel guide simply because… it's far from everything. From downtown, it will be a 20 minute drive. From the south end, 30 minutes with no traffic if you're lucky. I don't go to Ballard often besides the occasional brunch.

But then one of my best friends moved there. As I drove through central Ballard on a summer evening, we took a turn down the most beautiful streets lined with twinkling lights. As we drove, we continued to pass the cutest freaking restaurants with happy people clearly loving life….and all I could do was yell "Noooooo I love it here, nooooooo"! At that moment, I knew that I simply could not NOT include Ballard. I love it here and I want to move here.

It's like, if LA and the PNW had a baby…it would be Ballard. Fanciful boutiques, restaurants created by chefs who travel extensively for inspiration, lots of young couples in their 30's, lots of love for outdoor spaces, and as safe as it can get. Everyone who is here is happy and well-fed.

A little history before the Ballard love session begins: Ballard began as a gritty Scandinavian fishing village, founded by immigrants in the late 1800s who were drawn to the area's rugged coastlines and bountiful waters. Over time, this small port town grew into a major player in Seattle's shipping industry, with a culture deeply rooted in Nordic tradition and a hardworking, maritime spirit. You can still feel these origins in the architecture, the cobbled streets, and in the neighborhood's pride for its history.

Today, Ballard's mix of heritage and sass has made it a magnet for Seattle's new creatives. Here, history lives alongside some of the city's most imaginative restaurants, innovative breweries, and trendy boutiques. It's a place where you can explore Seattle's past while enjoying the vibrant, ever-evolving pulse of the present.

This chapter is a collection of the best recommendations from myself – but more importantly, from my friends who live in this neighborhood.

# Areas to Know

## BALLARD AVENUE

The heart of Ballard's dining and shopping, where historic brick buildings reflect its Scandinavian roots and host boutiques, bars, and eateries.

## BALLARD LOCKS AND FISH LADDER

Opened in 1917, these locks connect Lake Washington and Puget Sound. The adjacent fish ladder provides a fascinating view of salmon migrations in season.

## GOLDEN GARDENS PARK

A waterfront retreat with sandy beaches, trails, and breathtaking sunsets over Puget Sound—a go-to spot for a classic Seattle sunset.

## PHINNEY RIDGE

An extension of Ballard's charm, this is a separate yet connecting neighborhood with local cafés, unique shops, and stunning Olympic Mountain views, plus easy access to the Woodland Park Zoo.

## DISCOVERY PARK

While not directly in Ballard, this is as close as you're probably gonna get to Discovery Park. It's just a 20-minute drive south to Seattle's largest park, offers breathtaking, jaw-dropping views of Puget Sound, miles of hiking trails, and the iconic West Point Lighthouse. Weave this into your itinerary, perhaps before you go to Ballard.

## BOOKS SET IN WASHINGTON

**1. The Twilight Series by Stephenie Meyer – Forks;** misty, forested town

**2. Alone in Wonderland by Christine Reed – Wonderland Trail;** rugged Mount Rainier

**3. Firefly Lane by Kristin Hannah – Seattle;** scenic city life

**4. Snow Falling on Cedars by David Guterson – Puget Sound;** secluded island

**5. Fifty Shades of Grey by E.L. James – Seattle;** urban and upscale

**6. The Baker's Apprentice by Judith Ryan Hendricks – Seattle;** cozy bakery

**7. The Great Alone by Kristin Hannah – Seattle/Alaska;** wilderness survival

**8. The Absolutely True Diary of a Part-Time Indian by Sherman Alexie – Spokane Reservation;** rural landscape

# Best Things to Do

## EAT, DRINK AND WANDER

Back to my "Noooo" moment: Ballard is literally a wonderland of boutique experiences. Chefs, jewelers, book collectors, bespoke tours, energy healers, and candle makers who say prayers over their essential oil blends - they all really give a shit about what they are doing and why. This is the world I want to live in...if I had a tech salary. If you're on a budget though, maybe don't come here. It's a wonderfully bougie neighborhood with prices to match (best money ever spent though).

## BALLARD FARMERS MARKET

Dating back to the early 2000s, the Ballard Farmers Market has become a Sunday staple, drawing crowds for fresh produce, artisan goods, and unique crafts. It's one of the few year-round markets in Seattle, making it a lively gathering place even in the cooler months.

♥ **Pro Tip:** Arrive early to beat the crowds and grab fresh pastries or coffee to enjoy as you wander.

🏷 **Cost:** Free to explore, but bring cash for local treats!

🕐 **Hours:** Sundays 9 AM – 2 PM

🌐 **Visit:** ballardfarmersmarket.org

## THE BALLARD LOCKS

Built in 1917, the Ballard Locks are where saltwater from Puget Sound meets the freshwater of Lake Union, creating a fascinating transition. Watch boats rise and fall as they pass through the locks, and keep an eye out for the fish ladder where salmon leap out of the water as they migrate.

♥ **Pro Tip::** Visit during the summer for the best salmon viewing. The adjacent Carl S. English Botanical Garden makes for a peaceful stroll.

🏷 **Cost:** Free

🕐 **Hours:** Open daily

🌐 **Visit:** ballardlocks.org

## CARKEEK PARK BEACH

Carkeek Park Beach is a natural wonder where forested trails meet a stunning, rocky beach along Puget Sound. Once a salmon migration and tribal fishing site, it's now a place to enjoy Ballard's coastal beauty, spot wildlife, and explore the unique marine ecosystem. The beach offers stunning views of the Olympic Mountains, plus picnic tables if you're making it a day trip. Consider grabbing a

Mean Sandwich before coming here.

 Walk the Pipers Creek trail in fall to see the salmon returning to spawn.

📣 **Cost:** Free
🕐 **Hours:** Daily, 6 AM – 10 PM
🌐 **Visit:** seattle.gov/parks/all-parks/carkeek-park

## GOLDEN GARDENS PARK

Located right on the waterfront, Golden Gardens is a favorite spot for beach lovers and sunset watchers. With sandy beaches, forested hiking trails, BBQ pits, and panoramic views of Puget Sound, it's a fantastic place to relax by the water, cook up some fresh salmon and drink a bottle of wine. Ps. Take photo of your beach adventure and tag me in it @sologirlstravelguide

📣 **Cost:** Free
🕐 **Hours:** Open daily
🌐 **Visit:** seattle.gov/parks/all-parks/golden-gardens-park

## WOODLAND PARK ZOO

Founded in 1899, the Woodland Park Zoo is an award-winning, ethically operated zoo! Known for its dedication to sustainable practices, the zoo has earned recognition for ethical animal care and habitat design, providing enriching and natural environments for its residents! You'll see everything from grizzly bears and penguins to tropical birds and elephants in beautifully crafted exhibits designed to mimic their native habitats. After exploring, take some time to unwind in Woodland Park right next to the zoo. This green haven offers serene walking trails and scenic picnic spots. Bring a book and stay a while.
**Cost:** $24.60 for adult

🕐 **Hours:** Daily 9:30 AM – 4 PM
🌐 **Visit:** zoo.org

## NATIONAL NORDIC MUSEUM

Opened in its current building in 2018, the National Nordic Museum celebrates Ballard's Scandinavian heritage, dating back to when Nordic immigrants settled in the area during the late 1800s. The museum's exhibits explore Nordic history, culture, and art—everything from Viking history to modern design.

♥ **Pro Tip:** Stop by the museum's café for traditional Nordic treats and coffee after exploring the exhibits.
📣 **Cost:** $20 for adults, $15 for seniors, free for kids under 5
🕐 **Hours:** Tues - Sun 10 AM – 5 PM
🌐 **Visit:** nordicmuseum.org

# Where to Eat

## BREAKFAST, BRUNCH & COFFEE

### PICO CAFE AND BAKERY

Pico Café is for the early risers who crave a morning pastry and a coffee in a serene garden setting surrounded by flowers. This French-inspired bakery has flaky croissants, airy baguettes, and rich coffees that will transport you straight to a Parisian morning. Locals love to start their morning here, often meeting friends after a neighborhood walk.

♥ **Pro Tip::** Order the Apple Strudel.
☉ **Hours:** 6:30AM - 5PM
♥ IG: @pico_cafe_and_bakery

### HONEST BISCUITS

Get your Southern comfort fix at Honest Biscuits, where the homemade biscuits are legendary. This breakfast spot serves up hearty Southern-style biscuits that have become a local favorite. Try the "McGregor" with fried chicken and bacon gravy. Ps. They have gluten-free buscuits!

☉ **Hours:** Fri-Mon, Wed-Thurs 8 AM–2 PM; Sat-Sun 8 AM–3 PM; Tues Closed
⊕ **Visit:** honestbiscuits.com

### JOIE COFFEE

The cutest Vietnamese coffee shop! It's pink and girly with flowers on the walls, and the drinks are just as cute — and delicious. Try the Pandan Matcha or the Sea Salted Cream Latte. The store is tiny so fingers crossed that you'll get a seat. This place is best for a fun coffee stop (if you've got a car, preferably) during your busy day.

☉ **Hours:** Daily, 8AM – 4PM
♥ IG: @joie.thecupofjoy

## LUNCH & DINNER

### *Casual*

### SABINE CAFÉ & BAR

Don't be fooled by the long line! There is a secret to getting seated! It doesn't look like it but you can bypass the line and go straight to the bar! We love a bar! Expect Mediterranean-inspired plates with fresh, locally-sourced ingredients! Try the Shakshuka with house-made Labneh! Ps. This is also a great brunch spot!

☉ **Hours:** Fri-Sat 8 AM–11 PM; Sun-Mon 8 AM–3 PM; Tues-Thurs 8 AM–9 PM
♥ IG: @sabineseattle

## MEAN SANDWICH

Mean Sandwich is tucked just off the main drag in Ballard, the kind of spot you'd walk past if you didn't know any better. Don't. The signature Mean Sandwich is a powerhouse of thick-cut corned beef, tangy red cabbage, yellow mustard, and just a hit of mint—it sounds odd, but it works so well you'll crave it after. For sides, the Skins & Ins (crispy fried potato bites) are half-skin, half-magic. This is best for a takeout or a quick meal as seating is limited.

⊙ Hours:Daily, 11AM – 3PM
⊕ Visit:  meansandwich.com

## LITTLE CHINOOK'S

Little Chinook's at Fishermen's Terminal is a seafood spot that nails the classic Seattle fish and chips. Their wild salmon, cod, and halibut are fried to crispy perfection and make for a delicious waterfront lunch right by the fishing boats. The salmon tacos are a personal favorite—light and full of flavor—but if you're hungry, go for a seafood combo with fries and their creamy tartar sauce.

⊙ Hours:Daily, 11:30AM - 6PM
♥ IG: @chinooks_anthonys



## BRIMMER & HEELTAP

Wine snobs, this is your spot! The team at Brimmer & Heeltap are obsessed with finding the most beautiful wines to pair with lunch and dinner. Their happy hour is one of the best in town with half-priced wine by the glass and oysters so cheap they're practically free. Their menu is poetically small with fresh, seasonal ingredients – and make sure to ask for a wine pairing recommendation. The best place to sit? Their back patio feels like a secret garden, but it's popular so make a reservation.

⊙Hours: 4PM-9PM (closed Mon- Tues)
⊕ Visit:  brimmerandheeltap.com

## DELANCEY

Delancey is all about wood-fired pizza and stellar wines for a date that's casual yet polished. Their fennel sausage pie and white pie are top picks, each with a perfectly blistered, chewy crust. And with a well-chosen wine list, this spot has you covered for pairing a new glass with each slice. Cozy lighting, chic vibes, and those just-out-of-the-oven pies make Delancey the place to linger and savor.

⊙ **Hours:** Sat 4:30–10 PM; Sun 4:30–9 PM; Tues-Fri 5–10 PM; Mon Closed
♥ IG: @delanceyseattle

## BAKER'S

This is a popular date spot! It's casual, low-commitment and a bucket-list spot to tick. Here's what you're going to do: Head to Baker's in Ballard's Sunset Hill and likely stand in line (it's worth it, trust me). When you and your date sit down, order everything. This cocktail bar does tapas-style plates meant for sharing, so try the sardines on baguette and the beef dip sandwich—both get consistent rave reviews.

⊙ **Hours:** 4PM-10PM (12AM on Fri-Sat)
♥ IG: @bakers.seattle

## THE WALRUS AND THE CARPENTER

This Ballard gem is an oyster lover's paradise with a mix of French-inspired seafood and rustic charm. Expect fresh oysters on ice, served with shallot mignonette and seasonal varieties from Washington waters. The space has a beachy cottage feel, and the back patio is a cozy spot to sip Muscadet and slurp oysters. Besides oysters, the menu has standouts like grilled sardines, smoked trout, and potted crab—excellent for sharing with friends over a crisp glass of wine.

♥ **Pro Tip:** This is perhaps the most popular restaurant in Ballard and reservations are not accepted. So arrive early or late for less of a wait.
⊙ **Hours:** Daily, 4PM-9PM (10PM Fri - Sat)
♥ IG: @thewalrusbar

## RUPEE BAR

Rupee Bar in Ballard brings Sri Lankan and South Indian flavors into a cozy, stylish space that's perfect for adventurous palates. With a small but spot-on menu, it serves standouts like the Kerala fried chicken, a golden-crusted delight seasoned with a special Sri Lankan chili blend and paired with creamy aioli. The cocktail menu is equally exotic, featuring tropical ingredients like curry leaf and tamarind! The menu itself gives you lots to talk about even on an awkward date.

⊙ **Hours:** Fri-Sat 4–10 PM; Tues-Thurs 4–9 PM; Sun-Mon Closed
♥ IG: @rupeebar

# Where to Drink

## BALE BREAKER AND YONDER CIDER TAPROOM

Yonder Cider started out as one woman's dream in her garage, and now it's a Seattle staple. Teaming up with Bale Breaker Brewery (they make great Hazy IPAs), these two have created the most welcoming tap room experience! On sunny days, this is the spot—think outdoor summer camp for grown-ups, with picnic tables, cold drinks, and total relaxation. And when it gets chilly? Fire pits in a back-yard setting are ready to keep you warm, drink in hand. Love the drinks, love the people, love everything about this place.

⊙ **Hours:** Fri-Sat 12–10 PM; Sun 12–9 PM; Mon Closed; Tues-Thurs 3–10 PM

⊕ **Visit:** yondercider.com

## REUBEN'S BREWS - THE BALLARD TAPROOM

Reuben's Brews is so Seattle legendary that you can grab a six-pack in nearly every Seattle grocery store. Founded in 2012 by a husband-and-wife team, Reuben's offers a rotating tap list of innovative, award-winning beers. From IPAs to barrel-aged sours, there's always something new to try. I recommend ordering a flight and seeing what you like! Also, they have events, food trucks and trivia nights! Check their website and Instagram to see what's going on.

⊙ **Hours:** Daily 11AM-10PM

⊕ **Visit:** reubensbrews.com or @reubensbrews

## HAZLEWOOD

I've decided that this is my favorite bar in Ballard. Hazlewood is a tiny, divey gem with vintage charm and a sense of humor. Think velvet couches, candelabras and strange tapestries on the wall. Very medieval in a hauntingly romantic way. Check their Instagram to see what DJs they have spinning. Those are the nights where you're guaranteed to make a new friend or two.

⊙ **Hours:** 4PM – 2AM (closed Mon)

♥ **IG:** @hazlewoodbar

## TRACTOR TAVERN
### Live Music Alert!

One of the best live music venues in Seattle. This is as local as it gets, as it was recommended to me by one of the vendors in Pike Place Market! Tractor Tavern has been a local favorite for over 25 years booking incredible artists! Shows do sell out, however, so I recommend checking out their line up and grabbing tickets. Great drinks but they don't have a kitchen, so plan to grab a bite before!

⊙ **Hours:** Mon - Fri 8PM –2 AM
⊕ **Visit:** tractortavern.com

Hey - want a shortcut to meeting people while exploring Ballard?

**Join the Viking Beer Crawl**

---

♥ **STORYTIME:**

Emilia and I went on a double date in Ballard in 2021 (like 2 nights before I met my boyfriend) and our dates were so bad that we ended up hiding in the back of the restaurant while the waitresses brought us free tequila shots. It turns out, the staff has been watching how badly this date was going and felt so badly for us! Surprisingly, the waitress was also like, "Hey, aren't you The Solo Girl's Travel Guide?" That was cool! The point being: Ballard is a great first-date neighborhood where you can ask for help at any time! And if you and your date drive here together and you want to leave, just get in an Uber.

---

# Need a podcast for your flight?

Listen to our podcast, True Crime Travelers.

Listen at
truecrimetravelers.com ☞

# Beauty & Wellness

## SOUL

### SACRED RAIN HEALING CENTER

A spiritual oasis offering a mix of holistic treatments in Ballard. Think of it as a bathhouse for the soul. Their range of services includes everything from relaxing massages to reiki and chakra balancing. You can book a Spiritual Bath Ritual for deep relaxation, where healing techniques and mineral-rich baths are combined to promote energetic cleansing. For a full mind-body reset, try their combination packages, which mix massage and energy healing for a truly immersive experience.

⊙ **Hours:** Mon–Thurs, Sun 10 AM – 8 PM; Fri–Sat 10 AM – 10 PM
📍 **Location:** 1100 NW 50th St, Ballard
🌐 **Visit:** sacredrainhealing.com

## BODY

### LADIES ROOM 206

Ever made friends while topless? Here's your chance (but full swimsuits are welcome if you prefer). Ladies Room 206 in Seattle is a top-optional escape with plunge pools, saunas, and steam rooms designed for max relaxation in a body-positive, women-only space. Tuesdays are for unlimited spa time—take it easy and stay as long as you like. On All Gender Wednesdays, everyone's invited to unwind in this blissful space. Check out their happy hour from 12–4 PM on Wednesdays, Thursdays, and Fridays!

⊙ **Hours:** 10 AM – 8 PM; Closed Mon
📍 **Location:** 1121 E Union St, north of Phinney in Greenwood
🌐 **Visit:** ladiesroom206.com

## NAILS

### PINK POLISH SEATTLE

Pink Polish Seattle specializes in nail art that's on another level—if they can perfect intricate designs, you know their classic manicures and pedicures are going to be flawless. Their Ballard studio is a bright, welcoming space, where the nail techs are known for paying close attention to detail. Whether you're stopping in for a quick polish change or treating yourself to custom nail art, they make sure every nail is gorgeous.

⊙ **Hours:** Mon–Fri 10 AM – 7 PM; Sat 9:30 AM – 6 PM; Sun 10 AM – 6 PM
📍 **Location:** 907 NW Ballard Way Suite 118, Ballard
🌐 **Visit:** pinkpolishseattle.com

## PINK RUBY SALON

Ballard's go-to for curly hair and bold color. The stylists here know how to work with natural curls and can bring vibrant colors to life with confidence. If you're looking to change it up with fantasy colors or just want your curls looking their best, Pink Ruby Salon has a reputation for delivering. They also specialize in cuts that work with texture, so every curl is well-shaped and defined.

⊙ Hours: Wed–Sat 10 AM–6 PM; Closed Sun–Tues

Location: 1416 NW 46th St #301, Studio 20,7

♥ IG: @pinkrubysalon

## HOW TO GET TO BALLARD FROM DOWNTOWN:

▸ Car: ~15 min via 15th Ave NW.

▸ Bus: Route 40 or RapidRide D Line (~25-45 min, $3).

▸ Bike: ~30 min via Burke-Gilman Trail.

▸ Rideshare: ~15 min, $15-$25.



# Shopping

## BALLARD FARMERS MARKET

For an authentic Ballard experience, visit the Ballard Farmers Market, a bustling open-air market filled with local produce, handmade crafts, and fresh-cut flowers. Vendors are primarily local farmers and artisans, creating a community-driven experience that brings Ballard's small-town feel to life. It's perfect for those who love fresh, seasonal produce and supporting local markets.

⊙ Hours: Sundays, 9 AM–2 PM

Location: Ballard Ave NW between 20th and 22nd Ave

## BALLARD SQUARE SHOPPING MALL

Ballard Square is a small shopping center with a carefully curated mix of specialty stores, including Classic Consignment for unique vintage finds, KAVU for outdoor-inspired clothing and accessories, and Clover Toys for creative, thoughtfully selected children's toys. Known for its peaceful vibe, Ballard Square is ideal for a leisurely shopping day without the crowds, excellent for those who prefer a variety of boutiques in one place with a laid-back ambiance.

⊙ Hours: Daily, 5AM – 1AM
♥ Location: 2232 NW Market St

## BALEEN

I have this girlfriend who is a lawyer and always looks flawless. This is the jewelry store she recommended to me. Baleen is a must-visit jewelry shop that designs and handcrafts minimalist, sustainable pieces right here in Ballard. Owned by husband-and-wife team Leah and Billy, Baleen's jewelry is both affordable and ethically made, reflecting their commitment to beauty with a low environmental impact. If you love sleek, understated jewelry or need a unique gift, this is your place.

⊙ Hours: Fri-Sat 11 AM–6 PM; Sun-Thurs 11 AM–5 PM
♥ Location: 6418 20th Ave NW

## BALLARD ORGANIC SKINCARE

My bathtime sessions typically involve a decadent treat by Brooke from Ballard Organic Skincare. Fun Fact: I did a life-changing psilocybin retreat recently and Brooke, the owner of this incredible skincare line, was my guide (aka my spiritual babysitter). Needless to say, her products are more than skin-deep. She infuses intention and practicality in everything she makes so that your day to day life is more balanced and nourished. I love her and I love what she creates. You will, too. I adore her collection of beauty serums, cleansers & hydrosols! Shop Online at ballardorganic.com.

## SECRET GARDEN BOOK SHOP

A beloved independent bookstore, Secret Garden Book Shop has been a Ballard staple for decades. Owned by Phinney Books since 2021, it retains its community feel and passion for local authors and children's literature, making it a hit for families and book lovers alike. If you're searching for a hidden gem or a cozy corner to flip through books, Secret Garden offers the perfect ambiance. **Pro Tip:** Call ahead and ask if they have any signed copies of my books (The One-Way Ticket Plan or the Seattle Guide).

⊙ Hours: Mon, Tues, Thurs, Fri 11 AM–7 PM; Sat 11 AM–6 PM; Sun 11 AM–5 PM
♥ Location: 6418 20th Ave NW 2214 NW Market St

♥ Find Seattle tutorials and guides at @SoloGirlsTravelGuide on Instagram

# OUTSIDE SEATTLE



## CHAPTER THIRTEEN

# Day Trips, Hikes & Camping

**Oh, Washington's great outdoors!** They've been calling to adventurers since long before REI started peddling flannel shirts and headlamps. Even if you're not the "outdoorsy" type, I'm going to guide you to some outdoor adventures that are low-commitment, high-impressive.

The Pacific Northwest is a wonderland of animals, edible forests and secret gardens. From the ancient old-growth forests filled with towering Douglas firs and western hemlocks to the understory blanketed in a kaleidoscope of ferns, mushrooms, and mosses, each trail reveals nature's intricate layers. Washington's forests are famously rich in mushrooms—morels, chanterelles, and boletus among them—which emerge in abundance with the autumn rains, drawing foragers and enthusiasts who know to tread lightly and responsibly. Wildlife spotting is practically guaranteed, whether it's orca whales, harbor seals, black bears, bald eagles, or river otters.

Washington's wildlife, forests, and coastal ecosystems are accessible to you right now – no matter the season–, offering a perfect way to escape, reset, and reconnect with the natural world—even if only for a day trip or a brief hike into the wild.

**For more details on these adventures, visit my blog** 🌐 **Alexa-West.com/Seattle**

# Sleepovers Outside Seattle

**The beauty of Seattle is that it only takes a quick drive to feel like you've been transported to another world.**

## GIG HARBOR

I grew up here. Gig Harbor is a quaint maritime fishing village with "Downtown Gig Harbor" being one big walkable loop around the water where fishing boats and sailboats glide by against a backdrop of the majestic **Mount Rainie**r. In the early days, Gig Harbor was settled by Croatian and Scandinavian immigrants who built a thriving fishing and boat-building industry, shaping the town's identity. The "downtown" area preserves this heritage with restored buildings, maritime museums, and a waterfront where you can feel the town's nautical roots.

Today, Downtown Gig Harbor is lined with charming restaurants, artisan shops, and local breweries, offering everything from fresh seafood to damn good BBQ (elevated, of course). You must visit Jerisich Park and walk down the dock. When the weather is nice, you can rent kayaks and **paddleboards** to get up close to marine wildlife (look for seals).

It was a treasure growing up here, and I'm thrilled to share this slice of Pacific Northwest magic with you.

🏠 **Stay:** The Waterfront Inn
⊙ **Play:** Kayak on the harbor, drive to Narrows park for a picnic, restaurant hop the harbor.
✳ **Eat:** The Tides (sit on the deck or at the bar) and order the fish and chips.

## WOODINVILLE

Wine at the vineyards. Concerts at Chateau Ste. Michelle Winery. The original farm to table restaurant, Herbfarm. And the most gorgeous PNW-style lodge called The Willows Lodge. This is the perfect weekend destination for a solo girl, couples or a group of friends, guaranteed to be one of the highlights of your trip. In fact, this is where lots of local girls go for their mischievous yet classy bachelorette weekend; it's that iconic. If you have the time, consider spending "24 Hours at the Farm" with HerbFarm where you get to see every step from harvest to plating. And check out Chateau Ste. Michelle's event calendar and tasting experiences!

**Stay:** Willows Lodge
**Play:** ste-michelle.com/visit-us/experiences
**Eat:** Von's 1000 Spirits
**How to get there:** 45-minute drive or an $40-$70 Uber.

## TREEHOUSE POINT

Picture luxury in the treetops: plush bathrobes, silky sheets, and breakfast (yes, cheesy scrambled eggs!) delivered right to your treehouse door. Treehouse Point, just a **30-minute drive** from Seattle, offers the chance to sleep in the trees at one of **seven treehouses** built by Pete Nelson from Treehouse Masters on the Discovery Channel. The **two-night minimum stay** means you'll have plenty of time to relax or venture out to nearby spots like Snoqualmie Falls or the Hazel Wolf Wetlands. Rates vary by season, I've seen treehouses starting around a couple hundred bucks a night.

**Stay:** You can choose from seven different styles!
**Play:** Snoqualmie Falls or the Hazel Wolf Wetlands
**Eat:** At the treehouses or drive 15 minutes to Gianfranco Ristorante Italiano
**Web:** treehousepoint.com

## THE SAN JUAN ISLANDS

The San Juan Islands are pure magic—a Pacific Northwest dream where rocky shores meet deep blue waters, and whales glide through like something out of a storybook. Just a quick ferry or thrilling seaplane ride from Seattle, these islands are fabulous for adventurers and relaxation seekers alike. In **Friday Harbor,** the main town, you'll find cozy inns, charming cafes, and an unbeatable gateway to nature.

The best time to visit is **May through September,** when the islands come alive with wildlife and outdoor activities. Imagine spotting orcas, humpbacks, and gray whales right off the coast, hiking lush trails, or paddling through kelp forests as eagles soar above. Each season reveals a new side of the San Juans, but summer is the ultimate highlight reel. Ready for the perfect itinerary? **Check out Alexa-West.com/Seattle for tips on where to stay, eat, and play in this unforgettable paradise.**



▶ Fly: Take a seaplane with **Kenmore Air** from Seattle's Lake Union or Boeing Field, arriving in Friday Harbor in about **45 minutes**. Prices range from **$150–$200 each way**.

▶ Ferry: The **Washington State Ferry** departs from Anacortes, taking **60–90 minutes** to reach Friday Harbor. Tickets are **$13.25 per adult** and **$6.60 for youth** (round-trip, walk-on).

Once there, a car isn't mandatory—Friday Harbor is walkable, and you can rent bikes or use shuttles to explore. But if you want to visit the other islands, like Orcas Island or Lopez Island, having a car makes it easier to fully explore.

## VICTORIA, BC (CANADA)

**Yea, go to Canada!** I'm not kidding. Seattle is super close to Vancouver Island in BC. Consider spending one or two nights there. Explore the famous Butchart Gardens, historic downtown, enjoy high tea at the Fairmont Empress Hotel and go to a hot pot restaurant with a robot server! BC is another world. Don't forget your passport!



▶ By Car: It's about a 2.5- to 3-hour drive (140 miles) from Seattle to Vancouver, depending on border wait times. The fastest route is taking I-5 North to the Peace Arch border crossing. Gas and tolls will cost around $30–$50 USD round-trip.

▶ By Train: The Amtrak Cascades runs from Seattle's King Street Station to Vancouver's Pacific Central Station. The journey is approximately 4 hours and costs $35–$55 USD each way.

▶ By Clipper Ferry: This doubles as such an adventure! **The Victoria Clipper** offers seasonal trips through the Puget Sound directly from Seattle to Vancouver, giving you a scenic, stress-free ride up the coast. The ferry departs from **Seattle's Pier 69** and takes about **3.5 hours** to reach Vancouver's downtown waterfront. Prices range from **$100 to $150 USD** round-trip depending on the season and seat selection.

☞ No car option: You do not need a car for this trip. The Clipper ferry drops you off in downtown Vancouver, where public transportation and walking are excellent options for exploring the city.

☞ More details on this crazy adventure at Alexa-West.com/Seattle

# Day Hikes Around Seattle

**(in order of how far from the city and how much of a hike)**

## 01. NACHES PEAK LOOP

When my best friend came to town, this is the hike my Seattle-local boyfriend insisted we take her on – and it did not disappoint. It's stunning, not too difficult and takes around 1.5 hours. The Naches Peak Loop is a scenic 3.4-mile trail in Mount Rainier National Park that treats hikers to some of the most iconic views of Mount Rainier, vibrant wildflower meadows, and serene alpine lakes. With moderate elevation gain (aka not too step, can do it in sneakers), this loop is accessible for most skill levels. Pro Tip: Hike the loop clockwise for epic views of Mt. Rainier on your descent.

⇥ **How to get there:**
From Seattle, take I-5 south to Enumclaw, then follow State Route 410 east. Continue to Chinook Pass, where you'll find the trailhead parking near Tipsoo Lake.

⚠ **Need to know before you go:**
▸There's a toilet at the trailhead.
▸Pets are not allowed on the Mount Rainier National Park portion of the trail.
▸ Visit in late July through early September for peak wildflower season and optimal trail conditions.

## 02. MOUNT RAINIER NATIONAL PARK

Mount Rainier, an active volcano and Washington's tallest peak, stands at 14,411 feet. It's the centerpiece of the national park, which offers stunning meadows, alpine lakes, and over 260 miles of hiking trails. You can visit **Paradise** for wildflower-covered meadows in the summer or head to Sunrise for unbeatable mountain views. In winter, it's a wonderland for snowshoeing.

### Skyline Trail (_Paradise Area_)

▸ **Distance:** 5.5 miles round trip
▸ **Difficulty:** Moderate to strenuous
▸ **Time Required:** Approximately 3–4 hours
▸ **Highlights:** This iconic trail offers panoramic views of Mount Rainier, wildflower meadows in summer, and dramatic glaciers. The trail passes scenic points like Myrtle Falls and the overlook

at Panorama Point, where you can often see nearby peaks on clear days.

## Nisqually Vista Loop
### (Paradise Area)

▶ **Distance:** 1.2 miles round trip

▶ **Difficulty:** Easy

▶ **Time Required:** About 45 minutes to 1 hour

▶ **Highlights:** A short, accessible trail ideal for families and casual hikers, the Nisqually Vista Loop provides stunning views of the Nisqually Glacier and alpine landscapes. It's especially popular during wildflower season in late summer.

## Sourdough Ridge Trail
### (Sunrise Area)

▶ **Distance:** 2.5 miles round trip

**Difficulty:** Moderate

▶ **Time Required:** About 1–1.5 hours

▶ **Highlights:** This trail provides excellent views of Mount Rainier, the Emmons Glacier, and the surrounding alpine landscape. Starting at the Sunrise Visitor Center, the trail follows a gentle ridge with panoramas that are especially beautiful at sunrise or sunset.

Want to join a group of explorers at Mount Rainier? Join this group tour ☞

**How to get there:**
Mount Rainier is about 2 hours from Seattle. Take I-5 south to SR-7, which will lead you to either the Paradise or Sunrise entrances.

**⚠ Need to know before you go:**
▶ You'll need a National Parks Pass ($30 per vehicle).
▶ The park is open year-round, but some roads close during winter. Check for road conditions before you go.
▶ Arrive early, especially in summer, as parking lots fill up fast.
▶ Don't step off the trails, we don't want to smoosh the fields.

## 03. RATTLESNAKE LEDGE

Just 45 minutes east of Seattle, Rattlesnake Ledge offers a moderately **challenging 4-mile round-trip hike** with sweeping views of Rattlesnake Lake and the Snoqualmie Valley. It's a popular trail for locals and tourists alike, so expect company. On clear days, you'll get an incredible vantage point of the Cascade Mountains. This hike takes **2-4 hours.**

**How to get there:**
Take I-90 east from Seattle, then take exit 32 toward 436th Ave SE. Follow the signs to Rattlesnake Lake Recreation Area.

**⚠ Need to know before you go:**
▶ No pass required.
▶ It's a busy trail, so start early to avoid crowds.
▶ Trail can be steep in some areas—hiking boots recommended.

## 04. SNOQUALMIE FALLS & TWIN FALLS

Snoqualmie Falls is a breathtaking **268-foot waterfall** located just 40 minutes from Seattle. You drive there, park, and walk to a lookout point over the falls with paved pathways leading to multiple viewpoints. Spend about **30 minutes** feeling the mist on your face, then go for a hike!

Nearby, the Twin Falls trail offers a moderate 3.6-mile round trip hike with stunning waterfalls framed by lush Pacific Northwest forest. This hike will take 2-2.5 hours.

### ⏩ How to get there:
Head east on I-90, take exit 25, and follow the signs for Snoqualmie Falls. For Twin Falls, continue east to exit 34, and park at the Twin Falls trailhead.

### ⚠ Need to know before you go:
- Snoqualmie Falls is free to visit.
- For Twin Falls, you'll need a Discover Pass ($10 per day or $30 annually).
- Snoqualmie Falls has a lodge with dining options if you want to make it a full-day outing.

## 05. WALLACE FALLS STATE PARK

Wallace Falls offers a 5.6-mile round trip hike with views of nine stunning waterfalls surrounded by mossy forests. The park is about an hour northeast of Seattle and is known for its beautiful old-growth forest and the powerful waterfall views from various points along the trail. This is a great spot for both seasoned hikers and families.

### ⏩ How to get there:
Take Highway 2 east toward Gold Bar, then follow the signs to Wallace Falls State Park.

### ⚠ Need to know before you go:
- You'll need a Discover Pass.
- The trail is popular, so start early for the best parking options.
- Bring layers, as the trail can be cool and misty even in summer.

## 06. LAKE 22

Located on the western slopes of the Cascades, Lake 22 is a stunning 5.4-mile round trip hike that takes you through dense old-growth forest to a tranquil alpine lake. The trail can be steep at times, but the views of the lake nestled beneath towering cliffs make it worth the effort. On a clear day, you'll be surrounded by snow capped peaks, even in summer.

### ⏩ How to get there:
From Seattle, take I-5 north to SR-92, and follow signs to the Mountain Loop Highway.

### ⚠ Need to know before you go:
- Discover Pass required.
- Parts of the trail can be muddy and slippery, so wear proper hiking boots.
- Get there early to secure parking, as it fills up fast on weekends.

### BONUS HIKES:
- Cascade Pass Trail
- Snow Lake Trail
- Kendall Katwalk

# Ferry Trips

**Look at the Puget Sound!**
See all those channels and islands?! You can explore those via ferry!

Ferries are cheap, safe and comfortable - but they're not always the quickest so embrace that the ride is the adventure. Put on your comfy shoes, pack a day bag with a water bottle + your Solo Girls Sticker and explore the nearby islands for an easy day trip. Check the Washington State Ferries website for real-time schedules.

The **Seattle Ferry Terminal** is located at **Pier 52** on the Seattle Waterfront, at 801 Alaskan Way. It's within walking distance of downtown Seattle attractions like Pike Place Market and Pioneer Square, making it convenient for visitors. You can catch ferries here to Bainbridge Island, Bremerton, and Vashon Island. Returning is easy and convenient with frequent return trips throughout the day. ☞

## DAY TRIP TO BREMERTON FROM SEATTLE

The **Bremerton Ferry** offers an ideal day trip from Seattle, with a scenic 60-minute ferry ride across Puget Sound, providing beautiful views of the city skyline and mountains as you head west. Bremerton, known for its small-town charm, offers a waterfront packed with things to see and do, all within walking distance from the ferry terminal.

Once you dock in Bremerton, grab a coffee or breakfast treat at **Honor Coffee** or **Bremerton Bar & Grill.** Wander through the Bremerton Boardwalk, where you can explore the waterfront and check out the **USS Turner Joy.** Dive into local history at the **Puget Sound Navy Museum**, which is free and just a short walk from the terminal. Stroll through **Evergreen Rotary Park** for scenic views of the Sound and a beautiful, grassy spot to relax. Grab lunch with a water view. Then go do a mini brewery hop at **Local Boys Tap Room** and **Dog Days Brewing. OR book a massage** at one of the many massage studios walking distance to you. You're not in a hurry, right?

➠ **Return to Seattle:** Head back to the ferry terminal for an easy return trip. The Bremerton ferry departs every 2-2.5 hours throughout the day, including weekends.

⊙ **Ferry Times:** Every 2-2.5 hours from 5:30 AM to 12:50 AM

⊙ **Duration:** 60 minutes each way

🎟 **Cost:** $9.45 per adult (walk-on round-trip)

## BAINBRIDGE ISLAND

Bainbridge Island is a laid-back, scenic island with hiking trails, charming cafes, and the **Bainbridge Island Historical Museum** (it's free and right there when you get off the ferry). Don't miss the opportunity to **play pickleball at Battle Point Park**, where pickleball was invented. They have paddles and balls you can rent. If you're more of a wine enthusiast, Bainbridge also boasts some fantastic wineries.

✳ **Fun Fact:** The Seattle-Bainbridge ferry route is particularly popular for its views of the Olympic Mountains, Mount Rainier, and the Seattle skyline. It's a must for photographers!

☞ **No car option:** You don't need a car for Bainbridge Island. You can walk on the ferry and either rent a bike or explore on foot. Literally get off the ferry, follow the people, walk 7 minutes to downtown where you can walk, shop and eat.

⊙ **Ferry Times:** Every 45-60 minutes, 5:30 AM – 12:55 AM

⊙ **Duration:** 35 minutes each way

🎟 **Cost:** $9.45 per adult, $4.70 for youth (walk-on round-trip)

Don't forget the ferry trip to San Juan Islands that I've mentioned in the last section.

And be sure to re-read the West Seattle ferry adventure on page 195.

## KINGSTON

Kingston is a quaint waterfront town with easy access from Seattle, offering scenic views, cozy cafes, and a small-town vibe on the Kitsap Peninsula. Walk just minutes from the ferry to **Mike Wallace Park,** where you can watch the boats come and go or take in the sunset over Puget Sound. Kingston's small downtown area is filled with local gems, from **Borrowed Kitchen Bakery** for coffee and pastries to **J'aime Les Crepes** for delicious sweet and savory options.

☞ **No car option:** No car needed! The town center is just a short walk from the ferry, and bike rentals and public transport are available for exploring further.

⊙ **Ferry Times:** Every 45-60 minutes, 5:20 AM – 11:10 PM

⊙ **Duration:** 30 minutes each way

🎟 **Cost:** $9.45 per adult, $4.70 for youth (walk-on round-trip)

# KNOW BEFORE YOU GO

### ☞ Snag the Perfect Spot:

For Seattle skyline views, sit on the stern (back) of the ferry as you depart Seattle. For mountain views, head to the upper deck for a 360-degree look at the Olympics and Cascades.

### ☞ Watch for Ferry Traffic Alerts:

Check the Washington State Ferries app or website for live updates on ferry departure times, delays, and parking availability, especially during summer months when routes fill up quickly.

### ☞ Buying Your Ferry Ticket

*Online (Recommended):*

Buy your ticket ahead of time on the Washington State Ferries website or through their app. You'll avoid ticket booth lines and can track ferry delays or schedules in real time. For routes like the San Juan Islands, online reservations for vehicles are essential.

*At the Terminal:*

Purchase tickets at the terminal kiosks if you're more spontaneous, but lines can be long during peak times. Walk-on tickets rarely sell out, but arriving early is still wise.

### ☞ Best Times for Fewer Crowds:

Weekday mornings and midday offer lighter crowds, as do the shoulder seasons (spring and fall).

---

## *Be ready!*
# WILDLIFE SPOTTING

### ▸ Orcas:

Best viewed in May through September in Puget Sound, especially around Bainbridge and Bremerton routes. Orcas tend to frequent the Sound in search of salmon.

### ▸ Gray Whales:

Seen mostly in March and April during migration, particularly on the Edmonds-Kingston route.

### ▸ Harbor Seals and Sea Lions:

Seen year-round, often lounging on buoys or rocks near the ferry routes.

### ▸ Bald Eagles:

Common sightings along the Bainbridge and Bremerton routes, especially from April to July when they're nesting near the coastline.

Here during Whale Season? Join a whale watching tour! ☞ 

### MARINE WILDLIFE FUN FACT!

Puget Sound is home to diverse marine life. Passengers frequently spot harbor seals, sea lions, and even orcas from the decks.

# Day Trips & Scenic Drives

## CHUCKANUT DRIVE

Chuckanut Drive is one of the most scenic coastal drives in Washington. Located about 90 minutes north of Seattle, this 21-mile stretch of road offers stunning views of the San Juan Islands and lush forests. There are hikes, view points and most importantly, incredible restaurants that allow you to spend your afternoon with the most jaw-dropping water views. Stop at Taylor Shellfish Farms for fresh oysters, and be sure to explore Larrabee State Park for coastal hiking trails.

**How to get there:**
Take I-5 north from Seattle and exit onto Chuckanut Drive just south of Bellingham.

**Need to know before you go:**
▸ A Discover Pass is needed if you plan to explore Larrabee State Park.
▸ Chuckanut Drive is a narrow road with sharp curves, so take your time to enjoy the views safely.

## FORKS (AKA TWILIGHT)

Forks, Washington, gained worldwide fame as the gloomy, rain-soaked setting of the Twilight series. Whether you're a die-hard fan of the books and movies or just curious about the iconic Pacific Northwest town, Forks offers a fun, unique day trip. Explore Twilight-themed landmarks, the surrounding lush forests, and immerse yourself in the misty atmosphere that captivated millions. Forks' rainy, moody vibe makes it a perfect backdrop for a day of vampire-themed nostalgia.

**Morning:** Start Your Twilight Adventure, Drive to Forks

**How to get there:**
From Seattle, drive about 4 hours (via WA-104 W and US-101 N) to Forks. It's a scenic journey across the Olympic Peninsula, with plenty of lush forest views and Pacific coastline to set the Twilight mood.

I have the whole blog ready for you at Alexa-West.com/Seattle

**Need to know before you go:**
▸ **Park Pass:** No pass needed for Forks or La Push.

## DECEPTION PASS

Deception Pass is a breathtakingly scenic destination connecting Whidbey Island to Fidalgo Island, famous for its dramatic bridge, rugged cliffs, and the swirling tidal waters below. The park, named by early explorers, is one of Washington's most visited state parks, offering endless opportunities for outdoor adventures. Walking across the Deception Pass Bridge is a must for a terrifyingly beautiful view of the churning waters below. The park itself covers over 4,000 acres of pristine forest, beaches, and trails. Bowman Bay and Rosario Beach provide serene spots for picnicking, tide-pooling, and beachcombing, with rocky shores perfect for exploring marine life up close. For hikers, the Goose Rock Trail offers panoramic views of the San Juan Islands and the Olympic Mountains.

**➠ How to get there:**
From Seattle, drive north on I-5 to Highway 20, then follow signs to the Deception Pass Bridge. The trip is about 1.5 to 2 hours by car.

**⚠ Need to know before you go:**
▸ **Park Pass:** A Discover Pass is required for parking.
▸ **Weather:** Deception Pass can be windy; layers are recommended even on warmer days.

## THE OLYMPIC PENINSULA (IN GENERAL)

The Olympic Peninsula is a paradise for outdoor lovers. One must-visit is the Olympic Game Park, where you can drive through and see wildlife like bison, elk, and even bears up close. If you're feeling more adventurous, visit Hurricane Ridge for panoramic views or hike the Hoh Rainforest for a lush, green experience unlike any other. Pick a spot on the map and just drive.

**➠ How to get there:**
From Seattle, take a ferry to Bainbridge Island or drive around via Tacoma. The Peninsula is about 2-3 hours from Seattle, depending on your destination.

**⚠ Need to know before you go:**
▸ **Park Pass:** You'll need a National Park Pass to access certain areas of Olympic National Park. The Olympic Game Park charges $20 per person for entry.

# Over-Night Car Camping

The most beautiful parts of the Pacific Northwest are hidden, best explored after you've set up your tent. Don't have a tent?

**Rent:** You can rent camping gear including the sleeping bag, mat, tent, and chairs: https://www.back40outfitters.co

**Buy:** If you are moving here, you need your own camping gear. I love the camping gear I use from Natural Life. Easy to set up alone. I'll list my camping gear on <u>Alexa-West.com/Seattle.</u>

Yes, it's worth it. And yes, it's safe to do it alone or as two women.

**FACTS:** Washington hasn't seen any campground-related serial killers in decades! (#WashingtonHumor). The state's national parks and campgrounds, especially in popular spots like Mount Rainier and the Olympic Peninsula, have excellent safety records with few reported violent crimes. Statistically, national parks in the U.S. experience about 1 violent crime per million visitors annually, making them safer than most urban areas.

Remember that I am the **queen of travel safety!**
I wrote a Seattle safety blog for you at <u>Alexa-West.com/Seattle</u>

♥ **FERRY FUN FACT!** The Washington State Ferry system is the largest in the United States and one of the largest in the world, transporting over 24 million passengers each year.

# 01. ORCAS ISLAND – MORAN STATE PARK

Orcas Island, the largest of the San Juan Islands, offers some of the best camping and outdoor adventure opportunities in Washington. Moran State Park, located on the island, is a paradise for nature lovers, with over 5,000 acres of pristine wilderness, including old-growth forests, cascading waterfalls, and breathtaking viewpoints.

### ⚠ Need to know before you go:

Moran State Park features 151 campsites spread out around its lush forest and serene lakes. The park's crown jewel is Mount Constitution, the highest point in the San Juan Islands, offering stunning 360-degree views of the surrounding islands, Mount Baker, and even Vancouver. You can hike, swim in Cascade Lake, or kayak during your stay.

### ⏩ How to get there:

To reach Orcas Island, you'll need to take a ferry from Anacortes, WA. Ferries run multiple times a day, and it's recommended to make a reservation in advance. The ferry ride is about an hour and a half, and once on the island, it's a 30-minute drive to Moran State Park.

⊙ **Ferry Times:** Typically every 2-3 hours, with more frequent trips during summer.

✏ **Cost:** About $30-$50 for a vehicle and driver, and $15 per passenger (prices vary by season).

♥ **Pro Tip:** Book your ferry reservation in advance, especially during summer or weekends.

☞ **Ferry Reservations:** Washington State Ferries

⊕ **Website:** Washington State Parks – Moran State Park

# 02. LA WIS WIS CAMPGROUND

Gifford Pinchot National Forest
I feel like I'm giving you my best kept camping secret. La Wis Wis Campground is a hidden gem near Mount Rainier National Park. Set among towering old-growth trees, there is a magically blue river and swimming hole that make this campground so special (look for Blue Hole Trail on GoogleMaps). Spend the day on the shore swimming, reading and eating. Just clean up really well when you leave.

### ⚠ Need to know before you go:

The campground has 122 sites, many of which are shaded and located right by the river. It's a family-friendly spot with access to both Skate Creek and the Cowlitz River for fishing and water activities.

### ⏩ How to get there:

Take US-12 from Seattle for about 2 hours and 30 minutes, passing through the scenic Gifford Pinchot National Forest.

♥ **Pro Tip:** La Wis Wis is also

the best base for visiting the Packwood flea market which is this huge vintage market that feels like a county fair with butter on a stick. It's a little redneck...and that's why I love it. Lovely people, weird food and even weirder thrifting finds.

▸ Held over Memorial Day and Labor Day weekend

☞ Reserve: <u>Recreation.gov</u>

## 03. LAKE WENATCHEE STATE PARK CAMPGROUND

The classic summer lake getaway. This lake is ideal for kayaking, swimming, paddleboarding, and fishing. During the summer, the campground fills with families and outdoor adventurers. In the fall, look for Morel mushrooms. In the winter, the area transforms into a snowy wonderland, perfect for snowshoeing and cross-country skiing.

**How to get there:**

Located about 2 hours from Seattle, take US-2 East towards Stevens Pass.

♥ Pro Tip: For the best experience, head out for an early morning paddle when the lake is calm with reflections of the surrounding mountains!

✏ Cost: $20-$50 per night, depending on the type of site (tent or RV).

☞ Reserve: Washington State Parks – Lake Wenatchee

## QUICK GUIDE: Best Pacific Northwest (PNW) Weather for Camping

☞ **Best Time to Camp:**

**Late Spring to Early Fall (May - October):** Generally the most reliable weather with less rain, warmer days, and cooler nights.

☞ **Ideal Weather Conditions:**

▸ **May and June:** Light rain is common but usually manageable. Pack a waterproof tent and rain gear.

▸ **July and August:** Typically the driest months, ideal for lake and coastal camping.

▸ **September:** Rain may increase, but days are still warm—great for quieter campsites.

▸ **October:** Temperatures cool, with occasional rain; still pleasant but prepare for early-season storms.

☞ **Extra Tips for PNW Camping:**

▸ **Check for Wildfire Alerts (July - September):** Especially in eastern PNW regions.

▸ **Bug Protection:** Early summer is mosquito season, especially near lakes and wetlands.

▸ **Gear:** Waterproof tents, rainfly, and quick-dry clothing are essential for sudden weather changes.

# Packing for Seattle

 Ps. You can see my full Seattle Packing Guide at Alexa-West.com/Seattle.

Two things to consider when packing for Seattle:

#1: Seattle's weather can be unpredictable, so you need layers!

#2: Seattle is a city best explored on foot, so bring comfortable shoes.

When you think of Seattle fashion, you think of Nirvana grunge or sensible footwear made for your nerdy uncle who wears socks with sandals. But I'm here to save you from all that. I'm the queen of cute and sensible. Shop my go-to Seattle gear on my website at Alexa-West.com/Seattle.

## PACKING BY SEASON

## YEAR-ROUND ESSENTIALS

▶ **Tote Bag or Big Bag:** The #1 must for Seattle is a tote bag or a large bag. You'll need it to carry a sweater, scarf, or any layers you peel off as the day warms up. Plus, it's handy for any shopping you do at local markets

▶ **Comfy Shoes:** Whether you're walking through Pike Place Market or hiking in Discovery Park, you'll want something supportive. Sandals, boots or tennis shoes.

## SPRING ESSENTIALS
*March - May*

▶ **Rain Jacket:** The spring months can still be pretty rainy, so a lightweight, waterproof jacket is a must. Skip the umbrella—locals prefer rain jackets because they're more practical with the drizzle.

▶ **Layered Clothing:** Pack layers like long-sleeve shirts and sweaters. I love a tie-front shirt as a layer. Mornings and evenings can be chilly, but the afternoons might warm up.

▶ **An Umbrella:** JUST KIDDING. We don't use umbrellas in Seattle. The rain is often misty with occasional downpours. You need a waterproof jack for the mist and you need to duck into a coffee shop during the down pours.

## SUMMER ESSENTIALS
*June - August*

▶ **Light Jacket or Sweater:** Even in summer, Seattle evenings can be cool. Bring a light jacket or sweater that you can easily throw on.

▶ **Sunglasses:** Believe it or not, Seattle gets beautiful sunny days in the summer, so pack a pair of sunglasses.

▸ **Comfortable Sandals or Sneakers:** Walking around the city is a breeze in the summer, so bring a pair of comfortable sandals or sneakers that you can wear all day.

## FALL ESSENTIALS
*September - November*

▸ **Waterproof Boots:** Fall in Seattle means rain, so bring waterproof boots that can handle puddles and wet sidewalks. This is a must, I tell you.

▸ **Cozy Scarf:** A scarf is great for layering and adds warmth on those crisp fall days.

▸ **Midweight Jacket:** A midweight jacket, like a fleece or insulated layer, will keep you warm without being too bulky.

## WINTER ESSENTIALS
*December - February*

▸ **Heavy Rain Jacket:** Winters in Seattle are wet, so a heavy-duty rain jacket is essential. Make sure it's waterproof (not water resistant) and has a hood.

▸ **Warm Layers:** Pack sweaters, thermal tops, and a warm hat to stay cozy. You'll want to layer up since temperatures can drop.

▸ **Waterproof Gloves:** Keep your hands warm and dry with a good pair of waterproof gloves.

# DO YOU LOVE THIS BOOK?

As a self-published author – doing this whole publishing thing by myself – reviews are what keeps The Solo Girl's Travel Guide growing.

If you found my guidebook to be helpful, please leave me a review on Amazon.com

Your review helps other girls find this book and experience a truly life-changing trip.

Ps. I read every single review.

Leave me a review in the code below - it will just take a sec!

# Trip Planning for Seattle + Beyond



## 2-DAY SEATTLE ITINERARY

This is the itinerary I give my friends when they come to town. It includes the most exciting things to prioritize when ticking off your bucket list.

This itinerary is available and clickable on my website — along with more itineraries and planning support — at Alexa-West.com/Seattle

## DAY 1: DOWNTOWN & WATERFRONT CLASSICS

### ✱ Morning: Pike Place Market

▸ Start your day on a breakfast tour of Pike Place with Savor Seattle.

▸ Head to Storyville Coffee to give your feet a moment to rest.

### ✱ Midday: Seattle Waterfront

▸ Board an Argosy Harbor Cruise for a scenic tour of Seattle (no reservations required).

▸ Alternatively, visit the Seattle Art Museum.

▸ Have lunch at Matt's in the Market or The Pink Door

### ✱ Evening: Space Needle Queen Anne

▸ Mosey over to Seattle Center to see the Space Needle and, if interested, go up to the observation deck.

▸ Visit the Museum of Pop Culture (MoPOP)

▸ Dinner: Walk back to Umi Sake House and sit at the bar.

▸ Hit Roquette for an Espresso Martini, then visit The Crocodile for live music.

## DAY 2: SUNNY DAY ON LAKE UNION AND CAPITOL HILL

### ✱ Morning: Lake Union

▸ Brunch at Portage Bay in Lake Union.

▸ Walk to Lake Union Park

### ✱ Midday: Lake Union

▸ Explore MOHAI to learn about Seattle's history, innovations, and culture.

▸ Rent a kayak or paddleboard or take a Hot Tub boat out on South Lake Union.

▸ Alternatively, take a seaplane tour from Kenmore Air for an unforgettable aerial view of Seattle!

### ✱ Evening: Capitol Hill

▸ Dinner: Poquito's or Mario's Pizza Drinks at Foreign National and a/stir.

▸ Karaoke at Hula Hula
▸ Late night tacos at Carmello's (pre-plan a brunch in Georgetown for your hangover).

## DAY 2: RAINY DAY DOWNTOWN & ON CAPITOL HILL

### Morning: Downtown

▸ Have breakfast at Biscuit Bitch or Piroshky Piroshky

▸ Visit the Seattle Aquarium (the earlier the better)

▸ Take a ride on the Seattle Great Wheel afterwards

▸ Have a lunch at Post Alley Pizza

### Midday: Lake Union

▸ Hit the spa at Banya 5

▸ Head home afterwards to freshen up

### Evening: Georgetown

▸ Have dinner at Ciudad or grab a chirashi bowl and take it to a brewery

▸ Start your brewery and bar hop

▸ Every good night ends at Full Throttle Bottles

Looking for an adventure buddy? You can always ask in Girls in Seattle!

**Want to plan quickly?**

I have more Seattle Itineraries on my website.

⊕ Alexa-West.com/Seattle

---



# Directory

## EMERGENCY:

▸ **911:** For all emergencies requiring immediate police, fire, or medical response.

## NON-EMERGENCY:

▸ **Seattle Police Department Non-Emergency: (206) 625-5011**

Use for situations that require police assistance but are not life-threatening, such as reporting a theft, noise complaint, or suspicious activity.

▸ **Seattle Fire Department Non-Emergency: (206) 386-1400**

For general inquiries, burn permits, or to request information about fire safety.

## OTHER IMPORTANT NUMBERS:

▸ **Washington State Patrol: (206) 296-4100**

For incidents on state highways or for matters involving the State Patrol.

▸ **King County Sheriff's Office Non-Emergency: (206) 296-3311**

For non-emergency situations in unincorporated King County areas.

## PUBLIC UTILITIES:

▸ **Seattle City Light (power outages): (206) 684-3000**

▸ **Seattle Public Utilities (water, sewer, garbage): (206) 684-3000**

♥ **PRO TIP!** If the power goes out in the winter, use the Seattle City Light Outage Map to search for updates.

### PLANNED PARENTHOOD
**Central District Health Center**

- 🕐 Hours: Mon-Fri, 9 AM – 5 PM
- ☎ Phone: 800-769-0045
- 🌐 Website: plannedparenthood.org

### BIRTH CONTROL

Most pharmacies carry common brands. Brands to look for include Ortho Tri-Cyclen, Yaz, Lo Loestrin Fe, and Plan B for emergency contraception.

- 📍 Where: All major pharmacies like Walgreens, CVS, and Bartell Drugs.

### COMPLETE STD SCREENING

**Planned Parenthood – Seattle Health Center**

- 🕐 Hours: Mon-Fri, 9 AM – 5 PM
- ☎ Phone: 800-769-0045
- 🌐 Website: plannedparenthood.org

## MEDICAL RESOURCES

### SERIOUS INJURY / X-RAY HOSPITAL

**Harborview Medical Center**

- 🕐 Hours: 24/7 Emergency Services
- ☆ Specialty: Level I trauma center with full radiology services
- ☎ Phone: 206-744-3000

## STOMACH ISSUES OR FLU-LIKE SYMPTOMS

**UW Medical Center – Montlake**

- 🌐 Website: uwmedicine.org
- 📍 Where: 1959 NE Pacific St, Seattle, WA 98195
- 🕐 Hours: 24/7 for emergency care and urgent needs

**Indigo Urgent Care**

$200 will get you x-rays, stitches, and things they can do "in-house".

- 🌐 Website: indigohealth.com
- 📍 Where: All over Seattle
- 🕐 Hours:  24/7

## TRAVEL INSURANCE

Don't travel without travel insurance! I have options for you at:

- 🌐 alexa-west.com/safety

## EXTRA STUFF

### CAMERA REPAIR SHOP AND RENTAL

**Glazer's Camera**

- 📍 Where: Retail Store at 811 Republican St. and Rentals at 517 Dexter Ave N
- 🕐 Hours: Retail Store Mon–Sat 9 AM–6 PM; Sun 12 PM–5 PM
- ☎ Phone: 206-624-1100
- 🌐 Website: glazerscamera.com

# A little PepTalk...

**Why do we wait for someone else to give us permission to make big moves?**

To take a trip.
To chop our hair off.
To start a youtube channel, write a book, or create a business.

Because we all have the same fear: **what if my light shines too bright?**

Is that okay? Am I allowed to be shiny? Am I allowed to sparkle? Am I allowed to change?

Yes. Yes. Yes. And yes.

You are allowed to be all those things...because those things are already you.

So, next time you feel yourelf playing small to make someone else feel comfortable, remember this: Playing small doesn't serve you and it doesn't help anyone around you.

Be as bright as you can be, because when your light shines bright - you attract the right people into your life. Shiny people.

When you give yourself permission to live a shiny, sparkly and bright life, you wake up excited in the morning. You stop living in fear. And you inspire the people living in the dark.

Just in case you ever think a dream is too big, here's what I want you to remember...

**You don't need anyone's approval to fulfill your destiny. Don't let anyone get in your way.**

If you're reading this right now, understand that you are different than most people. If you're reading this, it means that you dream bigger and feel deeper than most people who live their whole lives in one place -- just going through the motions. But not you. You will never be satisfied with a provincial life.

So, give yourself permission to do everything you've always wanted to do. Give yourself permission to be the person you've always wanted to be. Starting with this adventure...

With love ♥

Alexa

**THIS TRIP.**

**THIS IS WHEN YOU DISCOVER EXACTLY WHO YOU ARE.**

**TRUST YOURSELF.**

# the Solo Girl's Travel

### ▸ 01. Be an Explorer, Not a Tourist.

Some people travel just for the photo. While others travel to find the unfamiliar, connect with strangers, expand their minds, and try new things for the sake of trying new things. Which kind of traveler are you?

### ▸ 02. Leave Room for Happenstance

Don't overstuff your itinerary. Slow down, be where you are and leave room for serendipity! Literally, schedule serendipity time so the universe can take the lead.

### ▸ 03. Vote with your Dollar

When possible, choose to support local businesses that operate ethically - aka businesses that respect the environment, benefit their local communities, don't take advantage of animals and just treat their staff really really well.

### ▸ 04. Look for the Gift

Love your mistakes! With every bump in the road comes a gift. Miss a bus? Look for the gift. Lose your room key? Look for the gift. Get dumped on your honeymoon? Look for the gift! There will always be a gift.

### ▸ 05. Stay Curious

Ask questions! Ask questions when you like something and ask questions when you don't understand something. Out loud or in your head. And whenever you feel judgment arise, replace it with a question instead.

### ▸ 06. More Stories, Less Photos

Take a couple photos and then put your phone away. While everyone else is taking shitty sunset photos that never look as good on camera…you are really there, experiencing every shade of color in real time. Take note in your head of the story you will bring home - of the people you see, the food you smell, the monkeys in the trees! Look up, not down.

### ▸ 07. Count Experiences, Not Passport Stamps

You can never "do" Mexico. You can go to Mexico 50 times and still each experience will be different than the last. Travel to live, not to brag.

### ▸ 08. Mind your Impact

Leave every place better than you found it. Take a piece of trash from the beach and be kind to people you meet. Bring your own water bottle, canvas bag, and reusable straw to avoid single-use plastics.

### ▸ 09. Avoid Voluntourism

People are not zoo animals. Playing with children at orphanages, temporarily teaching English in villages or volunteering at women's shelters hurt more than they help. Want to volunteer with a positive impact? Check out my blog at Alexa-West.com

### ▸ 10. Carry your Positivity

Ever had a crappy day and then a stranger smiles at you and flips your entire mood? Travel can be hard, but your positivity will be your secret weapon. Happy vibes are contagious. Even when we don't speak the local language, a smile or a random act of kindness tips the universal scale in the right direction for you and the people you meet along your journey.

### ▸ 11. Trust your Gut

Listen to that little voice inside you. When something doesn't feel right, back away. When something feels good, lean. Your intuition will lead you to beautiful places, unforgettable moments, and new lifelong friends.

**BONUS!**

### Drink where the Locals Drink, Eat Where the Locals Eat

Even if it's under a tarp outside a mini mart. This is how you discover the best food and make the most meaningful connections. It feeeeeeeels good to travel good.

**A CONFESSION:**

I bend the rules. Sometimes I stay in an all-inclusive resort instead of a locally owned guesthouse. Sometimes I go to McDonald's because I want a taste of home. And sometimes, especially when I'm tired or hungry, I'm not all sunshine and rainbows to be around.

But my moral travel compass does not bend for things that matter to me. I'll never leave a piece of trash on the beach. I'll never support elephant riding. I'd rather stay home than go on a Carnival Cruise even if it was free. Decide what matters to you now, let that guide you as you travel but let yourself be human.

Comfort yourself when you need comforting and eat the forbidden fruit sparingly. When you do make mistakes, brush yourself off and do better next time. No one's path is perfect but I'm proud of you for making your path better.

THE
ONE-WAY
TICKET PLAN
FIND AND FUND
YOUR PURPOSE WHILE
TRAVELING THE WORLD
ALEXA WEST
AUTHOR OF THE SOLO GIRL'S TRAVEL GUIDES

# PASS IT ON!

**THE SOLO GIRL'S TRAVEL GUIDE TO:** | **Seattle!**

**This guide book is meant to change lives.** Don't let it sit on a shelf forever and ever. Before you **give this book to a friend** who needs a travel push or before you **leave it in the hostel for the next travel girl** to find…This is your legacy, too

| DATE: | NAME + SOCIAL MEDIA ♥ |
| --- | --- |
| fall 2024 | alexa - @sologirlstravelguide |
|  |  |
|  |  |
|  |  |
|  |  |
|  |  |
|  |  |

# Where next?

**BALI**

**THAILAND**

**VIETNAM**

**SOUTH KOREA**

**PUERTO VALLARTA
& RIVIERA NAYARIT**

**CAMBODIA**

And More...

Get The Whole Collection.